Outstanding Primary Teaching and Learning

A journey through your early teaching career

To Katy,

Put the fun in
fundamental!!

Sj de
x

Outstanding Primary Teaching and Learning

A journey through your early teaching career

Sally Hawkins

 Open University Press

Open University Press
McGraw-Hill Education
8th Floor
338 Euston Road
London
NW1 3BT

email: enquiries@openup.co.uk
world wide web: www.openup.co.uk

and Two Penn Plaza, New York, NY 10121-2289, USA

First published 2016

A catalogue record of this book is available from the British Library

ISBN-13: 978-0-33-526366-0
ISBN-10: 0-33-526366-6
eISBN: 978-0-33-526367-7

Library of Congress Cataloging-in-Publication Data
CIP data applied for

Typeset by Transforma Pvt. Ltd., Chennai, India
Printed and bound by Bell and Bain Ltd, Glasgow

Fictitious names of companies, products, people, characters and/or data that may be
used herein (in case studies or in examples) are not intended to represent any real
individual, company, product or event.

Praise for this book

"There are few educational texts that you do not want to put down, but this one is! The book will encourage, motivate and inspire trainee teachers, recently qualified, early career and established teachers to reach the heights of their potential.

If becoming an outstanding teacher seems like an unattainable goal, this book will convince the reader otherwise. The author speaks to the reader, coaxing and encouraging, as if she was there by their side. She follows her own advice by creating innovative and stimulating sessions, but in text form.

The accessible structure with reflection sections, activities, prompts, checklists, further reading, and thought provoking quotes and extracts, provides an interactive resource, for all those who aspire to be the best possible teacher for their pupils. In simple terms, an outstanding book, that provides a pathway through the minefield that education can be."

Dr Tracy Whatmore, Senior Lecturer at the University of Birmingham, UK

"An easy to read book with sound practical advice underpinned by theory which every trainee teacher or early career teacher can dip into for guidance. It captures the essence of primary teaching through the metaphor of a coat and I'm sure readers will adapt their coats accordingly as they journey through the book."

Professor Vini Lander, Edge Hill University, UK

"Outstanding Primary Teaching and Learning is an absolute must-read for teachers of any age or experience who would like to become more outstanding in their practise. Written from a unique and highly reflective perspective of pedagogy as an art, a proactive and inspiring approach is taken to journey the reader along a personalised path, enabled through highly constructive and reflective opportunities.

Dedication

This book is dedicated to my late father and my two fabulous little-big boys, James and Eddie, without whom I would not be the woman I am. To past and, most importantly, to future generations.

Contents

Preface

Not so long ago I was stopped in a supermarket queue with a friendly 'Hello Miss Hawkins.' I turned to find the smiling face of a woman. I immediately recognized her as the mother of one of my pupils I had taught two decades ago. After a short chat about her daughter's success she said it was down to my belief in her child. I'm telling you this not to blow my own trumpet but to make you believe if you strive to be outstanding you really can change the paths of our children for the better.

This book was written to support trainee teachers and teachers wishing to enhance their practice. The structure of the book was inspired by Abraham Maslow's hierarchy of needs (my point of reference especially before lunch!) and Charles Handy's *Empty Raincoat* (a book my father gave to me in my twenties).

It is designed hierarchically and encourages you to build strong foundations for being a great teacher. It emphasizes the need to have these in place before building your fantastical skyscraper. You can, of course, start at any point and there is a signposting section in the Introduction to help you, or you may wish to start from the bottom and make your ascent gradually. Some days this ascent will feel like the north face of the Eiger – this is natural. The most important thing to remember is why you want to teach or are already teaching (and perhaps to invest in a tougher harness and more crampons).

This book uses a visual image of a perfect jacket to symbolize how essential it is you acquire and develop a clear sense of teacher identity that is professional, authentic and communicates who you are as an individual. My mother talked about sausage machines and how I should avoid turning out the same as everyone else. Sometimes I fear our educational system could produce sausages; fed the same diet, squeezed through the same hoops and squashed into the same mould. I encourage you to be an individual, be the best you can be and encourage each pupil you teach to do the same.

The book prompts and guides you on your journey to becoming an outstanding teacher through a range of reflection points, activities, teaching strategies and checklists embedded in each chapter. Reflection is placed at the apex of the pyramid (see Figure I.3, p. 5) but for you to successfully reach this height you must be prepared to critically look at and analyse yourself and your developing practice. Let's get started!

Acknowledgements

Thank you to Steven Popper for initiating the process. My special thanks to Alex for being an academic and creative muse; Marie Murphy for your encouragement; and James and Eddie for being an endless source of anecdotes, fun and your ineffable joie de vivre.

My thanks to the headteachers and staff of Epiphany Primary School, Westhill Park Independent School and Whiteley Primary School. Also to those teachers who very kindly completed interviews and questionnaires.

With specific thanks to Ginni Cooper, Carol Hughes, John Bills and Mark Bagust, and friends, family and colleagues for your support, ideas, proofreading and coffee! Also to Fiona Richman at Open University Press for your calm reassurance when needed.

A final thank you to Rock in the most fortunate of unfortunate games of rock, paper, skier!

Introduction

Introducing 'outstandingness'

> *The mediocre teacher tells. The good teacher explains. The superior teacher demonstrates. The great teacher inspires.*
>
> William Arthur Ward, 1968

A great teacher will have taught many of you reading this book. These are the ones that inspire, energize and engage us. As William Arthur Ward (1968) neatly points out, they go the extra mile to ensure that every pupil they teach has that feelgood factor and knows success. A great teacher with their infectious enthusiasm and substantive knowledge will bring out the best in all their pupils every day.

A rose by any other name . . . Over the last couple of decades we have used various superlatives, such as great, excellent, exceptional, superb or outstanding to describe the very best teaching and teachers. The chosen superlative for this book is *outstanding* simply because outstanding teachers STAND OUT!

What is outstanding?

Ask different people, and you'll get different answers. Teachers, pupils, headteachers, parents and inspectors would answer with a different emphasis. Let this book serve as your guide and through its range of valuable insights, reflective points, practical checklists and action planning you will learn what you can aspire to and what you can work on to enhance your practice.

 REFLECT

Let's begin to think about 'outstandingness' (noun: 'to be outstanding', as yet to appear in a dictionary!).

- What do you know already about outstanding teaching?

- What do you think an outstanding teacher does?
- Why should you aspire to be an outstanding teacher?

A good teacher will enable pupils to learn and develop necessary knowledge, skills and concepts, but an outstanding teacher has the capacity to change lives. To offer an individual pupil life chances that otherwise they may never be exposed to and aspirations to enable greater social mobility and a love of learning is a true gift.

We remember our teachers for different reasons but it is an outstanding teacher whose memory is cherished and has in some way moulded or influenced our lives. We often hear people say: 'They were inspirational'; 'They made me love school/a subject'; 'I loved their lessons'. These teachers create a judicious balance of fun and the fundamentals of learning (putting the *fun* in *fundamental*! Sigh!). There is an innate sense of enjoyment, humour, warmth, confidence and enthusiasm generated by such teachers.

An outstanding teacher plans great lessons with a richness and variety, drawn from excellent subject knowledge and an ability, confidence and passion to share this with their pupils; any observers will feel as involved and as carried along as the pupils, who do not want the lesson to end. An experienced salesman, at the cusp of my journey into teaching, reminded me of the old adage to 'always leave them wanting more!' Wise words indeed, so make sure your pupils are excited about your next lesson and arrive eager and ready to learn.

Outstandingness doesn't 'just happen' – it requires all pupils and adults in the classroom to have a clear vision and understanding of what constitutes outstanding teaching and learning. There will be risk-taking by teacher and pupil, exploration of new knowledge and concepts, and experimentation. Pupils are seen as unique and their potential identified and encouraged to make outstanding progress.

Outstandingness is not just for an observation by a mentor or tutor (a special occasion), *it's for life*. As was said of Sir Christopher Wren: 'If you seek his monument, look around you'. An outstanding teacher's vibrant and creative class-room can invite, with confidence, any passing observer to see a kaleidoscope of learning through excellent pupils' successes, stimulating displays, formidable feedback, timely interventions, stimulating dialogue and classroom dynamics giving every lesson the 'buzz' while leaving a lasting impression on all those involved.

While writing this section I reflected on my time as a primary school pupil and three very different teachers, in very different schools, immediately came to mind, who have never been too far from my consciousness throughout my career. My teacher, when I was 5, was caring and compassionate. She patiently helped me with my work, pulled out a hanky when I cried over my maths and sat with me with her soft voice comforting me. Then there was a teacher when I was 9 years old. He taught me for only one term but in that time I was engaged, I laughed and enjoyed each day because he made learning fun through his energy, enthusiasm, humour and spontaneity. My final memorable teacher, in my last year in primary school, embodied the traditional teacher. She was not whacky or gushing, but highly knowledgeable, consistent and very strict; everyone liked and respected Miss Parry! So, an amalgam of all three teachers would be my 'perfect' outstanding teacher: compassionate, caring, humorous, fun, enthusiastic, highly knowledgeable and with excellent classroom management. Ta da!

But it's not as easy as that! Teaching is more than a job; it's a vocation. Performing adequately is not enough, given your responsibility not only to your pupils but also to society as a whole. An outstanding educational system should demand that its learning experiences offer the very best to all learners. Therefore teaching makes *physical demands*: you are on your feet all day, rarely stationary, animated, dynamic and the embodiment of energy and enthusiasm (especially on wet and windy days!). To sustain such physical output is challenging. It makes *intellectual demands*: you must know and deliver the whole curriculum, understand and meet the needs of each individual in your class, and get to grips with new initiatives, policies and procedures. Sometimes your head will spin and your eyes will ache from time spent developing subject mastery and understanding curriculum changes. Finally, teaching makes *emotional demands*: pupils require compassion, care, empathy, sensitivity, respect, enthusiasm and understanding, which can deplete your own reserves (see Figure 1.1).

To be an outstanding teacher, you must be equal to all these demands. Imagine a great teacher without subject knowledge or compassion; or a teacher without energy and empathy – impossible!

Being cognizant of this *trilogy of demands* and having the necessary attributes and understanding, will prevent one or more sides pushing in and compressing you in the middle, until you implode!

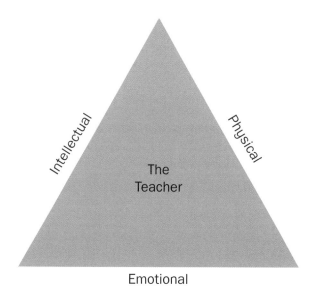

Figure I.1 Trilogy of demands.

Introducing this book

This book addresses the trilogy through *seven key themes* (Figure I.2), which form a core to enable you to more ably meet such demands. Reflecting upon and developing them within each chapter will guide you on your journey to becoming an outstanding teacher.

Figure I.2 The key themes.

- *Your teacher identity and philosophy* (addresses emotional demands as it keeps you centred, and more resilient to both change and challenge).
- *A sense of purpose in education* (addresses emotional demands and reminds you why you wake up in the morning).
- *A focus on well-being for you and your pupils* (addresses emotional and physical demands, prioritizing your personal physical and mental health and that of your pupils ahead of performance).
- *Knowing and meeting the needs of the unique child* (addresses intellectual demands as you develop the capacity to meet varied learning needs).
- *Creating an enabling and empowering environment* (addresses physical, intellectual and emotional demands as the learning environment influences all three aspects).

- *The need for self-awareness and critical self-reflection* (addresses physical, intellectual and emotional demands as it underpins all aspects of you as teacher and your teaching).

- *Continuous development as lifelong learners* (addresses intellectual demands as you build your mastery of knowledge and pedagogy).

This book has been designed hierarchically to support and enhance this journey. However, you may wish to focus on a particular chapter or section as you reflect upon your strengths and target areas for development.

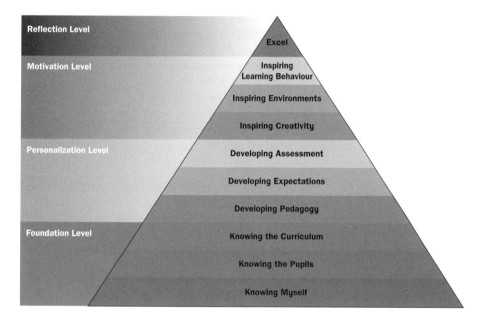

Figure I.3 The hierarchy of the book.

- *Foundation level (Chapters 1–3)*: The base of the pyramid supports the rest: without knowing yourself, the child, the curriculum and the subject matter, the subsequent levels cannot be fully realized.

- *Personalization level (Chapters 4–6)*: This level recognizes and addresses pupils' unique needs and ensures that these are met by both pedagogy and practice. Teaching strategies, planning, differentiation, assessment and high expectations for all are developed to equip you to personalize your teaching for the range of pupils you teach.

- *Motivation level (Chapters 7–9)*: As you move up the hierarchy it focuses on engaging and inspiring both you and your pupils through creativity, the learning environment and creating behaviour for learning.

- *Reflection level (Chapter 10)*: At the apex of the pyramid, you are explicitly guided toward ways to develop reflective practice and recognize how this impacts on, and is necessary for, the development and success of the underlying levels.

How do I become an outstanding teacher?

A list of top tips and strategies might produce outstanding learning experiences but will not empower and sustain you in being the outstanding teacher you aspire to be. The *Teachers' standards* (DfE 2012) call on teachers to consistently make teaching interesting, stimulating, inspiring, and challenging. However, outstanding teaching is not simply trying to do more 'good' things, it's doing things differently. Otherwise this may eventually lead to confusion, or even worse going backwards in desperation to tick too many boxes, or trying too hard to reach a seemingly elusive goal. This is a misguided approach as becoming consistently outstanding is about a shift in mindset, or as Dylan Wiliam says, 'giving up good things to do *great* things'.

What might these great things be? An outstanding teacher will inevitably create outstanding learning experiences for all pupils, leading to, as Ofsted (2015 para. 46) notes, 'successful learners' who show 'excellent attitudes to learning'. An outstanding lesson, although Ofsted no longer assigns grades, is one that would feature aspects such as:

- pupil engagement (see Chapters 3, 4, 6, 7);
- pupil progress (see Chapters 6, 8);
- mastery (see Chapter 5);
- pupil challenge (see Chapters 5, 6, 10);
- assessment for learning (see Chapter 6);
- independent learning (see Chapters 5, 8, 9);
- teacher innovation (see Chapters 5, 7);
- dialogic teaching (see Chapters 5, 6, 7);
- teacher self-reflection (see Chapter 10).

An outstanding lesson also has that 'wow' and 'feelgood' factor as pupils enjoy and achieve.

Evaluating your current practice

Based upon the *Teachers' standards* (DfE 2012), and this book's interpretation of outstanding, use the questions in Table I.1 to form a checklist for evaluating your current practice/understanding and as a guide to using this book most effectively.

- If you answered yes to all question, fabulous, you are already outstanding! Put this book down immediately and crack on!

Table I.1 Checklist to signpost needs.

No.	Question	Yes	No	Sometimes
1	Do you have a clear sense of teacher identity?			
2	Are you able to articulate your teaching philosophy?			
3	Do you recognize the necessity and impact of building positive pupil relationships?			
4	Do you reflect on child development theory to make informed decisions?			
5	Are you aware of your subject strengths and weaknesses and how this affects pupil progress?			
6	Do you have sufficient expertise of subject knowledge across the curriculum to enable all pupils to succeed?			
7	Do you use a range of inspirational teaching strategies matched to learners' unique needs?			
8	Do you promote deeper learning through effort, resilience and a growth mindset?			
9	Do your grouping and expectations allow all pupils to excel or do you limit some pupils' potential?			
10	Is the structure of the lesson clear and are pupils given sufficient time to respond, talk and think about their learning?			
11	Does the pitch and pace of the lesson reflect the learners' needs or follow a 'script'?			
12	Do you encourage rich and extensive pupil dialogue to enhance learning?			
13	Do you embed effective assessment for learning within your practice?			
14	Does your feedback enable each pupil to improve through setting clear next steps and targets?			
15	Do you feel confident to take risks and plan creative learning experiences?			
16	Does the classroom environment enable and empower all learners?			

(Continued)

Table I.1 (continued)

17	Are displays, technology and other resources strategically used to support and enhance teaching and learning?			
18	Do you plan for and communicate effectively with your teaching assistant (TA)?			
19	Are parents involved in their child's learning and the school?			
20	Do all pupils have a positive behaviour and attitude towards learning?			
21	Do you identify your own areas for development and actively reflect on your practice?			
22	Are you able to reflect while teaching and adapt your practice?			
	Total scores			

- If you answered no or sometimes to most or all questions 1–6, spend more time working through the foundation level, Chapters 1–3.
- If you answered no or sometimes to most or all questions 7–14, spend more time working through personalization level, Chapters 4–6.
- If you answered no or sometimes to most or all questions 15–20, spend more time working through motivation level, Chapters 7–9.
- If you answered no or sometimes to questions 21 and 22, spend more time working through the reflection level, Chapter 10.

Introducing the 'perfect jacket'

 In education we often refer to '*hooks*' to grab a pupil's attention. Hooks enable learners to make connections and engage with learning while they process information. As adults we could all do with a 'hook' now and again, so the hook in this book is a *coat hook* on which to hang the analogy of a 'perfect jacket'.

This analogy is used to represent the wealth of knowledge and skills that you acquire as a trainee teacher and teacher. The 'perfect jacket' is a symbol of your teacher identity, self-image, attitudes, values and professionalism. You must know what it truly means to be a teacher. Every day, as you enter school, you become a teacher. Your many other roles, such as a spouse, son or daughter, mother or father, are left at the gate until the end of the working day. You will spend most of your time interacting with pupils, colleagues and parents. However, your role extends much further. As a teacher, you are an important part of society; some may say the linchpin, educating the next generation and preparing them for life. As a teacher, you are playing a major role in the future social, political, moral, technological and economic state of the country. A weighty responsibility, and therefore your jacket needs to be both adaptable and durable!

A jacket and professionalism are often synonymous: a jacket selected for an interview, a meeting with governors or parents, or to make an impression. We often grab a trusted jacket before embarking on any journey, as you never know what the weather holds! At the end of the day a jacket can simply be taken off and hung up. This action symbolically signals that your teacher identity can be suspended until the morning, but neither discarded nor dismissed.

As you progress on your journey into teaching, you may repair the worn patches, embellish it, or decide to change the style and cut of your jacket completely as your educational philosophy and teacher identity are challenged and remoulded through your experiences. Your jacket will hopefully adapt to the prevailing circumstances so that over time it will be tailored to suit only you and is unique.

As you work through this book you will become more aware of how your jacket needs to be developed. Central to this are your pupils', parents', colleagues', headteacher's and Ofsted's expectations of how they want you to 'look' and 'act' in your jacket. These expectations are varied and can sometimes create tension as messages may be confused and conflicting. Parents will want you to bring out the very best in their children for their futures. Your pupils will have more immediate goals and want you to be a great teacher every day. The school will have its own culture and 'way of doing things' and will expect you to 'fit in'. Governments, both local and central, influence budgets and procedures in school, with which you must conform. Moreover, these expectations may not be consistent with the interpretation of what it means to be 'outstanding', which again can create potential conflict.

Your jacket needs to be fitted and prepared for such demands. Your jacket will become almost a 'smart' jacket! As you can see, developing your perfect jacket is central to your success.

The aim of this book is to give you the knowledge, skills, understanding and confidence to find your perfect jacket and become an outstanding teacher.

References

DfE (2012) *Teachers' standards*, www.gov.uk/government/uploads/system/uploads/attachment_data/file/301107/Teachers__Standards.pdf.

Ofsted (2015) *School inspection handbook*, www.gov.uk/government/ofsted.

Ward, W.A. (1968) *Thoughts of a Christian optimist*. New York: Grosset and Dunlap.

PART 1

The foundation level – knowing!

1

Knowing yourself – being and becoming a teacher

I've come to a frightening conclusion that I am the decisive element in the classroom. It's my personal approach that creates the climate. It's my daily mood that makes the weather. As a teacher, I possess a tremendous power to make a child's life miserable or joyous. I can be a tool of torture or an instrument of inspiration. I can humiliate or heal. In all situations, it is my response that decides whether a crisis will be escalated or de-escalated and a child humanized or dehumanized.

Haim G. Ginott, 1993

Our coat hook! We'll start with our analogy of the 'perfect jacket'. Let's consider its purpose. It should fit well, be comfortable, while communicating something about you and your professionalism. However, not all jackets are made equally, and not all individuals fit the same jacket; individualization and personalization must be considered in your selection process. Choosing a jacket is a complex business, so expect designing your jacket to achieve outstandingness to be as complicated. Consider something that suits you, performs a function, communicates the 'right' message for you and fits your budget. Your decision is influenced by many conscious and unconscious factors. However, as Ginott (1993) eloquently points out, you are the decisive element, and therefore the first step to finding your perfect jacket and being an outstanding teacher begins with knowing yourself, your teacher identity and philosophy.

This chapter explores these factors and the nature of professionalism, the complexity of competing agendas and the demands placed upon you as a teacher, and how best to manage these demands.

The key themes within this chapter prompt you to:

- understand how your *teacher identity and philosophy* can influence your journey to outstandingness;
- know why it is essential to have a *sense of purpose in education*;
- appreciate why a focus on *well-being for you and your pupils* is vital;

- reflect on how an understanding of professionalism enables you to *know and meet the needs of the unique child*;
- appreciate how an awareness of identity, professionalism and relationships supports creating an *enabling and empowering environment*;
- understand why *self-awareness*, *critical self-reflection* and being emotionally intelligent and mindful can impact on your practice;
- recognize why embracing *continuous development as a lifelong learner* is key to outstandingness.

This chapter addresses the following *Teachers' standards* (DfE 2012):

1 Set high expectations which inspire, motivate and challenge pupils
8 Fulfil wider professional responsibilities

Your teacher identity

To create yourself as the teacher you wish to be requires a strong sense of teacher identity – essentially, how you 'see' yourself as a teacher and your educational philosophy are absolutely necessary to sustain you throughout your journey in teaching.

 REFLECT

To define yourself as a teacher you must identify your beliefs and values, and how you see the purpose of education. Take a moment to consider the three questions below and the possible implications each 'position' may have for you and your teaching.

- Do you see education's role as meeting the needs of individuals or the needs of society?
- Do you see education as a way to develop individuals' sense of values, both morally and ethically, or their skills and competencies?
- Do you see education as preparation to fit into society, or equip individuals to change and develop it?

There is, of course, no right or wrong answer to these questions, but engaging in a deeper understanding of education enables you to begin to consider your role within it. The development of your teacher identity will not be instantaneous. It is a gradual process of defining, integrating and, most importantly, reconciling your beliefs and values with the demands of teaching. You may start your journey in teaching with preconceived notions or a 'picture' of who you might be as a teacher and your relationships with staff, pupils, parents and the wider community.

However, you may start to question whether or not this initial teacher identity (and choice of jacket) fits the environment you are in. This is when real and preconceived 'pictures' are misaligned, which may lead to tension, dissonance and internal conflict. As a young teacher I really wanted to change the world and had to reconcile my idealism with the pragmatic reality of the job; although I still believe a truly great teacher changes lives.

Understanding that teacher identity is influenced by both internal characteristics and external experiences (Pillen et al. 2013), and is both 'product and process' (Danaher et al. 2012), will enable you to appreciate that it is dynamic and not developed in isolation. Teacher identity is underpinned by confidence in who you are and how you see your teacher-self. Such conviction may not be a natural state for you, so step into the role of teacher as you put on your jacket and act confidently. Envisage how your perfect teacher in that perfect jacket looks, moves, talks, acts and responds. Take time to observe teachers you admire and note what defines them. With practice those gestures, posture, techniques and phrases will be part of you and a more secure teacher identity.

 REFLECT

An ability to clearly define your role, purpose and sense of teacher-self requires reflection. Consider the following.

- Does the environment within which you teach enable you to confidently explore your teacher identity?
- Have you felt conflict and/or tensions?
- Can you recognize the root cause(s)?
- Did you reconcile or resolve these conflicts and tensions?
- What enabled or prevented you from doing this?

Reflect on how the following situations could influence how you see your identity and consider whether they challenge/undermine or confirm/embed how you see yourself as a teacher.

- Meeting a new class at the beginning of the school year.
- Meeting the parents of a particularly challenging pupil for the first time.
- Meeting a school governor to discuss an aspect of the school.

New or unknown situations can make us more self-consciousness, and question our actions and attitude. Also, differing power dynamics may influence self-perception, and as a trainee or beginner teacher you may defer to a more experienced or knowledgeable other and so alter your own sense of identity in the process.

Self-efficacy

Your overall perceptions, beliefs, judgements and feelings are referred to as a *sense of self*, in which your teacher self or identity will be embedded. Questions such as: 'Are you an optimistic person? Do you like to be sociable? Have you got a particular strength?' will tell you something about yourself. However, this does not affect whether or not you will be outstanding. It is *self-efficacy*, a belief in your ability to succeed, that influences the levels of motivation, anxiety, effort, perseverance and resilience you apply to adverse situations; acting as an 'anxiety-buffer' (Bandura 1997). Consequently, teachers with higher levels of self-efficacy are generally more productive and more likely to adapt to the needs of diverse and challenging pupils (OECD 2009) and so influence their achievement.

Bandura (1977) identified concepts that enhance self-efficacy and thought it necessary to address one or more of them. Reflect on whether your experience of each has impacted on your sense of self-efficacy.

* *Performance accomplishments*: Has repeated success raised your mastery expectations or repeated failure lowered them, leading to avoidance behaviours?

* *Vicarious experience*: Has seeing others successfully perform an activity you perceived as threatening/impossible to achieve made you think you can do it with increased effort?

* *Verbal persuasion*: Has the suggestion from others that you can cope successfully with something that has previously overwhelmed you been successful?

* *Physiological factors*: Does your awareness of physiological arousal (e.g. blushing, sweating, increased heart rate) affect how you judge your anxiety and stress levels and either reduce or enhance performance?

A teacher's self-efficacy will influence their willingness to cope with change, embrace continuing professional development (CPD) and implement innovations, all of which can challenge and affect their teacher identity and philosophy.

Teaching philosophy

> *I cannot be a teacher without exposing who I am.*
>
> Paulo Freire, 1998

Your teaching philosophy is a means to promote professional growth as it requires you to, not only identify your values and beliefs, but articulate and contemplate how you deliver them in practice, so, in essence, as Freire (1998) states above, revealing your teacher-self (your belief, values, attitudes and philosophy) to those around you.

REFLECT

To develop your philosophy engage with the following questions and note down your responses to reflect upon as you work through this book.

How you see the learner and learning

- What does learning mean?
- How does a learner effectively learn?
- What are your beliefs about assessment?

Your understanding of teaching

- Do you encourage, for example, mastery, competency, learning, lifelong learning, creativity and critical thinking?
- What does an outstanding lesson look like? Why?
- What is your role as a teacher?

Your perception of an ideal pupil

- What does this tell you about your goals for your pupils?
- What outcomes of your teaching are reflected in pupils' knowledge, attainment and behaviour?

Experiences and/or theory that have informed your values and beliefs

- What learning and developmental theories and teaching strategies do you use?
- How are your values and beliefs realized in classroom activities?

Lifelong learning and self-development

- How important is professional and personal growth to you?
- What goals have you set for yourself and how will you reach them?
- How will you know when you become an outstanding teacher?

Your teacher identity shapes your teaching philosophy, and your teaching philosophy shapes your pedagogy that in turn determines the decisions you make in each teaching and learning context. The experiences you gain in the classroom and beyond will further refine your identity and philosophy; the cycle continues and is enhanced through a keen sense of self-awareness and critical reflection.

Remember, teaching is a journey and the development of professional identity and philosophy is an active and organic process, challenged and influenced by experiences, environment and those within it.

Teacher professionalism

Professionalism: The conduct, demeanour and standards that guide the work of professionals.

Evetts, 2006

Your understanding of teacher professionalism greatly influences your teacher identity. The term 'educational professional' gives prestige and status to the teacher and education policies make frequent reference to 'professional standards', 'professional development' and 'professional communities', and stress the need for professionalism; yet it is not so easy to pinpoint.

Professionalism can be seen as either *organizational* (based on structures and organizational success) or *occupational* (based on relationships and individual success) (Evetts 2009). An emphasis on one may create internal conflict as to how teachers see themselves, because a professional may be mismatched to their environment. For example, if a school's emphasis is on occupational professionalism and it promotes well-being over performance, but a teacher is concerned about external authorities such as Ofsted or government targets, they may believe the school will fail, which will reflect badly on them.

To further compound this lack of a clear-cut definition, teaching has changed dramatically over the last few decades. The late 1990s saw New Labour introduce a 'new professionalism', and the 'workforce remodelling' agenda. A decade later, Demos (2007) pressed for another *new professionalism* that sees teachers active in shaping and defining their own professionalism within their everyday lives. There is now increasing diversity within the profession, reflected in the range of routes available to enter teaching, such as School Direct, SCITT, Teach First, Troops for Teachers and higher level teaching assistants (HLTAs). The linear route into teaching and the traditional concept of the teacher has changed.

Regardless of these changes, the teaching profession holds a mandate based on the trust of the public and the government. Teachers who are competent and show integrity and dedication build this professional mandate. In this respect, the teaching profession is often referred to as a 'calling', and teachers have a significant responsibility to live up to this. Nevertheless, there are teachers who erode this trust and pay scant regard to the essence of professionalism. Such teachers are often 'unfortunate' enough to appear in tabloid headlines or 'gossip' magazines. I remember an article a few years ago about a male teacher supplementing his teacher salary as a stripper until he was 'spotted' and became a headline and an ex-teacher. There are numerous, less savoury or humorous, examples. Essentially, when joining this very noble profession, you must 'walk the talk'.

Knowing what, why, when and how to be that professional teacher is key, and developing your 'perfect jacket' will enable and affirm this.

 REFLECT

Consider how you might respond to this scenario.

A trainee teacher on school placement in a Year 6 class was finding a lively class difficult to manage as many pupils showed disinterest in the revision sessions she was told to teach. Despite her efforts to employ the school's behaviour management strategies she was finding this stressful. Over the weekend she reviewed the lesson content and planned a more creative approach using the outdoor environment based on problem-solving. She shared her lesson plans with her mentor but the response was that she must teach the school's pre-planned lessons as the school needed to reach the set target for Level 4 passes.

The above scenario illustrates a focus on organizational professionalism, driven by statistics rather than the well-being of the pupils and teacher. As a trainee teacher your own professionalism would require you to teach the required material, ensuring you do the very best job you can within the constraints dictated to you.

Teacher standards and professionalism

Teacher identity has undoubtedly been influenced by the introduction of the *Teachers' standards* (DfE 2012). Professionalism and standards have become intertwined, with a focus on measurement (Mahony and Hextall 2000). Arguably having such measurements will benefit the profession as they add to the homogeneity and assured level of competency within the body of teaching. Nevertheless, if the *Standards* are used to define professionalism this could potentially reduce a teacher's role to a series of practical skills of teaching, such as effective assessment and behaviour management. The teacher is then defined as merely a technician rather than a professional. Worryingly, a standard-driven perspective could also lead to 'nodding dog' syndrome. Here compliance and acceptance from teachers is sought rather than critiquing and questioning policy and curricula, and regarding critical reflection as a cornerstone of outstanding practice.

 REFLECT

Key competences are included in the *Teachers' standards* (DfE 2012) (www.gov.uk/government/uploads/system/uploads/attachment_data/file/301107/Teachers__Standards.pdf). Download the *Standards* and reflect on what it means to be an outstanding teacher.

- Is being a professional more than a list of skills to tick off from a prescribed set of standards?
- Could you attain outstandingness by solely working through these Standards?
- Do you think there are any gaps in the *Standards*?

Teacher characteristics

Whether the teacher is authoritarian, undisciplined, competent, incompetent, serious, irresponsible, involved, a lover of people and of life, cold, angry with the world, bureaucratic, excessively rational, or whatever else, he/she will not pass through the classroom without leaving his or her mark on the students.

Paulo Freire, 1998

As Freire indicates above, it is imperative you understand the influence your teacher-self has on those you teach. So let's widen the perspective of a *professional* and your teacher identity and deliberate the many characteristics of outstanding teachers. An outstanding teacher needs certain affective, cognitive and metacognitive characteristics. A significant factor that appears to be a predictor of teacher effectiveness is *personality*. Arif et al. (2012: 163) refer to the 'big five' personality traits needed for teacher effectiveness.

- *Conscientiousness*: dependable, hard-working, organized, self disciplined, persistent and responsible.
- *Emotional stability*: calm, secure, happy and unworried.
- *Agreeableness*: cooperative, warm, caring, good-natured, courteous and trusting.
- *Extraversion*: sociable, outgoing, talkative assertive and gregarious.
- *Openness to experience*: curious, intellectual, creative, cultured, artistic, sensitive, flexible and imaginative.

This list is not definitive. I might suggest that *extraversion* is a debatable trait, and would suggest *confidence* (either quietly or loudly confident, or both when needed) in its place. However, the list should encourage some self-awareness of and reflection on specific traits that effective teachers possess.

 REFLECT

Think about the characteristics listed and those of a memorable teacher, who may have helped forge your path into teaching. If you can think of more than one, what do these teachers have in common? Using Table 1.1, tick off those characteristics that made these teachers stand out. Then highlight or rate those that are the most important to you.

Table 1.1 Teacher characteristics.

Key feature	My memorable teacher features	My most important features
Purpose		
Enthusiasm and energy		
Wants to be with children and values their uniqueness		

Table 1.1 (continued)

Positive and encourages individuality		
Believes all children want to learn		
Makes learning joyous		
Holds high personal values and ethics		
Passion and desire to help children learn and grow		
Sense of calling		
Approaches to teaching		
Has mastery of knowledge and self-confidence		
Expectations are high, clear and consistent		
Promotes active pupil engagement		
Lesson structure maximizes learning for all		
Promotes critical thinking		
Personally accountable		
Creativity, flexibility and adaptability evident		
Provides challenge and support		
Plans for success		
Learning is interesting, of interest and motivating		
Relationships		
Communicates clearly and well		
Supportive and caring		
Reliable and dependable		
Actively listens		
Warm and friendly		
Uses humour to encourage rapport and engagement		
Helps children self-affirm		
Shows empathy		
Praise frequently given for a variety of purposes		

Table 1.1 (continued)

Motivates pupils through varied teaching approaches		
Shows mutual respect, trust and fairness; pupils know their teacher believes in and cares about them		

Source: Dunne et al. (2007); Sammons et al. (2008).

What does your response tell you about your core beliefs? For example, if you focused on characteristics from 'approaches to teaching' you may have a tendency to perceive assessment, target-setting and detailed lesson planning as your primary role. However, if most characteristics are from 'purpose' you may be focused on the role of education in society, and truly believe every child does matter. If 'relationships' received a greater weighting, you are likely to be child-centred in your approach, take time to really know your pupils and see teaching as truly vocational.

Demands on the teacher

The demands placed upon teachers are both constant and yet changing. For instance, in 2003 the 'Every Child Matters' initiative identified five desirable outcomes of education, which focused on being healthy, staying safe, enjoying and achieving, making a positive contribution and achieving economic well-being. Seven years later we saw the virtues of 'back to basics' being extolled by then education secretary Michael Gove. He instructed schools not to focus on 'peripheral' issues, such as children's moral, social and cultural development in the pursuit of academic excellence and economic benefit.

The teacher is often in a position of changing their approach, school policy and curriculum design to meet the national agendas. A focus on your core beliefs and forming a clear educational philosophy will sustain you through these shifts in culture. Revisit the sections on teaching philosophy and characteristics and identify what should be at the heart of teaching and education. Perhaps you may conclude, as Professor Richard Layard (2015) does, that a child's emotional health and happiness is far more important than achieving academic success. Meeting the demands of both economic and emotional well-being may not be as contradictory as first appears. The 'Broaden and Build' theory, by Fredrickson (2001), suggests emotional well-being should have cognitive advantages, such as greater open-mindedness and cognitive flexibility, and greater self-efficacy and motivation, linked to increased academic success. In addition, promoting potential economic well-being through increased attainment, as a byproduct of emotional well-being, sees higher levels of creativity and ability to tackle problems and challenges.

As illustrated in the Introduction's *trilogy of demands* (intellectual, physical and emotional) there will always be significant demands on the teacher. The challenge is how to manage them while defining and refining your own sense of teacher identity and professionalism.

REFLECT

- What are your main stressors?
- How has performance and accountability affected you?
- Identify those areas, within both personal and work life, that suffer due to time pressures.
- What are your fears or concerns in attaining and maintaining yourself as an outstanding teacher? Writing down your fears enables you to more pragmatically assess how you might best address them and whether or not you think them more distressing than they actually are.

Managing the demands

I believe that every human being has an innate desire for happiness and does not want to suffer. I also believe that the very purpose of life is to experience this happiness.

The Dalai Lama

If the Dali Lama is correct, and I hope this is true, your happiness and that of your pupils should be a core consideration. My equation is simple: *Happy teacher + happy pupils = happy parents + success*. However, the demands of teaching can undermine a sense of happiness as we focus on how to cope with them. It is the perception of how we balance our personal resources and the demands placed upon us which dictates whether these demands are doable challenges (resources and demands are equal) or stressors, triggering stress (demands exceed perceived resources). Recent surveys have revealed that stress levels are affecting the ability of teachers to perform successfully and many have considered giving up teaching due to workload; yet addressing teacher stress in the classroom remains a challenge. Teacher stress may be seen as an imbalance between demands at school and the resources teachers have for coping with them (Esteve 2000). Time pressures, in particular, can stifle creativity, reduce risk-taking and so suppress innovation and clarity of thought. Your personal well-being is core to coping with the demands. To illustrate the gravity of this I use the analogy of the oxygen mask. You must place your mask on firmly before attempting to tackle anything else. It's simple – if you don't save yourself, you can't save anyone else!

STRATEGIES FOR YOUR TEACHER TOOLKIT

Develop resilience and seek support

Although an individual's resilience is often seen as an inherent characteristic it can be developed and fostered through your own awareness, employing strategies and support provided by learning communities. Developing resilience will underpin being a great teacher. Your development is not linear. It will have its ups and down and there will be days when you want to curl up or throw the board writer in. It is your ability to cope through developing self-reflection and seeing the 'dips' as platforms to move forward and grow from that makes the difference.

 ACTIVITY

Try an online resilience test:

www.resiliencescale.com/your-resilience/test-your-resilience/true-resilience-scale-survey/true-resilience-scale-results/?eid=17395.

Shifting the onus from the individual teacher to their learning community can prevent a 'sink or swim' attitude as collegiate support and professional social networks will enable you to gain a fuller, and hopefully balanced, perspective on issues. Knowing when to enlist help comes from heightened self-awareness and the confidence to ask line managers, mentors and tutors for support.

Develop time awareness and ability to prioritize

Aim to do the 'basics' each week, define what the basics are (what is essential vs desirable) and list these to add clarity. If need be, reframe your priorities (list low-, medium- and high-priority) and ascertain what you need to focus on and what can wait. To support this you may want to shift your perception or revisit your teaching values and beliefs, and contemplate *measuring what you value and NOT valuing what you measure*. Use year planners, diaries and daily to-do lists to identify 'hot spots', for example coursework submissions, report writing or parents' evenings, and strategically plan your time.

Be aware of external pressures, such as Ofsted inspections or performance targets, but don't lose sight of the child; they are central to what you do; they are why you get up in the morning and why you're training to be a teacher. They're also why you are passionate about being an outstanding teacher who changes lives.

It is vital you develop the capacity of self-reflection and make time to do this (discussed in Chapter 10). Lack of teacher time and the day-to-day demands of teaching can impede your understanding of the underlying causes of stress. How often does a teacher feel like they are trying to fit a quart into pint pot (or metric equivalent)?

This then has the nasty habit of becoming self-perpetuating unless you identify the cause and break the cycle.

 ACTIVITY

Create a task list for the day and week and prioritize the activities. Evaluate how you use your time and consider how you can work smarter not harder. When do you feel most productive? Are there times in the day that can be better utilized?

Be proactive not reactive

Throughout my career I have always believed in proaotion rathor than rcaction; identify preventions rather than cures! (more in Chapter 9). By adopting such an approach, potential problems can be identified and solved before they arise, reducing the likelihood of stress developing.

Stress within the teaching profession has a negative impact on the health and well-being of teachers. Ongoing stress can create a sense of 'firefighting' as we flit frantically from one issue or task to another and never feel on top of the job. To prevent this, *knowing yourself* – your personality traits, your stress triggers and your calming strategies – is key.

Find and develop ways to feel empowered to be proactive and more self-aware. This sounds easy but in reality it takes time and your willingness to make it happen is crucial. Developing your sense of self-efficacy, well-being and confidence in your ability to manage stress and its effects will promote a healthy and effective classroom environment necessary for outstanding teaching and learning. Taking time to rest your mind and your body is vital. You will never *find* the time so you must *make* the time to do this.

REFLECT

Set up a reflective journal as this will increase your self-awareness and ability to foresee and prevent certain situations. Note down particularly stressful incidents or times as illustrated in Table 1.2. This approach will enable you to pinpoint patterns and specific stressors and more objectively identify strategies to prevent or cope with them. Models for reflection are discussed in Chapter 10.

Table 1.2 Recalling stressful incidents.

Date	Time	Incident	Response	Feelings

Mindfulness

The literature increasingly suggests *mindfulness* (described as paying attention to the present, on purpose, and without judgement) as a particularly helpful intervention for stress. Mindfulness has been linked to heightened activity in the prefrontal cortex, which regulates attention and emotion, including empathy and other pro-social emotions. As a result, mindfulness may make individuals less reactive to negative experiences and more likely to notice positive ones, as well as reducing emotional exhaustion and depersonalization (Gold et al. 2010).

A study based on the effects of teaching mindfulness-based stress reduction (MBSR) on primary school teachers showed improvement in anxiety, depression and stress as well as burnout. Teachers said of the course, 'The key ideas for me are being accepting and not judging'; 'It is very useful in times of crisis, like an invisible toolbox you can carry around with you'; 'Responding not reacting, it teaches us to take control'; 'It has been helpful for me to notice unhelpful thinking patterns and nipping them in the bud' (Gold et al. 2010).

If we approach emotions and attention skills as trainable, similar to skills such as music, mathematics or sports (Davidson and McEwen 2012), we may become more open to engaging in exercising and developing them. One of the first skills to learn is how to 'anchor' yourself in the present. The purpose of the exercise below is to avoid going into autopilot and to stay in the *now*, without flitting from past to future thoughts. We only have one life so we may as well be in the present.

ACTIVITY

Be in the moment! Take just two minutes and find somewhere comfortable. Close your eyes and bring your attention into your body, to physical sensations, such as your feet on the ground or the contact with the chair. Focus on the movement of your breath, the expansion of your ribcage and your breath in and out; don't try and change anything but see this breath as your 'anchor', your constant, the here and now. Your focus may move from the breath and thoughts will drift in and out. Aim to be non-judgemental and accept recognizing your thoughts as a first step in developing mindfulness.

Simply observing your breath and following it for a few moments can bring your attention to the now. It can remind us to make conscious choices, use our senses, be accepting and avoid slipping into habituated negative patterns. This technique can be used at any point throughout the day with you and your pupils to calm or to refocus attention.

Avoid autopilot

Being mindful means paying more attention to everyday activities. Recognize the moment you are in rather rushing through your day from one activity to the next. Be more mindful of activities you tend to do without focus, for example, brushing your teeth or eating your usual sandwich for lunch. Aim to slow down and focus on the moment, wake up from autopilot and use your senses.

So, how could this approach enhance your teaching? Reflect upon how often you are truly self-aware and mindful when you teach, especially subjects, specific lessons, strategies or routines you're familiar with. I used to wonder how I could read the class story while planning the next day, rehearsing for a meeting or compiling my shopping list. I certainly was not 'in the moment' and mindfully engaging my class; were they or I missing out? Both of us I feel. So, the message is clear – be proactive and don't lose yourself and the best part of a lesson as a result.

REFLECT

Choose a lesson or activity to 'observe' from the inside.

- Ask yourself if this is what you intended to do at specific points in the session.
- Observe whether or not you remain 'in the moment' throughout the whole session.
- At what points do you revert to autopilot, travel back to the past or forward to the future?

Consider small changes to break these routine habits and increase your focus on the now. Remember the breath is there to 'anchor' and remind you.

Further reading

Williams, M. and Penman, D. (2011) *Mindfulness: a practical guide to finding peace in a frantic world*. London: Piatkus. This guide offers very practical activities that build your understanding and ability to be mindful.

Emotional intelligence

Learning itself is an intrinsically emotional business.

Guy Claxton, 1999

As Claxton states, learning and cognition cannot be separated from emotions. If we reflect upon how well we learn, emotions play a significant role. They affect aspects such as enjoyment, enthusiasm, perseverance and retention. An outstanding teacher will optimally employ the emotional component of the teaching-learning experience to achieve outstanding lessons, which requires a high level of emotional intelligence (EI).

EI can be traced back to psychologist Edward Thorndike who, in 1920, believed that being able to 'act wisely in social relations' was a fundamental component of overall intelligence. In 1990, Yale psychologists Peter Salovey and John Mayer (1990) coined the term EI. Daniel Goleman (1996) then popularized EI in his bestseller *Emotional intelligence: why it can matter more than IQ*. Most importantly, Goleman considered EI not to be innate; instead he claimed it could be learned and developed.

He identified five key areas:

- *self-awareness*: recognizing feelings as they happen;
- *emotional control*: managing and controlling emotional reactions and impulses;
- *self-motivation*: using positive emotions to pursue goals;

- *empathy*: sensitivity to other people's feelings;
- *handling relationships*: using social skills such as leadership, teamwork and confidence in dealing with other people.

As a teacher, EI supports your ability to build relationships with pupils and adults. It will build key attributes, such as resilience and the ability to perceive, control and evaluate emotions, in oneself and others, which underpin professionalism.

Wong and Law (2002) used Mayer's EI dimensions (i.e. to assimilate feelings and to perceive, understand and manage emotions) as the basis for their scale (Wong and Law Emotional Intelligence Scale, WLEIS) (see Table 1.3), which can be used to assess EI. They found the people who scored highest were most likely to be satisfied with their jobs and those who performed the best used their EI in their work. Teaching is without doubt high in 'emotional labour' (one of the trilogy of demands).

Let's have a go . . .

 ACTIVITY

Table 1.3 WLEIS to assess EI.

	Score each statement 1–4 (4 being the highest)
1 Understand and express my own emotions	
I have a good sense of why I have certain feelings most of the time	
I have good understanding of my own emotions	
I really understand what I feel	
I always know whether or not I am happy	
2 Perceive and understand the emotions of others	
I always know my friends' emotions from their behaviour	
I am a good observer of others' emotions	
I am sensitive to the feelings and emotions of others	
I have good understanding of the emotions of people around me	
3 Regulate my own emotion	
I always set goals for myself and then try my best to achieve them	
I always tell myself I am a competent person	
I am a self-motivated person	
I would always encourage myself to try my best	

Table 1.3 (continued)

4 Use emotion to maximize performance	
I am able to control my temper and handle difficulties rationally	
I am quite capable of controlling my own emotions	
I can always calm down quickly when I am very angry	
I have good control of my own emotions	

Source: Wong and Law (2002); Whitbourne (2013).

Add up your score in each section of the table. The way you answered these questions can provide insight into your EI strengths and weaknesses.

- Were your strengths in reading yourself, or in reading others?
- Do you have the most difficulty regulating how you feel?
- Do you find it difficult to draw upon your emotional strength to achieve your best?
- How do your perceived EI strengths and weaknesses impact on you as a teacher?

For example, you may have greater strength in *social awareness* if you scored highly on understanding the emotions, needs, and concerns of others. You may be more adept at picking up emotional cues, feel comfortable socially, and recognize the power dynamics in your team or school.

To develop your EI is to be more aware of yourself. Our senses provide a wealth of information to our brain, however, when overwhelmed, instinct or habit will take over, limiting us to a flight, fight or freeze response. The amygdala (home to primitive feelings, such as fear) often responds before the neocortex (the site of more rational reactions) registers the situation. Thankfully the prefrontal cortex is there to mediate these emotional impulses generated by the amygdala and decide upon appropriate reactions (Hastings 2008). However, long-term stress may inhibit this ability. Learning to stay connected to the emotional and rational parts of your brain may enable you to draw upon emotional memory to reduce potential negative outcomes from instinctive or habituated responses. Take time to identify and understand the emotions you experience so that you can consciously channel your responses in positive ways. Negative emotions can affect relationships with others, so understanding your triggers can help you understand and control your responses.

However, reading your own emotions and having self-awareness can be a challenge, often when you need this skill the most. Time pressure, as experienced as a teacher, is immense; however, remind yourself to pause and take a step back. Ask yourself honestly how you feel and why, to gain insight into which emotions are influencing your behaviour. Developing an emotional toolbox (as simple as counting to 10) will provide you with choices and the ability to make appropriate decisions. Emotion regulation or self-management repeated regularly supports a more objective perspective, which will eventually become habituated and part of your teacher identity, giving you a greater sense of control.

Teaching with EI means planning for the emotional and physical experience of learners. This involves:

- dealing with pupils' expectations and being able to acknowledge and respond to their feelings;
- being self-aware, recognizing and handling your own feelings and showing them, as appropriate, to your pupils.

As a teacher it is important to note that the prefrontal cortex develops most rapidly between the ages of 3 and 8. Therefore using appropriate interventions and strategies to reduce stressors and increase coping abilities in your pupils is highly important. Moreover, efficacy of the prefrontal cortex is linked to working memory function and so will impact on learning, as discussed in Chapter 4.

 REFLECT – in the classroom

Identify the 'emotional temperature' of your classroom through reflecting upon the terms 'warm/supportive', 'cool/detached' and 'cold/antagonistic' (Pollard 2008). Take time to observe other teachers and use the terms to assess the 'emotional temperature' of their classrooms. As you observe consider the following questions:

- What does the teacher do and say which establishes the 'temperature' of the classroom?
- Is the temperature constant or does it change in the course of a lesson?
- If there are changes, what causes them?
- How did you recognize a change?
- Is the temperature the same for all pupils?
- How do the pupils respond to changes in emotional temperature?

Arrange for your mentor and/or colleague to observe your lesson.

- How aware were you of changes in your classroom?
- Was this change deliberate? If yes, why did you implement the change? If no, what caused the change and how did you and the class/individual pupils respond?
- Was your emotional temperature the same working with different groups or individual pupils?

Discuss the lesson observation and reflect on how emotion affects learning in your classroom.

EI should be recognized as an essential component of what an outstanding teacher offers. How you communicate and interpret communication from others can be deeply influenced by your emotions. Two aspects to take note of are 1) nonverbal communication, such as gestures, posture, how fast or how loud you talk, proximity to others and eye contact (discussed in Chapter 9); and 2) listening skills and developing a dialogic approach when teaching (discussed in Chapter 5). Make deliberate, conscious use of both and embed this in your own pedagogy.

A thought . . . to develop your identity, philosophy and ability to meet the trilogy of demands teaching places upon you requires experience, knowledge, support and reflection. This happens over time and requires effort; to be an outstanding teacher there are no 'quick-fixes'.

References

Arif, M.I, Rashid, A., Tahira, S.S. and Akhter, M. (2012) Personality and teaching: an investigation into prospective teachers' personality, *International Journal of Humanities and Social Science*, 2(17), http://www.ijhssnet.com/journals.

Bandura, A. (1977) *Social learning theory*. Englewood Cliffs, NJ: Prentice-Hall.

Bandura, A. (1997) *Self-efficacy: the exercise of control*. New York: W.H. Freeman.

Claxton, G. (1999) *Wise up: the challenge of lifelong learning*. London: Bloomsbury.

Danaher, P.A., George-Walker, L.D., Henderson, R., Matthews, K.J., Midgley, W., Noble, K., Tyler, M.A. and Arden, C.H. (2012) *Constructing capacities: building capacities through learning and engagement*. Cambridge: Cambridge Scholars.

Davidson, R.J. and McEwen, B.S. (2012) Social influences on neuroplasticity: stress and interventions to promote well-being, *Nature Neuroscience*, 15: 689–95.

Demos, with Craig, J. and Fieschi, C. (2007) *DIY Professionalism, Futures of Teaching*, GTC http://www.demos.co.uk/files/DIY%20Professionalism.pdf.

DfE (2003) *Every Child Matters*. London: The Stationery Office.

DfE (2012) *Teachers' standards*, www.gov.uk/government/uploads/system/uploads/attachment_data/file/301107/Teachers__Standards.pdf.

Dunne, M., Humphreys, S., Sebba, J., Dyson, A., Gallannaugh, F. and Mujis, D. (2007) *Effective teaching and learning for pupils in low attaining groups*, research report. London: DCSF.

Esteve, J.M. (2000) The transformation of the teachers' role at the end of the twentieth century: new challenges for the future, *Educational Review*, 52(2): 197–207.

Evetts, J. (2006) Introduction: trust and professionalism, challenges and occupational changes, *Current Sociology*, 54(4): 515–31.

Evetts, J. (2009) The management of professionalism: a contemporary paradox, in S. Gewirtz, P. Mahony, I. Hextall, and A. Cribb (eds) *Changing teacher professionalism: international trends, challenges and ways forward*. London: Routledge.

Fredrickson, B.L. (2001) The role of positive emotions in positive psychology: the broaden-and-build theory of positive emotions, *American Psychologist*, 56(3): 218–26.

Freire, P. (1998) *Pedagogy of freedom*. Lanham, MD: Rowman & Littlefield.

Ginott, H.G. (1993) *Teacher and child: a book for parents and teacher*. New York: Collier Books.

Gold, E., Smith, A., Hopper, I., Herne, D., Tansey, G. and Hulland, C. (2010) Mindfulness-based stress reduction (MBSR) for primary school teachers, *Journal of Child & Family Studies*, 19: 184–9.

Goleman, D. (1996) *Emotional Intelligence: Why It Can Matter More Than IQ*. London: Bloomsbury.

Hastings, S. (2008) *Emotional Intelligence*, https://www.tes.com/article.aspx?storycode=2042477.

Layard, R. (2015) *Action for happiness*, www.actionforhappiness.org/why-happiness.

Mahony, P. and Hextall, I. (2000) *Reconstructing teaching: standards, performance and accountability*. London: Routledge.

Pillen, M.T., Den Broka, P.J. and Beijaarda, D. (2013) Profiles and change in beginning teachers' professional identity tensions, *Teaching and Teacher Education*, 34: 86–97.

Pollard, A. (ed.) (2008) *Reflective Teaching*, 3rd edn. London: Bloomsbury.

Salovey, P. and Mayer, J. (1990) Emotional intelligence, *Imagination, Cognition, and Personality*, 9(3): 185–211.

Sammons, P., Sylva, K., Melhuish, E., Siraj-Blatchford, I., Taggart, B., Barreau, S. and Grabbe, Y. (2008) *The influence of school and teaching quality on children's progress in primary school*. London: DCSF.

Whitbourne, S. (2013) *Unlock your emotional genius, how emotionally intelligent are you, and why should you care?* https://www.psychologytoday.com/blog/fulfillment-any-age/201302/unlock-your-emotional-genius.

Wong, C. and Law, K.S. (2002) The effects of leader and follower emotional intelligence on performance and attitude: an exploratory study, *The Leadership Quarterly*, 13(3): 243–74.

2

Knowing the child – child development

Every child deserves a champion – an adult who will never give up on them, who understands the power of connection and insists that they become the best that they can possibly be.

Rita Pierson, 2013

Our coat hook! Returning to the 'perfect jacket' you may, with enhanced understanding gained from this chapter, adjust your jacket so that it fits and feels better. Select a few essential items to put in certain pockets that are necessary for your journey. This will enable you to make informed decisions with a greater depth of knowledge and understanding, and take comfort in the knowledge that support is easily to hand.

This chapter focuses on knowing the child and building positive relationships with children. It emphasizes developing an understanding of child development and learning theory, and applying the theory to practice.

The key themes in this chapter prompt you to:

- recognize how your *teacher identity and philosophy* can influence your preference for and use of theory;
- understand how your perception of the *purpose of education* interacts with the way you see and interpret child development theory;
- appreciate how a focus on *well-being for you and your pupils* impacts on how you respond to the demands of the pupil and the curriculum;
- understand why your knowledge of theory better enables you to *meet the needs of the unique child*;
- consider how your awareness of *creating an enabling and empowering environment* reflects on how you respond to and cater for the needs of each individual pupil;

- identify how your own *self-awareness* and *critical self-reflection* can enhance your understanding of pupils and how to enable them to develop their potential;
- understand how a rounded knowledge of theory focuses your need for *continuous development as a lifelong learner*.

This chapter addresses the following *Teachers' standards* (DfE 2012):

2 Promote good progress and outcomes by pupils.
5 Adapt teaching to respond to the strengths and needs of all pupils.

The unique child

You need to see your pupils as individuals and be their champion, as Rita Pierson (2013) urges us to. A champion will defend, support and guard and so a good starting point to develop this is to refer to the Early Years Foundation Stage, which focuses on the unique child. It recognizes that children develop and learn in different ways, at different rates, and consequently need the right environment to meet their individual needs and so be the best they can be.

It is vital that you get to know each pupil, see them as unique, and build that essential rapport, trust and respect (and dare I say, love). This entails spending time with every pupil to find out how they are, what's happening at home, in school and with their friends. Your belief in them and ability to identify and nurture their potential ensures the focus is on their well-being and happiness, which underpins their success and yours.

All too often this uniqueness is lost as we inadvertently or deliberately merge and label children into groups (HA, AA or LA), or worse assign a number (before the removal of levels in 2014) – 'Sandra is a 2b but she really should be a 3a!' Children may be labelled early in their school careers, which may remain with them for years: 'Jimmie is a Circle, shame he'll never be a Hexagon!'

So, how can we prevent this loss of insight? We might be quite adept at seeing how good a learner is at a subject but do we know what motivates, engages or induces worry in each of them? This understanding is at the heart of developing their learning capabilities and helps to prevent labelling.

I like to think of some children as being like onions! (They smell and make you cry . . . no seriously . . .). Some have a seemingly tough, protective outer layer; manifesting itself as, for example, poor behaviour, over-enthusiasm, acting the classclown, being withdrawn, lack of work or social issues. Your role as a teacher is to sensitively peel back those layers and see what is underneath, so as to avoid labelling a child because of what is shown and perceived externally. The pupil may not enable or allow you to gain this knowledge if you have not established trust, respect and rapport. Develop these to gain a genuine insight into each pupil; know your onions!

Teacher-pupil relationships

It is the quality of the teacher-learner relationship that is crucial. More crucial, in fact, than what the teacher is teaching, how the teacher does it, of whom the teacher is trying to teach.

Thomas Gordon, 1974

The first task as a teacher, as Gordon (1974) empathically states, is to establish these crucial relationships with all pupils as they influence their academic, social, behavioural and emotional development and well-being (Hattie 2009). It also helps establish a secure and nurturing space, enabling your pupils to explore their learning environment confidently (Hamre and Pianta 2001). Research has identified that calm, caring teachers who display sensitivity to pupils' personal and learning needs and provide affection and stability (Ofsted 2009) are those whose pupils gain most from their learning (Pollard 2010). Arif et al. (2012) also note that pupils scored better marks in subjects taught by teachers they liked the most. Be aware that a pupil's previous negative relationships or their attachment history can influence future relationships as well as their achievement (McGrath and Bergen 2015). Clearly, gaining an understanding of how your pupils perceive the relationship they have with you is important.

CHECKLIST for pupil-teacher relationships

- Start with the basics; get to know your pupils' names and something about them as individuals. These initial steps can make a school placement or school year either successful or challenging.
- Find out about your pupils' interests through planning opportunities and activities at the beginning of a school year or placement. Asking them to design their own 'coat of arms', pen-picture or zig-zag book, bring in a favourite book or artefact to discuss, or interview one another and create a display with posters, including biographical information, portraits or illustrations, will provide an insight into your pupils.
- Show a genuine interest and warmth and be self-aware when you talk, gesture, respond and listen. Your pupils will always 'see' more than you think you reveal.

ACTIVITY

Without referring to a register, write down the names of the pupils in your class.

Do you know who's in their family, the subjects they like and don't like, their friends? Note in which order you have listed your pupils and which names you found easier to remember. What does the order tell you about which pupils are more memorable than others, and for what reasons? Do you know what motivates them; what sparks their interest; when they feel fearful or unsure; when they are most and least productive; when and why they employ work avoidance strategies (a lost or blunt pencil, the need for the loo, a lost book or an argument with group member)? Bear in mind some strategies are very sophisticated and honed over years, and can almost go unnoticed.

Write down two or three words associated with each pupil. Identify any patterns that might exist: for example, whether some of the words relate more to boys than girls, or to pupils from a particular socioeconomic background, ethnicity or religion. Some comments may be related to academic ability, physical attributes or behaviour.

What does this tell you about how you focus your attention and time? Does your list reflect your philosophy? For example, you may have focused on affective characteristics suggesting you are more child-centred and nurturing in your beliefs.

Getting to know your pupils: building trust, rapport and respect

Understanding the core elements of these all-important relationships is necessary. Carl Rogers (1902–87) identifies these requirements: 1) **congruence** (knowing yourself and ensuring you are genuine, honest, trustworthy and that verbal and nonverbal communication is authentic); 2) **empathy** (understanding differing points of view and relating to how others feel); and 3) **respect** (accepting others' beliefs despite differences) (Rogers 1959). Applying all three elements would result in accepting a person without negative judgement or, with *unconditional positive regard*.

Building trust: congruence

Trust is built through being a 'real person' and not presenting a front or facade (Rogers 1969). A teacher, with a clear sense of self, identity and philosophy, makes relationship-building stronger as the 'messages' given to pupils are consummate with being a professional and so are consistent. Pupils will know 'where they stand' and what to expect.

 CHECKLIST for building trust

- Maintaining congruence, between body language and verbal communication, is vital (more on nonverbal communication in Chapter 9). Avoid saying 'I'm really pleased you did well at your tournament over the weekend!' while marking a book and sipping lukewarm coffee, or an enthusiastic 'Well done Michaela!' with no affirmation from your eyes or body language and a glance at the time.
- Be honest, but appropriate and professional, with your emotions and avoid presenting a facade.

REFLECT – in the classroom

An empowering strategy is to ask someone to video you teaching. If you have a trusted colleague or in a paired placement, do this, then find a quiet moment to analyse your interactions with your pupils.

- Did your verbal and nonverbal responses match and how did the pupils respond?
- Were your responses authentic and genuine?
- Could you spot any mixed messages or contradictions in what you say and do?

Building rapport: empathy

Developing and maintaining a good rapport with pupils can affect their motivation and engagement with a subject or learning. I remember disliking history at secondary school. My relationship with the teacher was distant and cold and so the subject matter became dull and impersonal to me and I remember very little of the content. However, as Rogers (1967) recognized, if teachers understand a pupil's reaction and how the pupil thinks and learns, then the learning is increased. Developing empathy, a key element of EI, and seeing classroom relationships and lessons through the child's eyes will inform and empower you. I think outstanding teachers listen to their inner child. If you fear you have lost yours, take steps to reaffirm childlike qualities. You may not feel comfortable avoiding the 'cracks in the pavement for fear of the snakes' but try to notice little things and people you pass, be curious, smile and laugh readily, learn a new joke, play catch or eat Haribos. Your inner child will support your relationships and give you an added insight into the behaviour, feelings and interests of your pupils.

 CHECKLIST for building empathy

- With a new group or class of pupils make eye contact as much as possible. Smile (ignore the 'don't smile until Christmas' myth!) until they smile back at you, without seeming intimidating. These seconds of connection will pay dividends in building a good rapport with your class.
- Become an orator and tell them stories that they can relate to or that amuse them. My children constantly request stories from my childhood, usually the ones involving humour and a moral code. These stories make the adult's life accessible and real so the pupils can connect with the adult more readily and so build empathy.

- Continue to tap into your pupils' interests, and build that knowledge into lessons, questioning, displays, classroom 'chit-chat' and humour. In one of my classrooms I would always end the day with 'joke of the day' so pupils would leave with a smile on their faces.
- Plan for circle time and opportunities for debate and discussion, using literature that develops a sense of empathy while acknowledging that people have differing views and feelings.

These approaches help convey the message that 'I care about who you are, what you do and how you feel'.

Building positive relationships and trust takes time. Your pupils need to trust that you will always do what you say, are fair and make informed and balanced decisions. If a pupil has a tough outer layer (that onion!), make time to gently and sensitively peel it away, without making them feel exposed.

REFLECT

- Do you have the ability to see the world through your pupils' eyes?
- Do you have a joie de vivre and awareness of how you communicate this to your pupils?
- How often and on what occasions do you use humour?
- Do you use well-formed questions that promote interaction and discussion?
- Do you know which 'buttons' to press, and when, for each pupil?

Building respect

The old adage 'respect is for those who deserve or earn it, not for those who demand it' is very true. A respectful teacher accepts the pupil for who they are and not for what the teacher wants them to be. Be aware of stereotypes or expectations that you may have which can affect how you view a pupil and prevent an authentic relationship developing.

CHECKLIST for building respect

- Be consistent, as this is, without doubt, a cornerstone for developing positive relationships. Inconsistency will undermine those relationships you may be working so hard to build. Children will very quickly let you know if you are not consistent. The classic 'That's not fair', and behaviour issues or lack of engagement can be a result of your inconsistency.
- Develop the right classroom culture through whole-class activities, such as circle time, which is a great way to achieve this. This addresses issues that can undermine acceptance and understanding of others and builds a cooperative and connected classroom.

- Demonstrate you are a role model of respect to help establish and build a classroom ethos of understanding and tolerance, which is paramount in today's society.

Further reading

Mosley, J. (1996) *Quality circle time*. Cambridge: LDA.

REFLECT

- How does good classroom management promote respect?
- Identify when and why you are not consistent.
- What effect does inconsistency have on your pupils?

ACTIVITY

Diary-keeping is an effective way to monitor and add perspective to your feelings about classroom relationships. It enables you to reflect on how things have gone and how you felt. It is common for such reflections to focus on specific behaviour issues or interactions with challenging pupils, so aim to keep focused. Ensure your diary is written professionally, mindful of ethical issues. Earmark specific blocks of time to keep a diary and then take time to read and reflect upon it objectively. Consider how this information can enhance your pupil-teacher relationships. This will give you greater awareness of particular issues, and facilitate critical analysis through tangible data. Discuss the issues you identify with a colleague to further your understanding.

Building strong and positive relationships will give you a deeper understanding of the many facets of the child and how these influence their development.

Understanding child development

An understanding of child development is essential for any teacher to fully appreciate the complexity of development from birth into early adulthood. A newborn baby enters the world with limited skills and abilities but as they grow they develop physically, cognitively, spiritually, morally, socially, emotionally, sexually and culturally.

As children grow they absorb information and learn to apply it, communicating verbally and nonverbally. They learn to interact, play and live with other people, such as family, friends and teachers, and recognize the difference between right and wrong. They begin to understand and appreciate there are different cultures within their communities and school. They form a gender identity and as they enter puberty they learn how their bodies work sexually. Some children may not grow within the expected parameters of development due to certain barriers. These can be *external* factors: those related to the community, family, previous and current school experience and peers (e.g. economic deprivation, family conflict, neglect or abuse, English as an additional language or high rate of mobility); and *internal*: those related to biological and psychological factors (for example special educational needs and disability – SEND – issues, illness, mental health or lack of nutrition).

A thorough and critical grasp of developmental theory underpins outstanding practice; it helps you to confidently explain, understand, predict and support pupils' responses that you observe and guides your formal and informal decision-making.

Some key developmental theories

Some theorists, especially those prior to our understanding of neuroscience, considered children's development to be dependent upon biological maturation. It was thought that the brain connections formed between nerve cells within what was termed a '*critical period*' or 'window of opportunity' during the first few years of life. For instance, it was argued that this critical period accounted for babies' and toddlers' brains being more receptive to language acquisition than older children's brains as this critical period has passed.

Advances in neuroscience have shown this to be a 'neuromyth'. Nevertheless, there may still be a '*sensitive period*', as Bornstein (1987) identifies, when a child can more readily acquire new skills. For example, learning a language appears relatively easy for children but becomes more difficult, although not impossible, for an adult.

Child development is rich, varied and enormously complex so you should not expect any single theory of development to do justice to this nebulous field. A more eclectic and analytical approach, whereby you gain an understanding of key theories and critically evaluate them will further your understanding of pupils' learning and developmental needs. Children's development doesn't happen uniformly. Keep this lack of developmental *sameness* in mind as you read this section.

Remember, theory informs how you interpret your observations, which detect patterns and specific behaviours as your knowledge of each unique child develops.

Table 2.1 provides an insight into some of the most influential theories. Each of the 'grand theories' of child development has considered the extent to which a child's development reflects maturation of individual genetic endowment (nature) and/or the environment in which their development takes place (nurture). However, it is not as simplistic as that: a collection of systems influence development and no one element dictates a child's developmental outcome.

Psychosexual theory

Sigmund Freud's (1856–1939) psychoanalytic child development theory stressed the *importance of childhood events and experiences*. He suggested that there are

Table 2.1 Summary of theories.

Sigmund Freud Erik Erikson	Psycho-sexual *Psychodynamic Psychosocial*	Behaviour is controlled by unconscious urges A series of stages of emotional and psychological development occurs
Ivan Pavlov B.F. Skinner	Behaviourist *Classical conditioning Operant conditioning*	Development and learning are attributed to environmental influences (nurture) and based upon stimulus (S) and response (R)
Albert Bandura	Social learning theory	A relationship is seen between environment, the learner's behaviour and cognitive development
Jean Piaget Lev Vygotsky Jerome Bruner	Constructivism and social constructivism *Cognitive theory Sociocultural theory*	Levels of intelligence or thought processes develop gradually through pupils' active involvement
John Bowlby Mary Ainsworth	Attachment theory	The nature of the attachment between baby and main carer affects behaviour
Abraham Maslow Carl Rogers John Dewey	Humanist theory *Progressive education*	Sees the uniqueness of individuals through the eyes of the observer, as well as through the person behaving
Noam Chomsky Howard Gardner	Nativist theory Information-processing theory Multiple intelligences	Intelligence is seen beyond narrow cognitive ability A belief in innate learning abilities
Reuven Feuerstein	Cognitive modifiability	Viewed human potential as having almost no limits.

three main structures to personality, which are the *id*, the *ego* and the *superego*. The id, present at birth, consists of impulses, emotions and desires, and demands instant gratification. Since this is unsustainable, the ego develops which mediates between reality and the desires of the id. The superego then develops to give a sense of responsibility and could be seen as our conscience.

Erik Erikson's (1902–94) psychosocial development theory (1963) proposed *psychosocial stages of emotional and psychological development that lasts a life-span and focuses on conflict and resolutions.* He considered the outcome, be it positive or negative, of each stage to be determined by the environment, nurturing, or experiences. Erikson's eight stages are:

- trust versus mistrust;
- autonomy versus shame and doubt;
- initiative versus guilt;
- industry versus inferiority;
- identity versus identity confusion;
- intimacy versus isolation;
- generativity versus stagnation; and
- integrity versus despair.

The *initiative versus guilt stage* (ages 3 to 6 years) sees a child developing initiative. If they continue to develop their self-concept they will have the confidence to try out and learn new things while gaining a sense of responsibility. The effective approach of plan-do-review, used in many schools, positively reinforces development through this stage. However, during this stage the child may develop a feeling of guilt if told 'no' continuously.

During the next stage, *industry versus inferiority* (ages 6 to 12), children will begin to be industrious, learn necessary skills and work towards their future careers and lives. Children within positive, nurturing environments will navigate their way through this stage with positive outcomes, while those receiving negative messages may become disaffected and develop low self-esteem.

As a teacher, be aware of the various stages, acknowledge each and aim to create a balance between opposing dispositions.

Some key teaching ideas from psychosexual theory are:

- be nurturing and responsive to the needs of young children so feelings of trust are established;
- encourage autonomy through an environment that promotes independence;
- allow exploration and self-expression and avoid unnecessary punishment or over-restriction;
- be aware of over-using 'no' and producing feelings of guilt, shame and inferiority.

Behaviourist theory

Development and learning from the behavioural perspective are attributed to environmental influences (nurture) and are based upon stimulus (S) and response (R). Teachers applying this theory would relate any difficulties a pupil has as being environmental and emphasize isolated skills, rote learning, teacher-directed and teacher-reinforced activities.

Ivan Petrovich Pavlov's (1849–36) *classical conditioning* saw behaviour *could be elicited by a neutral (unstimulating) stimulus because of its learned association with a more powerful stimulus*. This only applies to physiological reflex action and emotional reactions. For example, when food was presented to dogs at the same time a bell sounded, the bell would eventually cause a salivation response when presented on its own. Indeed, when I was a child my mother used a bell to signify a meal was ready, and sure enough, my brother and I would salivate at the sound! (I'm sure he still does!) Similarly, a child may quickly associate a certain stimulus with a response. The thought of going to the doctor or the dentist may induce fear if previous visits resulted in pain. Children may be fearful of school or particular subjects as a result of negative experiences.

Burrhus Frederic Skinner's (1904–90) *operant conditioning* highlighted the influence of environment upon a child's development rather than seeing the child as passive. His research, with rats, drew conclusions based upon his observations of continuous and intermittent reinforcement and identified the latter as more effective. Within the classroom, praise and rewards that are more judiciously given have a greater outcome than if continuously used. Skinner's contribution to education includes behaviour modification and programmed learning, both requiring correct responses.

Some key teaching ideas from behaviourist theory are:

- use positive feedback and other rewards to influence children's behaviour;
- create positive learning experiences for each pupil so a positive association is made with school.

Social learning theory

Albert Bandura (1925–) explains how *new behaviour is learnt through observing others*. Unlike the behavioural theories above, Bandura believed that both extrinsic and intrinsic reinforcement enabled learning. By observing the actions of others, including parents, peers and celebrities, children develop new skills and acquire new information. During the 1960s Bandura carried out the controversial Bobo Doll experiments proving that a child's particular aggressive behaviour might be reinforced vicariously. Through observing others a child may adjust their own behavioural limits based on perceived reinforcement.

Modern neuroscience has shed light on this theory and shown that neurons mirror the actions made by others (so-called mirror neurons) so when we observe others carrying out actions, some of the same cortical areas are activated as if we are carrying out the actions ourselves (Howard-Jones 2014). This process informs how a teacher's action influences a pupil's learning and supports their level of rapport.

A key teaching idea from social learning theory is:

- be highly aware of your influence as a role model and how your mood or teaching style can trigger or influence certain behaviour.

Constructivism and social constructivism

Constructivism emphasizes how children's thinking and reasoning change and how they actively contribute to their cognitive development by constructing their own understanding of the world.

Jean Piaget (1896–1980) proposed a *stage theory of cognitive development recognizing a child's active role in gaining knowledge.* He considered children as 'little scientists' who are active agents constructing their knowledge. He identified stages they pass through: the sensorimotor of infancy, the preoperational of early childhood, the concrete operations of middle childhood, and the formal operations of adolescence and beyond.

Piaget theorized that children learn by using existing knowledge to tackle new information (*assimilation*), which adds to and/or changes (*accommodation*) their prior understanding and knowledge (*schemas*). Schemata are cognitive frameworks or concepts that help people organize and interpret information, like index cards from which the child retrieves information. For example, my toddler would refer to certain animals as 'goat' as he experienced a goat on a farm trip, so for him he believed that all furry animals of a certain size with four legs were goats. On assimilating new information his schema for animals changed and over time he named other animals correctly.

Social constructivism focuses on how culture is transmitted through language and social interaction. From this perspective, knowledge is actively and socially constructed through interactions with others.

Lev Semenovich Vygotsky (1896–1934) suggested that *social interactions and the environment were responsible for a child's development.* He focused on the notion that children internalize feelings, emotions, ideas and language through social interactions. He saw children's '*intermental*' experience (based on social interaction) as shaping their '*intramental*' activity (based internally; the ways they think as individuals). Consequently, higher-order thinking skills are accessed more readily and developed through social interactions.

Vygotsky's proposed two key concepts were 1) the more knowledgeable other (MKO): anyone who has a better understanding or is more able than the learner; and 2) the zone of proximal development (ZPD), an area in which the child can most benefit from instruction with the help, or scaffolding, from the MKO, so extending the learning beyond the level of which they are independently capable. The teacher therefore becomes a facilitator and the learning process a reciprocal experience.

Jerome Bruner (1915–) emphasized the *connection between language and thought or the notion of instrumental conceptualization.* He viewed children as active participants in making sense of their world and, like Vygotsky, regarded cognitive development as a social process. He promoted the idea of discovery learning, the 'active search for meaning', where the environment provides the answers but the child makes the connections. Bruner was the first to apply the term 'scaffolding' to an educational context, seeing it as instructional support, often through dialogue and developing understanding. As the child acquires mastery of a task, the scaffolding can be removed. Hence he constructed the 'spiral' curriculum, enabling the learner to apply their own inquisitiveness and intuition to grasp basic concepts at an early age.

Key teaching ideas from constructivism and social constructivism are:

- consider how you can facilitate learning by providing ample opportunities to explore and by monitoring children to keep them safe;
- consider developmental needs rather than chronological age;
- begin from the concrete experiences and move towards the more abstract when meeting new concepts;
- take time to identify a pupil's ZPD;
- provide interesting experiences, ask questions, and pose challenges to actively solve problems, construct understandings through making connections and scaffolding their learning when a pupil is working in the ZPD;
- ascertain if your pupils have the relevant experiences or background knowledge to relate to your lesson.

Attachment theory

The most notable theorists linked with social development are John Bowlby and Mary Ainsworth.

John Bowlby (1907–90) believed that *early relationships with caregivers play a major role in child development and continue to influence social relationships throughout life.* He drew upon Freud's work whereby the mother acted as the infant's ego and superego and believed that children are born with a variety of behaviours that encourage parents and others to be near to them. These early proximity-seeking behaviours include laughing, gurgling and crying, as well as clinging and sucking. He concluded that the child strives to preserve the familiar and reduce their stress by developing these attachments to carers and 'home' settings. He claimed a well-loved, secure child may protest at separation from parents but will later develop more self-reliance.

Mary Ainsworth (1913–99) built upon Bowlby's theory and *experimented to test the nature of the attachment relationship between mother and child.* Ainsworth discovered that there are patterns of attachment that differ in degree of security and devised a test, the 'strange situation', to determine whether a child was *securely* or *insecurely* attached, *ambivalent* or *avoidant* of the parent. Securely attached infants cried less and seemed content to explore in the presence of their mother, and this correlated with great maternal sensitivity. Insecurely attached infants cried frequently, even when held, and explored very little. Ambivalent and avoidant attachments result in the mother being shunned, ignored or kicked and hit upon their reunion.

Key teaching ideas from attachment theory are:

- consider the pupil's background and how attachment to the caregivers affects them;

- identify how your understanding of secure attachment can support your relationships with pupils in the classroom;
- develop your classroom environment so that it is not inducing stress of the unfamiliar and feelings of insecurity – introducing known artefacts and systems will support a child's secure attachment.

Humanist theory

Abraham Maslow's (1908–70) approach focuses on the *individual's own subjective experiences, motives and desires presented as a hierarchy of needs*. Humanists argue that individuals have free will and are motivated to fulfil their potential, which Maslow referred to as self-actualization. The drive for self-actualization is not restricted to childhood but is present across the lifespan.

Maslow's hierarchy of needs is based on two groupings: *deficiency needs* and *growth needs*. Within the deficiency needs, each need must be met before moving to the next higher level. Once each of these needs has been satisfied, if a deficiency is detected, the individual will act to remove the deficiency. These are:

1   Physiological: hunger, thirst, bodily comforts, etc.
2   Safety/security: out of danger.
3   Belongingness and love: affiliate with others, be accepted.
4   Esteem: to achieve, be competent, gain approval and recognition.

Maslow's growth needs are:

5   Cognitive: to know, to understand, and explore.
6   Aesthetic: symmetry, order and beauty.
7   Self-actualization: to find self-fulfilment and realize one's potential.

Self-actualized people are characterized by: 1) being problem-focused; 2) incorporating an ongoing freshness of appreciation of life; 3) a concern about personal growth; and 4) the ability to have 'peak experiences'.

John Dewey's (1859–1952) *progressive education emphasized the need for active learning and a hands-on, discovery approach* (1897). Dewey felt that both teachers and pupils must learn together and the classroom environment should be democratic, with equal voice evident. Dewey identified the child as developing both the context and the framework to process information. However, if aspects of the curriculum and the child are not navigated well, with real connections made or links to prior knowledge, the child will simply be accumulating and reciting facts and not learning at a deeper level.

Key teaching ideas from humanist theory include:

- ensure that basics needs are met before attempting to meet higher ones;
- be aware of how home and school affects the different stages within Maslow's pyramid;

- review the timetabling of your teaching day – when those tummies rumble before lunch, or tiredness at end of the day – and address these deficiency needs;
- be aware of those pupils who are at risk, neglected, or have unstable home lives;
- consider ways to actively promote pupil voice and ownership of their learning.

Information processing or nativist theory

Noam Chomsky (1928–) focused on *biological dispositions, brain development and cognitive readiness suggesting that language is an inherent human quality and that children are born to acquire language.* He claimed that the important thing about language is its creativity. He considered firstly that mental function can be understood; and secondly, that the learner is an information processor. A young child will invariably add 'ed' to a word to make past tense. I often hear 'mummy I maked' or 'I winned!'; I'm forever gently correcting my boys, but marvel at their ability to connect and make patterns. This is not copying language but seeking to make sense of it and identifying rules.

Key teaching ideas from nativist theory include:

- be tuned into readiness and recognize the children who are striving to create patterns and make sense of the complexity of language;
- encourage discovery, pattern making and generalizations and unpack these with pupils.

Cognitive modifiability

Reuven Feuerstein (1921–2014) *viewed human potential as having almost no limits while recognizing that certain barriers may block a child's development.* He rejected the idea that intelligence is fixed and the view that 'present performance indicates potential'. This led to *structural cognitive modifiability* (SCM) and *mediated learning experience* (MLE) theory. He defined intelligence as 'the capacity of the individual to use previous experience to adapt to new situations'. This does not sound particularly ground-breaking and is akin to Piaget's notion of schemas. However, Feuerstein stated that traditionally regarded barriers critical periods, severity of condition and etiology (the causes of disease) to change could be overcome using cognitive modifiability interventions as the brain has plasticity. He coined the rather catchy phrase 'believe to achieve' and believed that all children can learn at any age.

Key teaching ideas from cognitive modifiability theory include:

- break glass ceilings that stop pupils achieving their potential and sign up to 'believe to achieve';
- avoid doing 'more of the same' and hoping for change; try different approaches and strategies;
- consider that behaviour shapes the nature of the brain, so develop the right behaviours.

Learning style theory

Learning styles have been under debate for a while. The popularity of identifying a particular child's learning preference was tempting for teachers and thought to potentially enhance practice. Presented below are two related theories, which, with a critical perspective, may help deepen your understanding of the learning process.

1 Multiple intelligences

Howard Gardner (1993), influenced by the work of Erikson and Bruner, *proposed the theory of multiple intelligences*. Traditional views of intelligence favoured particular cognitive processes, including certain types of problem solving (mathematical-logical intelligence) and language abilities (linguistic intelligence). Gardner moved beyond this narrow perspective and focused on how learners absorb information. He recognized that other intelligences – musical, visual-spatial, bodily kinaesthetic, interpersonal, and intrapersonal and naturalistic – must also be considered. Multiple intelligences theory has raised awareness in developing appropriate practices for pupils who do not fit the traditional view of intelligence and may not excel in the cognitive domains of maths or literacy.

 REFLECT

Use Table 2.2 to assess your strengths (1 weak to 10 strong) according to the different intelligences. How do your strengths and weaknesses reflect in your teaching, and your beliefs and values in education?

Table 2.2 Gardner's multiple intelligences.

Mathe-matical-logical	Linguistic-verbal	Musical-rhythmic	Visual-spatial	Bodily kinaes-thetic	Interper-sonal	Intraper-sonal	Natural-istic

2 Learning styles model and experiential learning theory (ELT)

David Kolb (1984) *identified learning as a cycle, which emphasized the internal cognitive processing of learning*. His learning theory identifies four stages of learning, namely *experiences, reflective observation, conceptualization* and action or *active experimentation*. The learner is engaged through their experiences that provide the basis for reflection. This is then assimilated into abstract concepts, which can be acted upon, thereby creating new experiences.

He viewed these four elements of learning as continuums forming two axes. The first, the x axis, is the processing continuum (a task is approached through *doing* and *watching*; grasping the experience), and the *y* axis is the perception continuum (how a learner *thinks* and *feels* about the experience).

 ACTIVITY

Mark your position on the axes of learning depicted in Figure 2.1. How does this inform you of your preferred learning style and impact on how you teach?

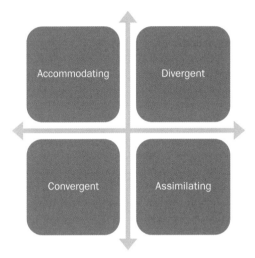

Figure 2.1 Kolb's Axes of Learning.

Kolb identified each quadrant as diverging (*feel and watch*); assimilating (*think and watch*); converging (*think and do*); or accommodating (*feel and do*). A divergent learner may, for example, prefer to watch rather than do and will gather information and use imagination to problem solve. On the other hand learners with an accommodating learning style prefer an experiential approach and enjoy working in teams to complete a task.

 REFLECT

Knowing every pupil and understanding their preference helps you meet their needs – therefore consider:

- How will this insight into learning style theory support your planning and delivery of an outstanding lesson?
- How might this influence how you group pupils?
- Will this awareness enable you to plan more effective scaffolding and stimulating pupil participation?

Learning styles discussion

Keenness to 'label' and 'prescribe' pupils has resulted in the sometimes narrow or extreme use of learning styles in classrooms. Proponents of the visual, auditory and kinaesthetic (VAK) style, for example, see it uncritically advocated as an essential component of classroom learning. There is evidence however that there are no benefits to learners from presenting information in their preferred learning style (Howard-Jones 2014). Moreover, it is important not to label primary age pupils or for them to believe that their lack of success is due to their learning style (EEF 2015).

So, you *could* ignore the idea of learning styles altogether. *However*, if the basic tenets of Gardner's and Kolb's theories are correct, this theory supports the assertion that everyone sees the world differently with their own disposition to learning. Go into any Early Years environment and you cannot fail to notice the evidence of Gardner's learning styles or Kolb's learner preferences being accommodated within a play-based curriculum. Children will be actively engaged using all their senses to learn – looking, handling, exploring artefacts, textures and sounds, listening to others, working in different groupings or independently, and using self-talk to refine their thinking. A multi-sensory approach that presents information in varied and imaginative ways, such as images, movement, auditory experience, physical explorations or concrete experiences, will engage all learners. Therefore, it is helpful to understand the content of the different learning styles frameworks discussed here when planning to meet the needs of all pupils of all ages.

Theory and practice

Let's use an example to help clarify the connection between theory and practice.

 REFLECT

Imagine that you observed the following.

Marcus is sitting at a table working on a group project. Fatima looks over at Marcus and tells him he's doing it wrong. He starts scribbling over his work and when the others object he jumps up and knocks his chair over and cries out 'Whatever!' He screws up his work and throws it across the room. Before his teacher can reach the table, he pushes Fatima as he storms past her.

Think about the multiple theoretical perspectives that can be used to interpret Marcus' behaviour.

Each theory used to interpret Marcus' behaviour will lead to a different way to address or resolve this situation. For example:

1   A teacher informed by *psychosocial theory* might conclude that Marcus is struggling with the conflict of industry versus inferiority. He is demonstrating

his application and development of skills in undertaking the activity but is experiencing conflict with respect to his ability and self-esteem. This teacher might decide to help Marcus to learn strategies for developing his self-confidence when working with others and his resilience in the face of criticism or challenge.

2   A teacher reflecting *social learning theory* may consider that Marcus has learned this response from observing models in his environment. He is imitating an observed behaviour, which in this case is aggressive. This teacher will most likely actively model non-aggressive strategies for solving problems and may focus on developing his EI and social interaction through role play, circle time, literature and discussion.

3   A teacher focusing on *cognitive developmental theory* may consider that Marcus has constructed from his past experiences a schema that involves solving problems through avoiding failure and/or becoming aggressive. This teacher might provide concrete experiences in which non-aggressive solutions are highlighted and discussed and resilience and self-esteem developed to cope in uncomfortable situations, thereby enabling him to accommodate and so change his schema for solving problems. The teacher may also reflect upon his ZPD and ensure they scaffold the learning to enable success.

4   A teacher focusing on *learning styles theory* based upon Kolb's convergent learner may consider that Marcus is uncomfortable in independent group tasks and prefers to work in a more structured and supported way. The teacher may scaffold the process, employ greater use of modelling, and clearly delineate tasks within the group, matched to skills and preferences.

The theories identified above may not address Marcus's issues and it may take multiple attempts to find the root cause of the problem. Liken this to troubleshooting an electrical circuit; you have to know at the outset what the potential problem may be, then systematically test each component part until the problem is found. It can then be resolved. The theories shed light on why a pupil exhibits certain behaviour and provide a greater understanding when analysing how to implement change. Without an understanding of theory it is unlikely that your pedagogy will be as effective and your decisions as informed.

 ACTIVITY

Identify three to five pupils in your class and create a table as shown in Table 2.3. Against the pupils' names reflect upon and pinpoint which theories help inform how you respond to and teach each pupil. In the third column, note down key observations and describe how you interact with, plan for, resource, support, nurture, extend and so on based upon that theory.

Table 2.3 Reflection on theory.

Sanjay	Attachment theory	He is reluctant to leave his mother and takes half the morning to settle. He becomes anxious as the end of the day nears and begins crying again	Ensure he is met by myself every morning and given a distracting/ settling task to do. Develop a home-school relationship to ensure communication is consistent and strong
Jessica	Sociocultural theory	Will not stretch herself without adult support. Finishes work quickly and generally accu- rately	Enable her to tackle more challenging tasks with strategic adult intervention. Build self-esteem on successes

Theory and self-reflection

You must be willing to use critical self-reflection and examine your educational philosophy, core beliefs and practices in relation to the theory. Outstanding teachers are reflective practitioners who know the importance of examining their professional beliefs and practices so that they are visible to both themselves and others (Rinaldi 2001). If you were unable to express your philosophy of education, devote time to reflect upon your beliefs and values (see Chapter 1). Ask yourself, 'How do I believe children learn and develop?'

 REFLECT

Take a moment to reflect on the different theories described in this chapter. Which theories resonate with you? Why?

A thought . . . No single theory can comprehensively explain the complexity of child development and learning; moreover, the aspects of child development are interrelated. For example, an infant's acquisition of a new motor skill enables them to explore their environment in different ways, which in turn affects their awareness, understanding and social interactions. Understanding the theory will enable you to take an eclectic and more analytical approach to understanding child development and its many factors, which either support or impede your pupils' development.

References

Arif, M.I., Rashid, A., Tahira, S.S. and Akhter, M. (2012) Personality and teaching: an investigation into prospective teachers' personality, *International Journal of Humanities and Social Science*, 2(17).

Bornstein, M.H. (1987) *Sensitive periods in development: interdisciplinary perspectives.* Hillsdale, NJ: Erlbaum.

Dewey, J. (1897) My pedagogic creed, *School Journal*, 54: 77–80.

DfE (2012) *Teachers' standards*, www.gov.uk/government/uploads/system/uploads/attachment_data/file/301107/Teachers__Standards.pdf.

EEF (Education Endowment Foundation) (2015) https://educationendowmentfoundation.org.uk/toolkit/toolkit-a-z.

Erikson, E.H. (1963) *Childhood and Society*, 2nd edn. New York: Norton.

Gardner, H. (1993) *Frames of mind: the theory of multiple intelligences*, 10th anniversary edn. New York: Basic Books.

Gordon, T. (1974) *Teacher effectiveness training*. New York: Peter H. Wyden Press.

Hamre, B.K. and Pianta, R.C. (2001) Early teacher–child relationships and the trajectory of children's school outcomes through eighth grade, *Child Development*, 72(2): 625–38.

Hattie, J. (2009) *Visible learning: a synthesis of over 800 meta-analyses relating to achievement*. London: Routledge.

Howard-Jones, P. (2014) *Neuroscience and education: a review of educational interventions and approaches informed by neuroscience: full report and executive summary*. Bristol: University of Bristol, EEF.

Kolb, D.A. (1984) *Experiential learning: experience as a source of learning and development*. Upper Saddle River, NJ: Prentice Hall.

McGrath, K.F. and Bergen, P.V. (2015) Who, when, why and to what end? Students at risk of negative student-teacher relationships and their outcomes, *Educational Research Review* 14: 1–17.

Ofsted (2009) *Twelve outstanding secondary schools - excelling against the odds*. London: Ofsted.

Pierson, R. (2013) *Every kid needs a champion*. www.youtube.com/watch?v=SFnMTHhKdkw.

Pollard, A. (ed.) (2010) *Professionalism and pedagogy: a contemporary opportunity. A commentary by TLRP and GTCE*. London: TLRP.

Rinaldi, C. (2001) Infant-toddler centers and preschools as places of culture, in *Project Zero and Reggio children. Making learning visible: children as individual and group learners*. Italy: Reggio Children.

Rogers, C. (1959) A theory of therapy, personality and interpersonal relationships in the client-centered framework, in S. Koch (ed.) *Psychology: a study of a science*, vol 3, *Formulations of the person and the social context*, pp. 184–256. New York: McGraw-Hill.

Rogers, C. (1967) *On becoming a person*. London: Constable & Robinson Ltd.

Rogers, C. (1969) *Freedom to learn: a view of what education might become*. Columbus, OH: Charles E. Merrill.

3

Knowing the curriculum – curriculum and subject knowledge

What we want is to see the child in pursuit of knowledge, and not knowledge in pursuit of the child.

George Bernard Shaw

 Our coat hook! You now need to get to know how functional your jacket is. It will become more than attire; it is developing as a resource that, hopefully, you increasingly value. You are now used to wearing your jacket, but does it fit well enough to wear all day, every day?

This chapter addresses curriculum and subject knowledge. It does not tell you how to teach each subject (there is already a plethora of resources available), but instead emphasizes the need for you to be highly competent and confident in the subject matter you teach and find that inner 'fire' to deliver outstanding lessons. To create lifelong learners your pupils should, as George Bernard Shaw succinctly states above, want to learn and actively pursue knowledge.

The key themes in this chapter prompt you to:

- recognize how your relative strengths and enthusiasm in each subject reflect *your teacher identity and philosophy*;
- consider how your *sense of purpose of education* reflects in your teaching of each curriculum subject;
- appreciate how a *focus on well-being for you and your pupils* reflects how you teach the curriculum subject content;
- understand how you develop your subject knowledge and how it influences your *ability to meet the needs of the unique child*;
- appreciate how confidence and enthusiasm in your teaching of each subject *creates an enabling and empowering environment*;

- recognize the extent of your *self-awareness* and *critical reflectiveness* when teaching each subject so your preferences and strengths do not adversely influence your pupils;
- identify areas of subject knowledge to support your *continuous lifelong development*.

This chapter addresses the following *Teachers' Standard* (DfE 2012):

3 Demonstrate good subject and curriculum knowledge.

The curriculum: changes and challenges

The curriculum is the difference between failure and success in education.
Siegfried Engelmann, 1992

Education should ideally reflect society and contribute to it, and therefore the vehicle to enable this is the curriculum, which should determine whether pupils' present and future needs are met. The effectiveness of this curriculum will inevitably, as Engelmann (1992) notes, lead to success or failure. Undeniably what is taught and learned should be worthwhile, however, with our diverse and rapidly changing world it is hard to pinpoint the worthy requirements of a curriculum.

Despite significant changes over the past few decades, primary schools still echo the nineteenth century utilitarian education designed 'for the masses' with the three Rs forming the basic curriculum. However, the basics have not always been seen as the answer to education. The Plowden Report (DES 1967) warned against 'educationally harmful practices' as 'at the heart of the educational process lies the child' (p. 7). The concept of child-centred learning (referred to as progressivism and liberal romanticism), which Plowden alludes to stems from the romantic ideologies of self, creativity, freedom and equality. These are noble and desirable educational aspirations, which theorists such as Rousseau and later Froebel and Dewey publically endorsed. However, this approach was much criticized and associated with a laissez-faire approach to teaching considered lacking in rigour or focus. This subject-centred vs child-centred debate remains today; as does the 'basics'-led curriculum.

Curriculum design

A national curriculum sets out what should be taught and aims to ensure each pupil receives the same standard of education, but the centrally controlled nature undoubtedly reflects and promotes certain values and priorities of those who construct it (Pollard 1996). Optimistically, the National Curriculum (from 2014) has given schools greater freedom in terms of planning and assessment and encourages them to respond to local agendas and needs.

Regardless, an effective curriculum should be the *sina que non* of an educational system and capable of delivering quality education to all (Engelmann 1992), essentially making it fit for purpose (Alexander 1992).

If we reflect upon our own conceptions of a curriculum it promotes our understanding of its purpose. Eisner and Vallance (1974) identify that a curriculum should:

- develop processes or skills, especially in the cognitive domain;

- exploit technology and technological approaches to maximize outputs;

- reform and revolutionize society to bring about greater justice and benefits for all;

- maximize the humanity of individuals by helping them develop their full potential;

- identify and deliver values, academic knowledge and intellectual development.

If we unpack that further and focus on our educational goal, which should be well 'educated' children, knowledge must lie at the heart of education. Take a moment to ponder Young and Muller's (2013) notion of knowledge. They distinguish between '*knowledge of the powerful*', the knowers of knowledge, and the educationally desirable '*powerful knowledge*', concerned with the intrinsic power of knowledge as an entitlement for each pupil. Teachers with great knowledge and respect for knowledge can accelerate the achievements of all pupils and avoid the *Matthew Effect*, whereby the gap between those with knowledge and skills and those without widens over time (Hirsch 2006). Consider this effect in pupils' reading ability: those with a wider vocabulary can access and understand more of the curriculum, are exposed to more interesting reading material and understand more complex spoken language. Inevitably the gap widens between these pupils and those with limited vocabulary who plod through uninspiring reading schemes, simplified worksheets or instructions. If knowledge is the power to close gaps we should, as Hirsch (2006) recommends, adopt a knowledge-oriented mode of schooling ensuring all pupils have equal access to it.

 CHECKLIST for curriculum design

Take the following principles into account to support more effective curriculum planning and delivery and avoid the Matthew Effect:

- learning is 'context based';
- the curriculum connects with pupils' experiences of home and community;
- mastery orientation is promoted;
- dialogue is promoted through group work and collaborative learning;
- pupils' existing understandings, prior knowledge and experiences are built upon;
- flexible learning occurs across the curriculum;
- teachers' subject knowledge and professional development is excellent.

Subject knowledge

If you can't explain it simply, you don't understand it well enough.

Albert Einstein

To be an outstanding teacher, knowing your subject matter is fundamental. A litmus test for us all, as Einstein ably states, is our ability to succinctly and coherently explain the information we hold. Depth of subject knowledge builds confidence and enables you and your pupils to engage more fully in learning. Subject knowledge has proved to be the most secure foundation for innovation, creativity and invention. Critical thinking skills require background knowledge and cannot be separated from it. Without background knowledge higher-order thinking skills would be harder to attain because analysis and problem-solving requires this level of embedded knowledge to facilitate deeper thinking.

However, this knowledge, imperative within education, is still understated. The *Teachers' standards* (DfE 2012) place teachers' first requirement to inspire, motivate and challenge pupils and the third as subject knowledge-based. This arguably emphasizes 'processes' (a teacher's range of skills and learning approaches) over subject knowledge. McCabe (2011), an expert who reviewed the National Curriculum, appears to agree, reflecting that when interviewing newly-qualified teachers, they talk about classroom processes rather than the subject they will teach. She considered that the quality of teaching starts with good subject knowledge. Likewise, Mitchell Chester, education commissioner for Massachusetts, USA (the highest performing US state in national tests) and Pilvi Torsti, State Secretary for the Minister of Education in Finland (European high performer in Pisa's tests) both agree subject knowledge is at the core of good teaching.

As a trainee teacher in England you are required to gain at least a Grade C in GCSE mathematics and English and pass the skills tests before you are accepted on an initial teacher-training course. However, this may not guarantee that you have sufficient subject knowledge for teaching the breadth of the curriculum. Without doubt pupils feel more confident with, and respect a teacher more, if they show they really know what they're talking about. There are no short cuts, you need to read and research because if you don't know the content in sufficient depth and fully understand the teaching sequences, you won't be able to plan for and respond to the varied needs in your classroom.

 REFLECT

Use the set of questions below for self-evaluation before you teach your next lesson.

- Do you sufficiently understand the subject content to explain it clearly to your pupils?
- Can you clearly identify and plan for the next steps in learning?
- Will you be able to use probing, effective questions that promote learning?
- Will you be able to answer more challenging/tangential questions?

Remember, you are the deciding factor in the classroom and have the power to influence all your pupils' learning. Without depth of understanding and appreciation of the curriculum you will disadvantage them.

Your subject knowledge audit

Gaining a depth of knowledge across the whole curriculum is a prerequisite for all teachers. However, this requires both time and effort to gain sufficient confidence and mastery so that your 'powerful knowledge' enhances pupil achievement. Below is a brief summary of the 2014 National Curriculum, which offers just a taster of the knowledge you must acquire and acts as a platform, or memory jogger, to support your own subject audit shown in Table 3.1.

Maths, for example, requires pupils to learn their 12 times table by the age of 9. Basic fractions, such as half or a quarter, are taught to 5-year-olds. By the end of Year 2, pupils should know the number bonds to 20 and be precise in using and understanding place value.

English, for example, expects pupils between the ages of 11 and 14 to have studied two of Shakespeare's plays. Word lists for 8- and 9-year-olds include complex words such as 'medicine' and 'knowledge', and by 10 and 11 pupils should be able to spell 'accommodate' and 'rhythm'.

Science emphasizes hard facts and 'scientific knowledge'. In Key Stage 2, for example, knowledge of the solar system, speed and evolution is included; Key Stage 3 includes climate change and a clearer delineation of physics, biology and chemistry.

Computing aims to teach pupils how to, for example, write code and 5- to 7-year-olds are expected to 'understand what algorithms are' and to 'create and debug simple programs'. By the end of Key Syage 2 pupils will 'design, use and evaluate computational abstractions that model the state and behaviour of real-world problems and physical systems'.

Design & technology is linked to innovation and digital industries. Pupils learn, for example, about 3D printing and robotics. Food and nutrition is emphasized.

History focuses on British history from the Stone Age to the Normans and a later era, such as the Victorians. 'Significant individuals' such as Elizabeth I, Neil Armstrong, Rosa Parks and Emily Davison are studied.

Geography encourages contextual knowledge of different locations and key processes in physical and human geography; it emphasizes geographical skills such as interpreting a range of sources and communicating geographical information, for example through maps.

Art & design aims to encourage pupils to produce, explore and record their creative ideas and become proficient in a range of media, as well as evaluate works of art using appropriate language and an appreciation of historical and cultural developments.

PE aims to develop confidence within a broad range of activities for sustained periods of time. The focus is on competitive sports and healthy, active lives.

Music aims to ensure that pupils perform, listen, review and evaluate a range of music as well as understanding and exploring how music is created.

Modern languages focus on how to understand and respond to spoken and written language and speak with increasing confidence, fluency and spontaneity. Pupils can write and appreciate a range of writing in the language studied.

ACTIVITY

Consider your strengths and weaknesses identified at the beginning of Chapter 1 that may help or hinder you from achieving outstandingness. How aware are you of the importance of subject knowledge? Carry out this internal subject audit to establish your depth of knowledge and feelings toward each subject you teach.

Rate each subject in terms of your enthusiasm 1–5 and expertise 1–5.

Table 3.1 Subject audit.

	Enthusiasm	*Expertise*
Maths		
English (speech and language, writing, reading, phonics, drama)		
Science		
Computing		
D&T		
History		
Geography		
Art & design		
PE		
Music		
Modern languages		
RE		
PSHE and citizenship		

- Does assessment and/or performance indicators/targets influence the time and quality you give to each subject?
- Do the subjects you rated in enthusiasm match your level of expertise? Why?

Developing your subject knowledge

Teachers need to understand subject matter deeply and flexibly so they can help students create useful cognitive maps, relate one idea to another, and address misconceptions. Teachers need to see how ideas connect across fields and to everyday life.

Lee S. Shulman, 1987

Ideally you need to have a sense of mastery over the whole curriculum in order to develop your depth of understanding, as Shulman notes above. Nevertheless, we undeniably love teaching some subjects and plan and deliver great lessons with little effort, but other subjects don't inspire us and it feels like hard work. It is imperative, therefore, that you light that inner fire and make those sparks fly, regardless of the subject matter, through developing your subject knowledge.

A friend of mine who used to sell houses said, 'Some houses you fall in love with. When you show people around you can't help but wax lyrically and potential buyers also fall in love with them. However, when trying to sell houses I really didn't like I made sure I knew every detailed fact so I could feel confident and engage the viewer.' A great analogy; teaching *is* like sales, you are essentially *selling* the curriculum, making the consumer, your pupils, buy into what you are teaching them. So, be the best salesperson! Top salespeople possess common attributes: empathy, determination, energy, passion, self-confidence, enthusiasm, customer and product knowledge (BASIS international 2002; Sardar and Patton 2002). Reassuringly, these are all reflected in the characteristics of an outstanding teacher described in Chapter 1, but it is your deep knowledge of both the child and the subjects that is vital to your confidence and effectiveness.

The challenge is how to master and deliver *all* the requirements of the curriculum. Your *self-awareness* and ability to be *critically self-reflective* are fundamental in identifying, valuing and developing subject knowledge. People often ask us to 'open the black box', 'think outside the box', or undertake 'blue sky thinking'. In each case this requires a wealth of knowledge you can apply creatively, innovatively and confidently. An outstanding teacher needs both substantive (knowing what) and syntactic subject knowledge (knowing how to connect concepts together). In addition, a strong sense of self-efficacy, as discussed in Chapter 1, is required to underpin your confidence and ability to develop subject knowledge. This is best developed through *mastery* of the subject (Bandura 1997). When you succeed at something, you are more likely to attempt it again.

However, to be an outstanding teacher simply imparting subject matter is not enough – it is also, as Shulman (1987) identifies, about understanding *connectivity* and planning meaningful links. For example, you may know all the key facts, concepts and principles about forces in science but be unable to make concrete, real-life connections to meet the needs of your pupils. You cannot have substantive knowledge without syntactic knowledge because an outstanding teacher needs to have an in-depth understanding of the underlying concepts, principles and ways of thinking that underpin that subject (Pollard 1996) to truly support pupils' learning.

The Cambridge Primary Review (Alexander 2009) points to clear international research showing that domain, subject and pedagogical content knowledge – or the teacher's depth of understanding of what is to be taught – is one of the key attributes that distinguish the best teachers from the rest. The research reinforces what is common sense and what the children also tell us, and is summarized in the following checklist.

CHECKLIST for excellent substantive and syntactic knowledge

- Anticipate and identify misconceptions and address them.
- Use effective analogies and practical examples in explanations.
- Ask questions you don't know the answer to; encourage pupils to teach you; and so modelling that learning about a subject never stops.
- Field pupils' more probing questions.
- Refer pupils to extra sources of information to extend their learning – the more current, the better.
- Keep up to date, refer to new developments in specific subjects and embrace CPD.
- Make learning relevant, purposeful, cross-curricular and linked to real-world events.
- Encourage collaborative sharing of new knowledge through forums, wikis, texts or school noticeboards.
- Actively consult literature sources including the internet (such as EEF, TDA, TTRB, Teachers' TV), textbooks and newspaper articles.
- Read around how subjects and subject specific skills are taught (and their impact on the next key stage) to develop understanding of progression.
- Reflect on previous knowledge gained in degree or prior experience.
- Challenge higher attaining pupils.
- Show little reliance on external schemes of work.
- Productively work with colleagues.

Further reading

A good starting point to develop your subject expertise is through TDA (2007) *Developing trainees' subject knowledge for teaching: a way of looking at subject knowledge for teaching*, http://dera.ioe.ac.uk/9688/.

REFLECT

- How do you identify your pupils' current knowledge to help you plan the next steps they need to take?
- How can you create contexts based in real life and prior knowledge and experiences, such as the local environment?
- How can you increase opportunities for pupil collaboration and talk?
- How can you identify opportunities where cross-curricular approaches are effective (e.g. drama, history and science; mathematics and design & technology, or English and science)?

A thought . . . expect the unexpected! Pupils will ask tangential or taxing questions or pursue an unpredictable idea, so you need this depth of knowledge to cope with challenging or novel situations. However, you are not omniscient and the all-knowing 'sage on stage'. Consider yourself a 'guide on the side' (the socio-constructivist perspective). As the learning journey is lifelong, be the lead learner in your classroom and develop your mastery, confidence and credibility.

Further reading

A useful DfE website provides guidance across the curriculum:
https://www.gov.uk/government/uploads/system/uploads/attachment_data/file/358070/NC_assessment_quals_factsheet_Sept_update.pdf.

References

Alexander, R. (1992) *Policy and practice in primary education.* London: Routledge.

Alexander, R.J. (2009) *Children, their world, their education: final report of the Cambridge Primary Review.* London: Routledge.

Bandura, A. (1997) *Self-efficacy: the exercise of control.* New York: W.H. Freeman.

BASIS International (2002) BASIS: your portal to e-business, http://www.basis.com/advantage/magv4n2/portal.html.

DES (1967) *Children and their primary schools. A report of the Central Advisory Council for Education* (the Plowden Report). London: HMSO.

DfE (2012) *Teachers' standards,* www.gov.uk/government/uploads/system/uploads/attachment_data/file/301107/Teachers__Standards.pdf.

Eisner, E.W. and Vallance, E. (1974) *Conflicting conceptions of curriculum, series on contemporary educational issues.* Chicago: National Society for the Study of Education.

Engelmann, S. (1992) *War against the schools' academic child abuse.* Portland, OR: Halcyon House.

Hirsch, E.D. Jr (2006) *The knowledge deficit.* Boston, MA: Houghton Mifflin.

McCabe, B. (2011) www.telegraph.co.uk/education/educationnews/8881987/New-teachers-struggle-to-communicate-subject-knowledge.html.

Pollard, A. (ed.) (1996) *Readings for reflective teaching in the primary school.* London: Cassell.

Sardar, A. and Patton, M.A. (2002) *What makes a great salesperson? Links between our heritage and the future,* cited in A. Ruth and A. Wysocki (2011) *Top sellers: characteristics of a superior salesperson.* Gainesville, FL: University of Florida.

Shulman, L.S. (1987) in *Teacher Knowledge & Behavior,* www.intime.uni.edu/model/teacher/teac2summary.html.

Young, M. and Muller, J. (2013) On the powers of powerful knowledge, *Review of Education,* 1(3): 229–50.

Summary of the foundation level

Your perfect jacket

This first level in the hierarchy focused on choosing your jacket, and making sure it fits and feels comfortable. You have begun to equip it with a few essential items and you now view it as a valuable resource as it has increased your sense of 'knowing': knowing what suits you; knowing your shape and size; and knowing what to choose to carry in your pockets.

Your professional knowledge

This level asked you to focus on your teacher identity and philosophy and to examine how self-awareness, mindfulness and EI informed this and your sense of teacher professionalism. The focus on child development and learning theory has hopefully given you a broader and more analytical understanding of pupils as unique individuals. Moreover, you should have gained an appreciation that a key to unlocking pupils' learning potential is through building relationships and being highly competent and confident in the subject matter you teach. Know how to find your inner 'fire' to inspire!

Your professional development and action plan

This section, at the end of each level, is aimed at identifying areas of strength and development. Connect the content of this level to the seven key themes. Reflect upon the extent to which you have achieved each statement. To support your journey to outstanding, rate each key theme in Table 3.2 from 1–5 (1 not confident to 5 most confident) to form actions points.

Table 3.2 Key themes confidence rating – the foundation level has prompted
you to . . . .

Key theme	Confidence level
Recognize how your *teacher identity and philosophy* influences: your sense of professionalism and your journey to outstandingness; your understanding and use of theory; and your strengths and enthusiasm for each subject	1 2 3 4 5
Understand how the *purpose of education* is reflected in: your developing teacher identity; your perception and interpretation of child development theory; how you teach all the aspects of the curriculum	1 2 3 4 5
Appreciate that *well-being for you and your pupils* is important: when meeting the demands of teaching; when understanding the development of the whole child; when meeting the demands of both the pupils and the curriculum	1 2 3 4 5
Understand how to *meet the needs of the unique child* through: your teacher professionalism; understanding learning and development theory; your strength of subject knowledge	1 2 3 4 5
Appreciate the need for an *enabling and empowering environment* to promote and nurture: your own teacher identity and professionalism; your pupil-teacher relationships and their development; your mastery of subject knowledge as well as your pupils	1 2 3 4 5
Recognize the need for *self-awareness and critical self-reflection* to enable: your teacher identity and professionalism to be defined; you to draw on theory and evaluate the best way forward; to increase the quality and depth of your knowledge to ensure pupils succeed	1 2 3 4 5
Embrace *CPD* to enhance: your understanding of professionalism, EI and self-efficacy; your knowledge of learning and development theory; your mastery of curriculum subjects	1 2 3 4 5
Total score	

Reflecting upon the above, identify key areas to address. This will serve as an action plan (Table 3.3) to bring about a desirable change, with a particular focus on knowledge, in your teaching.

Table 3.3 Action plan.

Desirable change	Perceived Barriers/risks	Time/support/ training required	Timescale
This could be focused on *managing the demands of teaching; your teacher-pupil relation-ships; your ability to fully connect theory to practice; or lighting your inner fire for all subjects*	List these and consider whether they are signifi-cant or insignificant. I have used the word *'perceived'* as sometimes we create *barriers* and amplify *risks*, resulting from fears: previous experiences, false perceptions based on hearsay or distorted opinions. Filter, as objectively as you can, these barriers	Identify support that might help you to address these barriers/risks, e.g. *'I need further training in . . . to increase my confidence'* or *'Increase my mastery of the subject . . .'*	These may be immediate, e.g. *'Next lesson I will . . .',* or longer term, e.g. *'By the end of the term I will . . .'*

Education should inspire and motivate pupils to want to learn and not insist they are simply there to be filled with knowledge. As such I would like to finish this level with a poetic quote from Yeats to spark your interest and to encourage you to see your role as someone who inspires and one that certainly requires more than one element (but maybe not an exothermic reaction!).

Education is not the filling of a pail, but the lighting of a fire . . .

W.B. Yeats

PART 2
Personalization level – developing!

4

Developing your pedagogy – teacher repertoire and strategies

The calling of the teacher. There is no craft more privileged. To awaken in another human being powers, dreams beyond one's own; to induce in others a love for that which one loves; to make of one's inward present their future; that is a threefold adventure like no other.

George Steiner, Lessons of the Masters

Our coat hook! The 'perfect jacket' has become an essential belonging but now it is time to ensure it is really comfortable. You may need to adjust the sleeves or the length so it doesn't hinder you by restricting your movement. This chapter calls for greater versatility of your jacket, enabling you to wear it with increased confidence. As you widen your teaching repertoire so too will you develop a range of 'tools' neatly tucked into your pockets, to draw upon when planning outstanding learning experiences.

This chapter explores pedagogy as science, craft and art, as well as aspects of motivation, growth mindset and neuroscience and its relevance to education, especially regarding memory and deeper learning. As Steiner states, you, like no other, can empower and enable your pupils to aspire to more, to grow and blossom knowing you have set them on their life adventures with open eyes, hearts and minds.

The key themes in this chapter prompt you to:

- appreciate how your *teacher identity and philosophy* influences your preference and use of teaching strategies;
- reflect how your understanding of the *purpose of education* is congruent with your pedagogy;
- consider how your focus on *well-being for you and your pupils* reflects how you respond to pupils' demands and how you deliver the curriculum;
- understand how your knowledge and understanding of pedagogy and teaching strategies enables you to *meet the needs of the unique child*;

- recognize how your awareness of *creating an enabling and empowering environment* is reflected in your lesson delivery;
- appreciate how your own *self-awareness* and *critical self-reflection* should be embedded into your teaching to enhance the strategies and approaches you choose;
- reflect how your understanding of pedagogy focuses your need for *continuous development as a lifelong learner.*

This chapter addresses the following *Teachers' standards* (DfE 2012):

2 Promote good progress and outcomes by pupils
4 Plan and teach well structured lessons
5 Adapt teaching to respond to the strengths and needs of all pupils

Pedagogy defined

The word 'pedagogy' is derived from the Greek *paidagogus* (or pedagogue), meaning someone who *tends to* the child. Pedagogy is about leading and guiding pupils purposefully to enhance learning. In a dynamic classroom environment a teacher makes decisions and actions informed by theory, evidence and research (science); their 'toolkit' full of strategies (craft); and through the more implicit, responsive and intuitive (art) element of teaching. The Teaching and Learning Research Programme (TLRP 2007: 5) defines pedagogy as science, craft and art, which 'helps us to understand the complementary needs for collectively created knowledge, professional skills and personal capacities'.

A fuller understanding of pedagogy goes beyond the assumption that children are 'empty vessels' waiting to be filled by the teacher imparting information. However, a teacher can be unwittingly pulled into this narrow mode of teaching. Consumed by day-to-day work, a teacher can focus on the 'doing' element of teaching (such as planning and assessment), rather than considering the pedagogy that should underpin and inform their decisions. An understanding of pedagogy will therefore enhance your day-to-day practice and serve as a source to develop your professional identity and philosophy.

Education in the twenty-first century requires teachers to, sometimes rapidly, adapt or develop their pedagogy in line with new innovations or research. Utilizing technology and real-world relevance, new pedagogies are needed in today's classroom. An understanding of concepts, such as brain plasticity, growth mindset, deeper learning, mastery, meta-cognition and embedded formative assessment and how these impact on learning is needed (Phew! Don't worry, all this is developed within this and subsequent chapters).

Classrooms where teachers embrace and understand the nature of pedagogy with a focus on the learner can lead to outstanding performance for all. By embedding this understanding into your thinking, language and practice, you can begin to talk the same language as your colleagues and the wider learning community. Participating in more critical and fruitful discussion enables self-reflection and enhances practice. For example, in Finland, consistently rated in the top few in PISA scores, teachers are invited to initiate discussions about pedagogy, and to evaluate and critique ideas (TLRP 2007). Whether in a school or teacher training institution it is through reflection and discussion that beliefs, values and theoretical knowledge can be examined which then shape the understanding of the strategies employed.

A willingness and confidence to engage in professional dialogue is needed, along with an acceptance that not knowing something and making mistakes are learning opportunities. As such, pedagogic discussion should prompt us to openly and honestly ask *why?* For example *'Why are we/you teaching/learning this?'*; *'Why did I/you use that strategy?'*; *'Why was that my/their response?'*; or *'Why did/ didn't this work?'*. This approach will develop an insight and ability to research, reflect and ensure that pedagogical approaches employed continue to be refined, evolve and, most importantly, become outstanding.

Pedagogy as science, craft and art

Pedagogy as science

> *There is no such thing as teaching without research and research without teaching.*
>
> Paulo Freire, 1998

Pedagogy as science is *knowing* and, as Freire (1998) rightly notes, necessitates using theory and research to inform practice and vice versa. However, conflicting political agendas and various dichotomies of teaching approaches, such as child-centred vs teacher led; progressive vs traditional; mixed ability vs whole class; independent vs group work; or knowledge vs discovery, have swung the education debate from one direction to another, influencing pedagogy each time. Often the result is confusion and dissatisfaction (and a certain dizziness).

It is important to develop an understanding of how learning theory influences pedagogy and day-to-day practice, which in turn impacts on pupils' achievement. Do note, there are no easy, 'right' answers (Alexander et al. 1992), so developing your knowledge and critical thinking is essential.

 REFLECT

Reflect upon the extent your personal style of teaching fits into a discovery, transmission or connectionist approach, illustrated in Figure 4.1. Interestingly, but not surprisingly, Askew et al. (1997) found that the teachers with the lowest pupil numeracy gains were mainly traditional or didactic (transmitting knowledge) or child-centred (discovery learning). *Can you explain why this is?*

Table 4.1 Teaching approaches and theory.

Approach	Teaching style	Summary	Associated theory
Transmission	Traditional and didactic	This approach is associated with teaching methods often found in preparatory and elementary traditions in primary education. Knowledge is transmitted to the pupil, who is the passive recipient and it is perceived to produce 'higher standards'	*Behaviourism*: based upon stimuli and response, sees the child as passive within the environment in which they operate
Discovery	Progressive and child-centred	This approach focuses on a child's perceived needs at a particular age and how they construct their understanding	*Humanism*: Maslow, Dewey and Rogers saw the role of a teacher as facilitating learning within a supportive learning environment that fostered a love of learning and promoted self-actualization *Constructivism*: based on children constructing understanding through interaction with their environment and experiences therein
Connectionist	Internal and external connections within the digital age	The environment and interactions influence learning. The rapid advance of virtual environments (instant messaging, blogs, wikis and other social media) creates tools to support greater connectivity, knowledge sharing, collaboration and interactions both local and worldwide. The teacher values such interactions and enables them to make connections through modelling, high-quality questioning and other technology	*Connectivism*: George Siemens (2005) proposed learning takes into account the way it has been and is influenced by new technologies *Social constructivism*: This approach draws upon constructivist ideas set within a social context to emphasize the influence of culture and interaction on learning

A reflection . . . in education, as illustrated in Table 4.1, we find contradictory styles at each end of a continuum. Adopting a single approach may not develop outstandingness, so consider how to draw out the very best from each side. For example, taking the continuum of the progressive versus traditional teacher: the child-centred approach of the progressive teacher when blended with a traditional approach could create an environment of choice and discovery set within clear expectations and learning goals.

REFLECT

Try 'blending' continuums (refer to 'child development theory', Chapter 2), for example, behaviourist (use of rewards and reinforcement) and socio-constructivist (scaffolding learning collaboratively), and see how it can enhance what you do.

Further reading

Grasha, A.F. (1996) *Teaching with style*. Pittsburgh, PA: Alliance. He describes five teaching styles: the expert, formal authority, personal model, facilitator and delegator.

Pedagogy as craft

> *We are so made, that we can only derive intense enjoyment from a contrast and only very little from a state of things.*
>
> Sigmund Freud

Freud advocates intrinsic motivation; he saw sameness as boring and advocated change that keeps us interested and engaged. Pedagogy as the *craft of teaching* implies that the teacher must master a wide repertoire of skills and practices to engage and motivate the unique individuals they teach. New teachers often want to know the 'recipe' for good lessons and there are a plethora of resources, which proffer for instance '100 excellent maths lessons' or the like. But to be outstanding this is not enough. With any 'recipe' critically analyse, evaluate and extract the elements that enhance what you already do and blend, mould and integrate them to suit you and your pupils.

Over the past few decades the teaching profession has been seduced by methodologies and 'solutions' to curriculum pressures that eventually became the norm. For example, the three-part lesson was introduced in the late 1990s as 'the way' to teach literacy and numeracy (NLS, NNS, 1998–9) or the QCA non-statutory guidance that *guided* almost all schools, or popular off-the-shelf maths schemes, such as the Hamilton Trust. Although conceived to raise standards and support teachers, arguably they have all limited the range of strategies and activities used and created a structure which is less responsive to pupils' needs.

Without a deeper understanding of *why* certain strategies are used your teacher 'toolkit' (your repertoire of teaching strategies and approaches) is likely to be a short-term fix or no use whatsoever (Korthagen and Vasalos 2005). Quality education does require teachers to have a breadth and depth to their toolkit, and the knowledge and understanding of how this impacts on pupil achievement. Try applying a 'magpie approach' when developing your toolkit and look for the 'shiny' things and steal them. I'm not advocating kleptomania but encouraging you to be constantly aware of excellent practice and ideas.

 ACTIVITY

Keep a reflective journal of these *magpie moments* and reflect upon how you could adopt and adapt them to enhance your practice. Remember copying an idea is likely to result in failure; instead, critically reflect on your philosophy and teacher identity and recognize how such a strategy or approach might mesh with and enhance these.

Reassuringly, Ofsted (2015) confirms there is no single 'right way' to teach. When observing teaching, inspectors should be 'looking at' and reflecting on the effectiveness of what is being done to promote learning (Ofsted 2015, para. 178). 'One size *does not* fit all' so it is imperative that you acquire and use a rich variety of teaching strategies. Understand it isn't just about *what* teachers teach but *how* they teach and being able to meet the needs of all pupils through selecting the right strategy.

● ●

 STRATEGIES FOR YOUR TEACHER TOOLKIT

There are a plethora of approaches to learning to add to your teacher toolkit, but the following are worth consideration.

Mastery-based learning

Research found that pupils learned more and felt better about themselves in classrooms where they were performing at around 80 per cent accuracy (Tomlinson 2000). This emphasis on mastery is embodied in the National Curriculum 2014, particularly in maths, and challenges the traditional three-way differentiation of tasks (the 'all, most, some' approach) seen in many classrooms. The focus is shifting toward whole-class teaching, with richness of task and collaborative learning. This sets higher expectations (the expectations pupils *can* rather than *can't* achieve a task) as the task is not restrictive and focuses on the pupils taking responsibility for helping each other within mastery learning (EEF 2015).

Inquiry-based learning

A pupil-centred approach with specific tasks or activities. This strategy develops a dialogic approach, higher-order thinking skills and independent learning with teachers coaching or guiding pupils through the process of discovery.

Collaborative-based learning

Approaches which promote talk and interaction between learners tend to result in the best gains (EEF 2015). This requires careful task design, as well clear guidance and expectations, to ensure actual collaboration rather than pupils working alongside others yet on their own.

Digital-based learning

Use technology to support learning through programs for pupils or technology for teachers, such as interactive whiteboards (IWBs) or learning platforms. Its effective use should be driven by learning and teaching goals and not seen as an end in itself. It should supplement not replace effective teaching, therefore critically reflect and evaluate its impact on learning (EEF 2015).

● ●

A brief mention regarding 'active learning' is pertinent to developing pedagogy. Ofsted (2015) recognizes pupils may be expected to sit and listen to a teacher and still be active in acquiring knowledge and understanding. If you want your pupils to learn something you have to get them to think about it, which can be achieved 'actively' or 'passively' (Willingham 2008).

A reflection . . . 'if the only tool you have is a hammer, you tend to see every problem as a nail' (Maslow 1966). Maslow's insightful quote is equally true of teaching strategies. The fewer tools (teaching strategies) in your toolkit (teaching repertoire), the less likely you will have the most appropriate tool (strategy) for the task at hand – an idea highlighted in TLRP (2007), the Cambridge Primary Review (Alexander 2009), and others. However, to avoid the pitfall of the strategy becoming the focus rather than the learning, ask yourself 'how' and 'why' it promotes learning. Develop pupil self-efficacy, which enhances efficient and effective learners, through opportunities to select their own strategies, especially those promoting metacognition (knowing about one's own thinking and learning).

Pedagogy as art

> *I feel it is necessary to overcome the false separation between serious teaching and the expression of feeling.*
>
> Paulo Freire, 1998

An extensive range of teaching strategies is of limited use unless you are cognizant of and responsive to your pupils' needs. Freire (1998) sees teaching and emotion as one, and to embrace the *art* of teaching you must be intuitive and responsive. This requires you to be self-aware and recognize your own feelings (as discussed in

Chapter 1), and not adopt an aloof, cold exterior that many might say you should employ (another myth busted!). Teachers have to be attentive to individuals but cope with and process the complexity and speed of information flowing moment-by-moment from each pupil and other adults within the classroom. Failure to do so can result in loss of learning, as aspects such as pace, engagement or behaviours are adversely affected. Wragg et al. (1996) found that teachers, who survive their first three years and become good teachers do so because they rapidly internalize practice knowledge every time they face a new situation or challenge, then draw upon it when needed. Knowing when, how and why to respond in that split second is an indeed an art.

Pupil motivation and engagement

If pupils are motivated and engaged with their learning they more willingly exert greater effort, furthering learning and building on successes. Pupil engagement on a *cognitive, emotional/affective* and *behavioural* level is, without doubt, required for all great teaching (Fredricks et al. 2004). A core element of pedagogy as art is knowing which 'buttons' to press to turn each level on. The art of teaching is know-ing when to use humour; when to affect different voices; when to use *that look*; when to step in and when to pull back; and when to give a little pat on the back which communicates more than words ever will.

Pupils who are motivated by their learning show enthusiasm, interest, curi-osity, resilience and perseverance to solve problems. Motivation is also deter-mined by whether pupils expect to succeed, and whether they value the learning goal. The 'expectancy-value theory', founded by Martin Fishbein in the 1970s, and more recently developed by Eccles et al. (1983) illustrates this as a formula, simplified as:

> *Value* (the value of the learning to the learner) x *Expectancy* (the extent to which the learner expects success in the learning) = *Motivation*

If the learner neither values the learning nor expects to succeed (placing either at zero) their motivation will be zero; as V and E are multiplied. This can be related to extrinsic or intrinsic motivation. The extrinsic motivator may be, for example, attaining a top mark because they have previously, to avoid a sanction or to meet parental, peer or teacher expectations. These pupils place little value on the sub-ject content and therefore have no motivation to extend, connect or apply their learning further. Conversely, the pupil who is intrinsically motivated will be absorbed in the task and be motivated to work (right through breaktime) as they are in the 'flow' (Csikszentmihalyi 2002). This pupil values the learning, strives for success and applies more effort. With understanding, support and richness of task, motivation moves from external to internal and develops the 'feelgood' fac-tor of learning. It is motivation and engagement that leads to mastery and success, or as Pintrich and De Groot (1990) state more succinctly, the *will* and the *skill* to be successful.

REFLECT – in the classroom

A 'litmus test' for an outstanding lesson is how pupils respond. Develop your ability to see the learning experience through the pupils' eyes (empathy). Take time to *really* look at your classroom, your pupil-teacher relationships, planning and the nature of the tasks. Identify if there is a 'buzz' created through your energy (your inner fire) and that of your pupils. Their sense of enjoyment and motivation, and yours, creates a positive environment and can literally be learning's 'on-off switch'.

CHECKLIST for pupil engagement

- Would I want to be a pupil in my class?
- Does the classroom 'buzz' feel good?
- Do my teaching style and strategies enable all pupils to engage with the learning?
- Do my pupils react positively to adults, other pupils, the school and me?
- Do my pupils try to overcome difficulties, show resilience and a mastery orientation?
- Do they value the task and feel they can succeed?
- Do my pupils respond to incentives, either extrinsic or intrinsic?
- Do they enjoy success?

Models for effective pedagogy

A bad curriculum taught well is invariably a better experience for pupils than a good curriculum taught badly: *pedagogy trumps curriculum!* It is pedagogy that needs to evolve to meet learners' needs. Pedagogical understanding is gained through questioning decisions and actions taken. However, you need to know what questions to ask in the first place. To gain an insight in developing your pedagogy reflect upon Shulman's (1987) 'model of pedagogical reasoning' which proposes a cycle of comprehension; transformation; instruction; evaluation; reflection; and new comprehension. Use this cycle, presented in more detail below, to identify your own areas for development.

CHECKLIST for effective pedagogy

Comprehension

You need to understand what you are teaching and why you are teaching it.

- How do you identify and address a pupil's misconceptions?
- Do you know how this knowledge builds upon prior learning and experiences?
- Are you aware of a pupil's readiness to take on new knowledge?

Transformation

Transform the body of knowledge within the curriculum into a form each pupil can access, participate in and achieve. For example through connecting prior knowledge, experience and interests, preparing resources including ICT, use of TAs, personalized activities, presenting concepts through analogies and metaphors, specific teaching strategies, groupings and differentiation.

- Do the activities and differentiation of tasks anticipate potential misconceptions?
- Do you make effective use of concrete, meaningful, real-life examples to aid understanding?
- Are your explanations and use of analogies accessible, well-formed and clarifying of understanding?
- Do the resources and targeted support enable pupils to achieve their potential within the lesson?

Instruction

Your exposition and the actual teaching activity.

- Does the lesson flow, have pace and make sense to the pupils?
- Are your instructions and explanations accessible, precise, logical and clear for every pupil?
- What humour and behaviour management do you use?
- Do you make links to other areas of the curriculum and pupils' experiences and knowledge?

Evaluation

Check for pupils' understanding through assessment for learning (AfL) (more in Chapter 6).

- Do you ask open, probing questions to assess understanding?
- Do you prompt your pupils to analyse their understanding?

Reflection

Critically review performance to adjust and enhance the teaching and learning experience of you and your pupils (more in Chapter 10).

- Do you critically reflect on pupils' understanding and analyse where and why there may be misconceptions (e.g. your explanations, type of activities, use of resources)?
- Does your own self-reflection enable you to move towards outstandingness?

New comprehension

Gain up-to-date knowledge and understanding of subjects and pedagogy.

- Are you able and active in identifying where and when to pursue new learning?
- Do you extend your subject knowledge as a result of a probing pupil question or interaction with colleagues, parents or an inspector?

Further reading

James, M. and Pollard, A. (2012) *TLRP, principles for effective pedagogy*. London: Routledge. This provides clear guidance to use as a checklist for developing your practice.

Pianta, R.C., La Paro, K.M. and Hamre, B.K. (2008) *Classroom assessment scoring system*. Baltimore, MD: Paul H. Brookes. Focuses on emotional and instructional support, and classroom organization.

Outstanding teaching should be seen as a synergistic relationship between various component parts to make a greater whole. How a teacher orchestrates this is an essential part of what makes them effective. Focusing on the separate constituent elements or behaviours will always be too limited (Sutton Trust 2014).

Fixed and growth mindsets

Research has increasingly shown that there is more to a pupil's success than cognitive ability, curriculum and instruction.

Carol Dweck, 2000

Dweck observed two divergent theories of learning: the *entity theory*, whereby intelligence or ability is static leading to decreased motivation and failure; and the *incremental theory*, whereby intelligence is malleable and can be developed with effort, leading to 'mastery orientated' performance. The pupil with *mastery orientation* will, as Dweck (2000) notes, find ways to enhance their competence and place learning as their goal. However, those with *performance orientation* will try to prove they're competent or clever. This led to the theory of growth mindset.

A pupil's mindset, or their beliefs about themselves and their environment, can affect whether they learn and succeed. Some pupils cannot see a relationship between effort and progress and their success. As a teacher we may often hear such pupils say, 'I'm no good at this!'; 'I'm stupid!'; or 'I'm not naturally talented'. This demonstrates a *fixed mindset*, whereby the pupil avoids challenges and lacks the necessary resilience to overcome problems. The pupil who holds negative beliefs about effort and achievement may also say or think, 'If I have to work hard, I'm not clever enough to do this!'; or 'I've never been able to do this!' Pupils may also conclude, 'People like me don't belong here' where cultural boundaries may exist, regardless of their cognitive ability and quality of teaching.

However, a growth mindset pupil perceives effort as positive, and may say 'Trying harder makes me cleverer' or 'I tried that but it didn't work so now I'm doing this'. Parents who praise the effort of their child rather than their ability also influence the growth mindset.

As a teacher, you may have strong, deeply held intuitions about what to say to pupils to boost their confidence and self-esteem. However, comforting struggling pupils, a natural response, by saying for example, 'It's okay, not everyone is good at maths' compromises their motivation and resilience; both outcomes of a fixed mindset. Well-intentioned praise, centred on encouraging or protecting lower ability pupils conveys a message of low teacher expectation and these pupils are more likely to attribute their failure to lack of ability (Stipek 2010). Likewise, person-orientated praise that focuses on cleverness, talent or mediocre performance, regardless of merit, reinforces a fixed mindset, communicating that at that point they are either intelligent and talented or not (Zentall and Morris 2010).

Responses, both verbal and nonverbal, indicate how you may perceive and value, for example, a pupil's ability or gender. To further understand the effect of feedback in relation to pupil achievement, it is pertinent to reflect upon Bernard Weiner's (1985) attribution theory. This is based on how individuals see their ability, effort, task difficulty and luck, set within three dimensions:

- *Within own control or out of own control* (internal vs external);
- *Stable or unstable* (changes vs unchanged over time);
- *Able or unable to control change* (causes one can control, such as skills or knowledge vs causes one cannot control such as luck or perceived intelligence/talent).

Teacher attributions can have a lasting impact on future learning. When teachers offer feedback to pupils it centres on either success or failure:

- An *ability-based attribute*, such as: 'Great work. It is clear you know this subject inside out!'
- A *task-difficulty attribute*, such as: 'You got 100 per cent, but it was easy!'
- A *luck-based attribute, such as*: 'Great job! This must be your lucky day!'

With such attributes the pupil will maintain or develop a fixed mindset (external, stable and unable to control). However, if a pupil attributes a success or failure as internal (within their control), unstable (changeable over time) and controllable (increase skills or knowledge), then motivation and engagement in similar tasks in the future will increase. An *effort-based attribute* may be: 'You worked hard, and if you practise this every day you will improve!' or 'Your success will depend on you choosing the right strategy'.

As a teacher you can influence a pupil's mindset by creating a classroom culture where mistakes are valued for their intrinsic value to the learning process; a growth mindset is promoted and the belief that a pupil can control and change their attributes creates positive change. One school I visited recently had a 'no rubbers' policy. Pupils were actively encouraged to keep and use their mistakes in their learning and not value 'unflawed' work. This had an empowering effect on the pupils as it reduced the fear of failure and increased a positive attitude to learning.

Underperformance has been linked to fear of failure for many years, as John Holt (1964) notes in his book *How Children Fail*. The underpinning factor is this inextricable link between cognition and emotion: success results in feelings such as happiness and pride, and failure in feelings of frustration or sadness. It is therefore essential that you understand your pupils' feelings and beliefs and how these impact upon their learning. Above all your *pupils need you to believe in their learning potential,* rather than complimenting them to raise self-esteem regardless of actual effort and worth.

REFLECT

Think about something you weren't good at initially which with practice you improved, or conversely something you tried and failed at and never gained competence in.

- What factors influenced you succeeding or failing?
- Can you explain how you became good or even talented?
- Did you experience failure within that process?
- How did you overcome this?
- What emotions did you feel?
- What effect did these emotions have on your success?

ACTIVITY

Which mindset scenario? A boy in your class has completed a short creative story/piece of art but he doesn't like it and wants to throw it away. Which category do the statements listed in Table 4.2 fall into?

Table 4.2 Mindset scenario.

Statement	Fixed mindset response	Growth mindset response
Don't be silly! This is an amazing story/picture; you've always been so good at writing/art!		
You've done your best – that's the main thing!		
Don't throw it away; I need it for the display!		
Your talent is really on the football pitch!		
Let's look at it together and discuss elements you like and ones you want to improve		
Don't worry; you're good at maths!		
What can you now do to move forward with this? Ask for support if you need it		

A typical growth mindset response would be, as Dweck (2006) advises, asking the pupil and yourself, 'What can I learn from this? What will I do next time?'

Further reading

Dweck, C. (2006) *Mindset: How you can fulfil your potential*. New York: Random House.

Neuroscience and education

We are now in an era where the fields of education and neuroscience are in alliance. Neuroscience has demonstrated the brain's potential to evolve, dismissing the myth that intelligence and talent are fixed and finite. The brain can change and develop physically, functionally and chemically as ability is acquired or improved. With this increased understanding it is useful to reflect upon how neuroscience might contribute to the development of pedagogy.

Neuroscience is without doubt exciting and enticing for those in education, but this has led to many 'neuromyths'. For example, labelling a pupil as left or right-brain dominant; the fascination with more commercial programmes such as Brain Gym; the popularity of VAK and considering learner preference as visual, auditory or kinaesthetic. All have been seen in classrooms. Neuroscience's allure has led many to more readily accept explanations that may allude to, but perhaps not accurately reflect, the actual scientific findings or be contrary to common sense. A study by Paul Howard-Jones (2014) revealed that teachers know very little about the brain and their knowledge is often poor or incorrect.

It is, however, unlikely that the popularity of neuroscience will diminish any time soon. By raising awareness in basic neuroscience, teachers should more confidently be able to critically evaluate and apply the findings to inform and enhance their practice rather than accepting the permeation of neuromyths and commercial 'quick-fixes'.

Further reading

Sylvan, L.J. and Christodoulou, J.A. (2010) Understanding the role of neuroscience in brain-based products: a guide for educators and consumers, *Mind, Brain and Education* 4: 1–7. This guides a teacher in how to differentiate between brain-supported, brain-derived, brain-driven and brain-inspired interventions.

Neurotransmitters and learning

To learn, the brain creates memories or templates through the release of various chemicals, the main ones being glutamate and dopamine. Dopamine, which we shall call *teacher's pet* (you'll see why), can be released through both stress and reward. Stress may inhibit learning and affect the areas of the brain concerned with memory (the prefrontal cortex). However, reward or anticipation of reward creates stronger connections and enhances not only learning but the rate of learning.

The level of challenge, incentive and involvement affects a pupil's emotional state and their potential success. Pitching a task too low creates no real reward and pitching too high may leave the pupil feeling helpless, the task unachievable and therefore without reward. We need to take a 'baby bear's porridge' approach – i.e. the task should be 'just right' to create a reward-based emotional response, which enhances what is learnt.

In addition, Skinner's research within the behaviourist field found that random reinforcement enhances learning. Uncertain rewards are more stimulating and this anticipation will release greater levels of our 'teacher's pet', dopamine. This explains the attraction of games and gaming with the element of chance (Howard-Jones 2014). This understanding of neural response and learning potential should motivate us to make lessons more rewarding for pupils.

The human memory

Why is it when you have taught something one day it can be forgotten only a few days later? Willingham (2008) suggests a number of reasons:

- *Attention*: you can't remember things you haven't paid sustained attention to;
- *Storage*: you have paid attention, but it hasn't made it into long-term memory;
- *Usage*: you can't remember things as they have faded through disuse;
- *Transfer*: your process by which things are drawn from long-term memory is prone to failure: transfer is difficult, because it's difficult to apply abstractions to new situations.

The majority of pupils do not learn over half of what is taught. If you want your pupils to really learn, the end goal is working towards long-term memory. Further insight into understanding how these memory templates are formed and embedded will help ensure your teaching time results in actual learning.

Working memory

Working memory (WM) is different from short-term memory (STM), which enables the pupil to hold information for a few seconds to record or repeat it, and long-term memory (LTM), which could be likened to a library of knowledge. Pupils initially use their WM – which literally *'works'* to process and filter information and construct meaning – when you are teaching them. Using the library analogy, it acts like a librarian who seeks and retrieves relevant pieces of information when required. However, it has limited space and can become cluttered with irrelevant information. This can often explain why some pupils misunderstand, can't remember key information or can't execute seemingly straightforward instructions. An overloaded brain drops in performance; it does not multitask (Klingberg 2009), the librarian becomes overwhelmed and ends up being unable to find any information or may grab the first book to hand (this could account for the pupil with the left field response).

Try this: *There are seven colours in the rainbow.* True or false? Your WM very adeptly delved into your LTM and enabled you to respond. You may have also visualized the colours and counted them in your head or used a mnemonic.

Baddeley and Hitch (1974) explained how WM functions with a model comprised of: a *phonological loop* (concerned with speech, lip/sign language and sound); a *visuo-spatial sketch pad* (concerned with colour, shape, spatial and kinaesthetic elements); and the *central executive* (the Fat Controller!) being the control centre. These parts, together with an *episodic buffer* (added in 2000), enable us to process information.

Now try this exercise to illustrate how it works: work out the number of desks in your classroom.

- The *visuo-spatial sketch pad* (inner eye) visualizes your classroom drawing from your LTM.
- The *phonological loop* (inner ear or inner voice) then counts the desks.
- The *central executive* takes this information from the two 'slave' systems and generates a strategy to problem solve with the *episodic buffer* acting like a workbench bringing relevant information from the LTM.

When WM is dealing with new information, it calls upon LTM for relevant background information to make sense of it – our schema (think back to Piaget's assimilation and accommodation model in Chapter 2). New knowledge retrieves and builds upon older information to form new connections making learning new topics easier. Once the WM has processed the information, understood it and made sense of it, there is a good chance that this information is committed to the LTM.

Why is WM worth knowing about?

WM is a good indicator of a pupil's potential to learn and their potential attainment. Unlike IQ, WM is not affected by factors such as socioeconomic status or attendance at preschool. Poor WM can easily go unrecognized and these pupils may fail to make progress regardless of interventions and support, and may be 'diagnosed' as having cognitive or behavioural issues, such as attention deficit hyperactivity disorder (ADHD) or dyslexia, or simply labelled as just plain lazy.

WM and classroom practice

Firstly, it is important to be aware of pupils' ability to retain instructions. Therefore, as Alloway and Alloway (2015) indicate, use a simple guide for the different ages as follows:

- 5–6 years: two instructions;
- 7–9 years: three instructions;
- 10–12 years: four instructions;
- 13–15 years: five instructions.

Reflect upon the number of the instructions you give during the school day, for example a common set of instructions is often 'Underline your work, tuck your chairs in and put your books in the red tray, then come and sit on the carpet'. A pupil with weak WM may keenly rush to be the first on the carpet but will then have to be reminded to carry out the rest of the instructions.

When planning, ensure that the intended learning and instruction matches a pupil's ability to process. Evaluate how you deliver instructions so they do not detract from the learning objective (LO). The idea is to reduce WM load so the LO or focus on that particular element of learning is met. Consider if, for example, the cutting, sticking, underlining, resourcing, date and title writing is enabling that pupil to focus on achieving the learning goal or not. Identify how you can reduce the number of peripheral aspects so the pupil can focus on the learning element which you then scaffold.

Identifying pupils with poor WM

There are screening tools on the market, for example a WM rating scale (WMRS) or the Automated Working Memory Assessment (AWMA) (Alloway and Gathercole 2006), however, certain behaviours may indicate a weak WM:

- pupils who frequently daydream, are disruptive, wildly guess at an answer or do not answer at all;
- pupils who have difficulty copying from the board, remembering text and writing it down, solving mental maths problems, remembering sequences of events or numbers, or recalling a sequence of numbers in reverse order (digit span).

Encouragingly, until our thirties WM is increasing in size, nevertheless identify which of your pupils have higher or lower than average WM. Both sets of pupils may become frustrated and disengaged from their learning.

Deeper learning and supporting pupils' WM

Knowledge and skills must be acquired in a way that makes the learning durable and flexible. This learning may be seen as deep or surface. Deeper learning is based on internal motivation, being engaged in the task and craving knowledge about a particular topic, while surface learning sees little interest in the task itself (Chamorro-Premuzic et al. 2007), in line with expectancy-value theory.

If pupils are simply reproducing or memorizing information and passively accepting this, with no demands for them to connect, apply or reflect, they are only engaged in surface learning with the likelihood it will be lost. The key is securing the surface learning to create opportunities for deep and profound learning. This is illustrated in Bloom's taxonomy (1956) with the higher-order thinking skills, such as analysis and evaluation, which promote deeper learning. At the heart of the deeper learning we should place opportunities for pupils to actively discover and think about their learning, as here they develop as thinkers who can be critical (convergent); creative (divergent) and reflective (metacognitive).

Deeper learning is also reflected in the popular adage 'If you don't use it you lose it'. If pupils don't revisit concepts, the connections or 'routes' to them become weaker and harder to retrieve. This could be likened to a road network: as the seldom-used roads become overgrown, access to the desired destination becomes problematic and fearful due to hazards. There is also a risk that if the breadth of learning experiences is restricted, the more frequently used roads become motor-ways as they become fast and direct. Gradually the minor roads become derelict, and so much of the countryside will never be appreciated or accessed freely. It is then harder for this pupil to be creative, critical, flexible, adaptable and innovative in their learning.

Encouragingly, Bjork and Bjork's *New theory of disuse* (1992) suggests that memory doesn't decay; instead we become less able to retrieve stored information. It means that the storage capacity of human memory is, for all practical purposes, limitless. He discusses LTM and its strength based upon two indices: *storage strength* (SS) – how well something is learnt; and *retrieval strength* (RS) – how accessible (or retrievable) something is. It is important to plan lessons which are high in both SS and RS. In simple terms, the better you learn something, the higher both SS and RS will be.

To illustrate this I recall revising for my GCSE physics exam and on the day I could access all the necessary key information indicating high RS, however this learning had low SS, as I can't for the life of me remember all the formulae now.

RS and SS also explain why I passed my oral French exam with flying colours but struggle (resorting to Franglais!) on my occasional trip to France. However, if I am there a number of days I feel more fluent; my French has high SS but low RS. It was mastered once but is now dormant, but can be remastered again. This explains that frustrating feeling of suddenly being unable to recall information we know we should know; the 'on tip of my tongue' feeling.

How can you help pupils remember what they've learned?

Let's reflect on the difference between good and outstanding teaching. An outstanding teacher brings about real change in the learner, opens up learning potential and deeper learning. Undeniably, a good teacher will ensure learning is obvious to all (although possibly only surface learning) and pupils feel success as they boost their RS in the short term leading to better *performance*. A performance focus sees teaching as safe and predictable and pupils having clear cues about the answers you're looking for. You are fairly happy, the pupils are fairly happy and an observer can tick the necessary boxes. However, the RS quickly evaporates and learning is lost.

'Desirable difficulties'

So how do you move to outstanding? Bjork's term *desirable difficulties* lie at heart of the counterintuitive nature of learning. These desirable difficulties will slow down *performance*, but lead to long-term retention and connections being made (increased SS and RS; deeper learning). This sounds contradictory in our current accountability and performativity culture, which sees 'pupil progress' (performance) making a good lesson. However, when learning has desirable difficulties pupils will make more mistakes in the short term, which may inhibit performance, causing even more mistakes and apparent forgetting. This is part of the learning process (Nuthall 2007).

It is, of course, undesirable for pupils to be struggling by the end of a lesson, but if real learning is the aim then you must move beyond safe, correct, meticulous outcomes and short-term performance indicators. The route to outstanding teaching requires more risk-taking and may feel uncomfortable, but desirable change in your pupils is made through deeper learning, rather than just performance, and it takes more time.

Further reading

Bjork, E.L. and Bjork, R.A. (2011) *Making things hard on yourself, but in a good way: Creating desirable difficulties to enhance learning*, in M.A. Gernsbacher et al. (eds) *Psychology and the real world: essays illustrating fundamental contributions to society*, pp. 56–64. New York: Worth Publishers, http:// bjorklab.psych.ucla.edu/pubs/EBjork_RBjork_2011.pdf.

John West-Burnham offers another explanation of surface or shallow (What?), deep (How?) and profound (Why?) learning. See Understanding deep learning, http://johnwest-burnham.co.uk/index.php.

STRATEGIES FOR YOUR TEACHER TOOLKIT

As you learn more about your school's curriculum and assessment systems you may like to consider if they were designed with the following principles in mind and how to apply these to your day-to-day teaching.

Framing

Use framing or goal-setting to start the lesson. This creates expectations as goal-orientated, which activates non-conscious processes, such as attention and motivation (Dweck 1986). The mind is naturally goal-oriented, and when the goal is achieved potentially it stops 'learning'. When goals are set at a higher level, the brain's goal-oriented systems are more likely to remain engaged (with careful scaffolding), drawing on more strategies until the goal is reached. This creates a cognitive reserve to carry a learner through the conscious/hard part of their learning (Schenck and Cruickshank 2015), so avoiding the 'book flying through the air' and the 'I can't do this' outcry.

Spacing

Hermann Ebinghaus, a German psychologist, demonstrated that it takes time for the memory of the learning event to stabilize. Information that is presented repeatedly over spaced intervals enhances learning. Essentially the 'pause' allows the pupil to reflect and make sense of the learning experience (Schenck and Cruickshank 2015). The pupil is given time and space to download without information bombardment (as I like to call it, a metaphoric 'dot-to-dot' as they can join the dots of their learning up).

Contrary to what we may think, forgetting benefits pupils in the long term as relearning forgotten material is significantly easier each time. This enhances memory and increases learning, therefore planning to revisit topics with an *optimal gap* between each can improve knowledge retention. Studies indicate the penalty for a too-short gap is greater than for a too-long gap (Howard-Jones 2014).

In addition, Kornell et al. (2009) found unsuccessful retrieval attempts enhanced learning and suggested that taking challenging tests, instead of avoiding errors, may be one aspect of effective learning. Using memory improves memory: the act of retrieval helps recall and recall in the future (Bjork 1975). Bjork found that multiple-choice tests have a higher effect as when pupils do not know the answer they try to retrieve information as to why the other answers are incorrect to find the correct response (Little et al. 2012). Try adding tests as a starter, mid-lesson activity or plenary when planning.

Repetition

As a child I watched a game show called *The Generation Game* and the most exciting part was to recall all the items on a conveyor belt. The items the contestant remembered (always a cut glass decanter and a cuddly toy!) would be given to them as prizes. A pupil with poor WM would struggle; they may recall the first and last item and then scrabble around for other items, often the ones that are repeated week after week (so guaranteed I would win that decanter and soft toy!). Ebinghaus (1850–1909) documented the *serial position effect*, which describes how the position of an item affects recall. The two main concepts are: 1) the *recency* effect which describes the increased recall of the most recent information as it is still in the STM; and 2) the *primacy* effect which increases memory of the first items in a list due to the opportunity for rehearsal (i.e. repeating it in our heads several times) and connects and makes meaning of that information, increasing its chance to commit to LTM.

The brain will also store information better the second, third or fourth time round and so retrieval strength improves, making sense of Bruner's spiralling curriculum whereby concepts are repeated throughout a pupil's education. It is repetition that supports the WM as information is moved to LTM. I reflected upon this when my 5-year-old was practising 'The 12 Days of Christmas'. Dutifully we rehearsed the song and I was word perfect until the sixth day . . . the primacy effect exemplified. Days one to five are repeated eight or more times but days 6 to 12 only seven times or fewer, so were not embedded as firmly in my LTM. Repetition may result in the 'But, we've done this before!!' wail, so, as with all things pedagogical, explain *what* you're doing and *why* you're doing it so they will be happy to (eat, sleep, learn) repeat.

Interleaving

Interleaving topics can increase how efficiently material is learnt and recalled. This strategy highlights difference ('discriminative-contrast' hypothesis) and so enhances inductive learning (Birnbaum et al. 2013). A typical strategy might involve a lesson being followed by practice problems drawn from previous lessons, so no two problems of the same concept appear consecutively. For example, at the end of a lesson about measurement, a teacher might alternate questions based on calculating and converting units of measurement with questions about volume or area of shapes.

Reducing distractions and anxiety

Be aware of the number of distractions that can overload memory, leaving the pupil overwhelmed as they struggle to filter the information. Consider the pupil who is easily distracted and unable to focus. Position this pupil in a less busy or potentially less distracting area, such as a quieter corner, away from the door or window. Structure the group so that fellow pupils are supportive and won't overload the pupil's WM.

Anxiety can have detrimental effects on WM as it clutters it with worry and stress, and pupils with poor WM are more prone to anxiety. Stress releases cortisol, which acts as an inhibitor in the neuron pathways between the hippocampus (LTM) and the amygdala (centre for emotion). As a result, these pupils can find it very difficult to control emotions and may find transition points, novelty and social interactions very difficult. Developing a pupil's ability and confidence to talk about the root of their anxiety helps to reduce and dispel concerns, whether social or academic, for them to more ably apply their WM to the task in hand.

Table 4.3 Deeper learning checklist.

Slow down and . . .	*Scaffold learning by . . .*
Distribute practice over time rather than cramming	Providing additional hooks for the pupil to refer back to
Allocate enough time to a task and build in mini-plenaries	Adding a number system to the sequence of a task
Match the complexity and number of instructions to pupils' ability	Modelling examples to give pupils a reference point
Monitor your speed of talking	Using displays and visual aides
Ask pupils to repeat the instructions back	Using mnemonics and imagery to connect with verbal or written information
'Chunk' up a task so WM is not overloaded	Concept mapping to promote connections
Ensure the task is seen as possible at the outset	Building upon a prior knowledge from their LTM
Overlearn material to develop a sense of *mastery*: an additional 20 per cent	Using strategic peer support through collaborative working

● ●

A thought . . . if these tenets of mindset interventions, deeper learning and memory are right, the main reason some pupils struggle with retaining and applying information is that the curriculum, delivery and assessment procedures are not designed with this in mind. It is therefore imperative that you plan and deliver each lesson with this knowledge of how to create that *desirable change* in your learners.

This level addresses these issues but it is believing in your pupils' potential and in them as individuals that also makes the difference to their success.

References

Alexander, R., Rose, A. and Woodhead, C. (1992) *Curriculum organisation and classroom practice in primary schools: a discussion paper.* London: DES.

Alexander, R.J. (2009) *Children, their world, their education: final report of the Cambridge Primary Review.* London: Routledge.

Alloway, T.P. and Alloway, R.G. (2015) *Understanding working memory*, 2nd edn. London: Sage.

Alloway, T. P. and Gathercole, S. E. (2006) How does working memory work in the classroom? *Educational Research and Reviews*, 1: 134–9.

Askew, M., Brown, M., Rhodes, V., Wiliam, D. and Johnson, D. (1997) *Effective teachers of numeracy: report of a study carried out for the Teacher Training Agency.* London: King's College, University of London.

Baddeley, A.D. and Hitch, G.J. (1974) Working memory, in G.H. Bower (ed.) *The psychology of learning and motivation*, pp. 47–89. New York: Academic Press.

Birnbaum, M.S., Kornell, N., Bjork, E.L. and Bjork, R.A. (2013) Why interleaving enhances inductive learning: the roles of discrimination and retrieval, *Memory and Cognition*, 41: 392–402.

Bjork, R.A. (1975) Retrieval as a memory modifier, in R. Solso (ed.) Information processing and cognition: the Loyola Symposium, 123–144. Hillsdale, NJ: Erlbaum.

Bjork, R.A. and Bjork, E.L. (1992) A new theory of disuse and an old theory of stimulus fluctuation, in A. Healy, S. Kosslyn and R. Schiffrin (eds) *From learning processes to cognitive processes: essays in honor of William K. Estes*, 2: 35–67.

Bloom, B.S. (ed.) (1956) *Taxonomy of educational objectives: the classification of educational goals, Hanbook I, cognitive domain.* New York: McKay.

Chamorro-Premuzic, T., Furnham, A. and Lewis, M. (2007) Personality and approaches to learning predict preference for different teaching methods, *Learning and Individual Differences*, 17: 241–50.

Csikszentmihalyi, M. (2002) *Flow: the classic work on how to achieve happiness.* London: Rider.

DfE (2012) *Teachers' standards*, www.gov.uk/government/uploads/system/uploads/attachment_data/file/301107/Teachers__Standards.pdf.

Dweck, C.S. (1986) Motivational processes affecting learning, *American Psychologist*, 41: 1040–8.

Dweck, C.S. (2000) *Self theories: their role in motivation, personality, and development.* Philadelphia, PA: Taylor & Francis.

Dweck, C. S. (2006) *Mindset: the new psychology of success.* New York: Random House.

Eccles, J.S., Adler, T.F., Futterman, R., Goff, S.B., Kaczala, C.M., Meece, J.L. and Midgley, C. (1983) Expectancies, values, and academic behaviors, in J.T. Spence (ed.) *Achievement and achievement motivation*, pp. 75–146. San Francisco: W. H. Freeman.

EEF (2015) The Education Endowment Foundation, https://educationendowmentfoundation.org.uk.

Fredricks, J.A., Blumenfeld, P.C. and Paris, J.H. (2004) School engagement: potential of the concept, state of evidence, *Review of Educational Research*, 74: 59–109.

Freire, P. (1998) *Pedagogy of Freedom.* Lanham, MD: Rowman & Littlefield.

Holt, J. (1964) *How children fail.* New York: Pitman Publishing Co.

Howard-Jones, P. (2014) *Neuroscience and education: a review of educational interventions and approaches informed by neuroscience full report and executive summary*. Bristol: University of Bristol, EEF.

Klingberg, T. (2009) *The overflowing brain: information overload and the limits of working memory*. New York: Oxford University Press.

Kornell, N., Hays, M.J. and Bjork, R.A. (2009) Unsuccessful retrieval attempts enhance subsequent learning, *Journal of Experimental Psychology: Learning, Memory, and Cognition*, 35(4): 989–98.

Korthagen, F. and Vasalos, A. (2005) Levels in reflection: core reflection as a mean to enhance professional growth, *Teachers and Teaching*, 11(1): 47–71.

Little, J.L., Bjork, E.L., Bjork, R.A. and Angello, G. (2012) Multiple-choice tests exonerated, at least of some charges: fostering test-induced learning and avoiding test-induced forgetting, *Psychological Science*, 23(11): 1337–44.

Maslow, A. (1966) *Psychology of Science*. New York: Harper & Row.

Nuthall, G. (2007) *The hidden lives of learners*. Wellington: NZCER Press.

Ofsted (2015) *School inspection handbook*, www.gov.uk/government/ofsted.

Pintrich, P.R. and De Groot, E.V. (1990) Motivational and self-regulated learning components of classroom academic performance, *Journal of Educational Psychology*, 82: 33–40.

Schenck, J. and Cruickshank, J. (2015) Evolving Kolb: experiential education in the age of neuroscience, *Journal of Experiential Education*, 38(1): 73–95.

Shulman, L.S. (1987) Knowledge and teaching: foundations of the new reform, *Harvard Educational Review*, 57(1): 1–21.

Siemens, G. (2005) Connectivism: a learning theory for the digital age, *International Journal of Instructional Technology and Distance Learning*, 2(1), www.itdl.org/Journal/Jan_05/article01.htm.

Stipek, D. (2010) *How do teachers' expectations affect student learning?* www.education.com/reference/article/teachers-expectations-affect-learning/.

Sutton Trust (2014) *What makes great teaching? Review of the underpinning research*. Durham: University of Durham.

TLRP (2007) *Principles into practice: a teacher's guide to research evidence on teaching and learning*. London: TLRP, Institute of Education, University of London.

Tomlinson, C.A. (2000) *Differentiation of instruction in the elementary grades*. ERIC Digest, http://ericir.syr.edu/plweb-cgi/obtain.pl.

Willingham, D. (2008) What will improve a student's memory? *American Educator*, 32(4): 17–25.

Wragg, E.C., Wikely, F., Wragg, E. and Haynes, G. (1996) *Teacher appraisal observed*. London: Routledge.

Zentall, S.R. and Morris, B.J. (2010) 'Good job, you're so smart': the effects of inconsistency of praise type on young children's motivation, *Journal of Experimental Child Psychology*, 107: 155–63.

5

Developing your expectations – teacher expectations and planning

Be a yardstick of quality. Some people aren't used to an environment where excellence is expected.

Steve Jobs, 2009

Our coat hook! Your 'perfect jacket' now feels better equipped with items, although some pockets may be overflowing. Review and refine what you are carrying and identify what is most useful and discard those items that are no longer of value to you and weighing you down. What is left must enable you to meet your expectations and needs, making your jacket enabling and empowering.

This chapter explores the learning experience with regard to teacher expectations and how to meet individual pupils' needs. You, as Steve Jobs (2009) pointedly stated, should be that yardstick of high expectation and communicate this in every aspect of your teacher-self. This chapter also discusses pupil engagement, independent learning and the role of effective dialogic talk, and how to effectively plan all aspects of a lesson.

The key themes in this chapter prompt you to:

- reflect upon how your *teacher identity and philosophy* influences the learning expectations of your pupils;
- appreciate how your understanding of the *purpose of education* is reflected in how you differentiate the learning within your classroom;
- consider how your focus on *well-being for you and your pupils* reflects how you plan for and respond to your pupils and your expectations of them;
- understand how your knowledge of effective lesson planning enables you to *meet the needs of the unique child*;
- appreciate how your awareness of *creating an enabling and empowering environment* reflects how you plan for the needs of each individual pupil;

- consider how your own *self-awareness* – for example, your individual expectations of or responses to pupils and your *critical self reflection* enhance your planning and delivery;
- identify how your understanding of teacher expectation, independent learning and dialogic teaching focus your need for *continuous development as a life-long learner.*

This chapter addresses the following *Teachers' standards* (DfE 2012):

1   Set high expectations which inspire, motivate and challenge pupils
2   Promote good progress and outcomes by pupils
3   Plan and teach well structured lessons
4   Adapt teaching to respond to the strengths and needs of all pupils.

Expectations

Rosenthal's study in the late 1960s, *Pygmalion in the classroom* (Rosenthal and Jacobson 1968) recognized the effect of teacher expectation on pupils' achievement. When a teacher has high expectations pupils do well; likewise when they expect them to fail, they will. In my experience, appropriately high expectations enable both pupil and teacher success and directly influence pedagogical decisions, such as pupils' ability, learning preferences and pace. As discussed in Chapter 4, expectations influence a pupil's mindset; moreover, a teacher's mindset is influenced by the expectations they hold. Understanding the factors that influence expectations enables us to create a framework for outstandingness. For example, if a teacher believes in success for all, treats all pupils as potential high achievers and actively plans to make this happen, a culture of high expectation is inevitable.

 REFLECT

- How do you communicate high expectations?
- How do you communicate your belief in your pupils' abilities to reach your expectations?

If you are not aware of your beliefs, values and possible preconceived notions regarding pupil ability, such as accent, socioeconomic status and behaviour, these can limit or have a negative effect on pupil outcomes. Consider adopting an 'expectation mind-set' and embed an awareness of your expectations in every aspect of your teaching. An expectation mindset is about *desirable change* in the learner as a result of carefully matched learning opportunities. The term 'desirable change' is distinct from the more familiar phrase 'pupil progress', which can narrow expectations to cognitive, performance-related outcomes. If our concern is for the well-being and whole development of our pupils, desirable change is a more appropriate term as it encompasses all aspects of pupil development. Raised self-awareness combined with an expectation mindset will prevent you limiting this desirable change through unintentionally communicating to pupils, 'That's good enough for you!' but 'I expect more from you!'

Have you heard 'Don't forget your Ps!'? (Perfect preparation prevents *particularly* poor performance!) Approaching a lesson with this mindset will support the mental rehearsal of the different elements, as well as maintaining high expectations to thoroughly plan for success of all pupils. Understanding and meeting the needs of all your pupils and extending these high expectations beyond the classroom to parents and the community will also build success.

However, your expectations and what you perceive as a desirable change may not match those of the pupils (or parents). It is therefore necessary to make expectations highly visible but tailored to pupils' needs, beyond the cognitive, to close the learning or developmental gap. Being responsive will enable you to adapt your expectations in a lesson. Despite the hours spent in careful preparation you do have to accept that some pupils may not respond as you predicted.

 REFLECT

View each lesson, day or week as a timeline of expectations. Review a lesson plan in the same way.

- How do you expect the pupils to enter your classroom?
- What expectations do you have for each pupil?
- Do you value and nurture each pupil's contributions?
- How do you expect your pupils to work?
- Are these moment-by-moment expectations informed and authentic?
- Do your expectations inadvertently place glass ceilings or fear of failure on some pupils?
- How do you expect each pupil to leave at the end of the day?
- Do your expectations consider cognitive, emotional, social, moral, spiritual, physical and cultural expectations?
- Does your nonverbal communication set the tone for high expectations across the whole class?

The independent learner

As educationalists, we strive to promote, among other attributes, resilience, confidence and independence. A phrase frequently used is 'independent learner' and associated terms such as 'personalization', 'child-centred learning' and 'ownership' of learning have been popularized over the past decade. Independence, to whatever degree, is a life necessity and without the ability to be an independent learner we would struggle to fulfil our learning potential or embrace lifelong learning. Independent learners often work to higher standards, are motivated, develop mastery, and have higher morale and self-esteem than others (Williams 2003). Therefore, at the heart of forming your expectations there should be the development of independence for every pupil.

When promoting independence, the teacher's role shifts to facilitator or coach, skilfully nurturing and negotiating strategies and processes with the pupil. However, becoming an independent learner is a gradual process and cannot be achieved without a strong and trusting teacher-pupil relationship (Alexander et al. 1992; Williams 2003), an enabling environment and engaging tasks. There is also a continuum of development, from dependent to independent learner, as pupils take increased ownership of and responsibility for their learning.

If independent learning becomes the norm, then challenge can be increased. This requires you to fully utilize your teacher toolkit to enable pupils to move beyond established set or norm expectations. However, for some pupils this development does not occur, especially if they develop a sense of *learned helplessness* whereby they perceive they have no control over their direct environment. Bandura (1977) identified that this occurrs due to:

- *A low sense of self-efficacy*: a pupil's repeated lack of success and their perception of fixed ability results in attributing negative outcomes to internal, stable and uncontrollable factors, as exemplified in Weiner's (1985) attribution theory (Chapter 4). This fuels further low self-concept.

- *A response-outcome expectancy*: an expectation that their behaviour has no effect, so the focus is on the response as an outcome. Too much support can place the focus on improving their performance and producing expected outcomes. TAs, who are task focused, support pupils to ensure they complete set tasks neatly and accurately but at the expense of promoting pupils' thinking, learning and independence. This can leave the pupil feeling disempowered and unchallenged. TAs should *facilitate* the learning and not *do* the task for the pupils.

To change this self-perception of helplessness the value of an individual's own competencies (Bandura 1977) must be restored. Think about baby bear's porridge ('just right!') or refer to Vygotsky's ZPD – pupil success is more assured (and the resultant dopamine released!). Setting expectations to produce desirable change sees the pupil making incremental progress. This is emotionally and intellectually satisfying, for you and the pupil, and each step the learner takes creates a new baseline from which to progress further.

Planning for independence

Independent learning can be achieved through pupils planning their own tasks, evaluating their learning, or having control within the pace and the direction of learning. This should enable pupils to develop and apply a range of skills, including:

- *cognitive* (memory, making connections, attention and problem-solving);
- *metacognitive* (how to learn and strategies needed to learn, such as listening, applying knowledge, self-assessment learning or enlisting support);
- *affective* (how to manage feelings and emotions and develop resilience, perseverance, cooperative and collaborative skills).

 CHECKLIST for independent learning

- Enable and invite pupils to make *choices* and own their learning.
- Set *purposeful* and *meaningful* tasks that relate to pupils' experiences.
- Set *clear* learning expectations, goals and targets.
- *Scaffold* learning through the teacher, TA or peers.
- Provide pupils with opportunities to *peer-* and *self-assess*.
- Offer models of independent learning through your *own actions* – i.e. showing resilience, reflection or collaboration.
- Allow pupils to *control* time and 'desired' outcomes.
- Develop a *language for learning* and vocabulary to explore the learning.
- Encourage pupils to gain 'mastery' over the learning through applying their understanding and skills to other contexts.
- Promote *higher-order thinking* skills through using a range of strategies, such as classifying, comparing or hypothesizing or use, for example, de Bono's 'thinking hats'.
- Use ICT to provide the tools for pupils to take *responsibility* for their own learning (but use it critically and strategically).

Further reading

Meyer, B., Haywood, N., Sachdev, D. and Faraday, S. (2008) *Independent learning, literature review*. London: DCSF. This report defines and comprehensively explores the many aspects of independent learning based on the findings.

Grouping pupils and expectations

An awareness of how to promote independence will influence how you group or organize your pupils. Classroom teaching is a combination of whole-class, group, paired and individual work. Additionally, pupils may also work across classes or year groups, in programmes such as Read Write Inc. The structure of grouping should fulfil a clear educational purpose and reflect the pupils' ability, background knowledge, social and emotional development, language, learning preferences and interests. Ability grouping can allow teachers to target a narrower range of pace and lesson content. However, research is not wholly conclusive regarding the effect on pupil attainment; moreover it can create an 'exaggerated sense of within-group homogeneity (sameness) and between-group heterogeneity (diversity) in the teacher's mind' (Stipek 2010 cited in Coe et al. 2014: 23) and so restrict expectations within certain groups.

The most successful countries, especially in Asia and the Pacific Rim, base schooling and grouping practices on growth mindset beliefs, communicating that learning requires time and effort (Boaler 2013). However, the UK and USA, in particular, remain focused on performance, and consequently ability grouping is prevalent. In particular, setting pupils communicates strong fixed ability messages, and commonly ability grouped English and maths subjects can place glass ceilings upon pupils. There may be the thought that 'Those pupils in "circles" will never attain what "hexagons" do!' or 'Sammy is in fiction group, he'll never be in encyclopaedias!' Unfortunately, pupils are all too aware of their 'level' among their peers (Boaler 2013; Marks 2013) and the hierarchy of the class, despite a teacher's best efforts to disguise this.

In addition, these ability groups are set early in the school year as a teacher draws conclusions regarding a pupil's strengths or weakness. If initial assessments are accurate reflections of ability and development this can lead to well-matched grouping and task setting. However, if these indicators are inaccurate and influenced by, for example, attractiveness, siblings, eloquence, behaviour, social, economic or cultural factors (Hattie 2009; Alexander 2010), grouping becomes, as Alexander concludes, 'a somewhat arbitrary affair'. To compound the problem these groups may remain unchanged for the term, a year, or worse a key stage. Misplaced teacher expectations lead to labelling pupils or groups, which can lead to a self-fulfilling prophecy and underachievement. To avoid such negative outcomes it is important to group dynamically; changing groupings as you assess and responding to pupils' specific needs as they engage with their learning.

When grouping, consider the following findings:

- high ability pupils either benefited or it made no difference;

- attainment of lower ability pupils is reduced in low ability groupings;

- lower ability pupils benefit most from mixed-ability grouping;

- pupils judged to be borderline between two ability groupings could be disadvantaged by being over-placed and not understanding the tasks, or under-placed and not encouraged to work to their full ability;

- ability groupings can develop and maintain educational, social and personal inequalities, creating, for example, an over-representation of pupils in working class families being placed into low ability groups; feelings of alienation, stigmatization and disaffection; and both groups can be the target of teasing;

- effective grouping is highly dependent on the quality of teaching, teaching goals and a safe and secure learning environment.

Further reading

Hallam, S., Ireson, J. and Davies, J. (2013) *Effective pupil grouping in the primary school: a practical guide*. London: Routledge. This book discusses the strengths and weaknesses of different groupings and offers guidance on how to implement effective grouping.

 REFLECT

Evaluate the groupings you have currently.

- Are these static (fixed lesson to lesson; term to term) or dynamic (change with the needs of the pupil and informed through assessment for learning)?
- What informs your choice of grouping?
- How do you communicate, both verbally and nonverbally, your expectations to pupils?
- How does this vary from group to group?
- How do you monitor the impact of ability grouping on pupils' attitudes to learning, their whole development, their engagement and learning outcomes?

Expectations within mixed ability classrooms will differ so all pupils make that desirable change in their learning. In classrooms we find statements such as 'All pupils will . . . or must . . .'; 'Most pupils should . . .'; or 'Some pupils could . . .'. These *differentiate* expected outcomes for each targeted group, but this might be limiting. So let's consider the term *differentiation*. What does it mean to you? Now replace it with *expectation*. Which term promotes greater aspirations for your pupils? Which promotes more specific feedback and guides intervention and engagement?

Our goal is to provide a learning environment that maximizes every pupil's potential for success and produces that 'feelgood factor'. Frame your expectations by considering all pupils *can* rather than they *can't*. If you differentiate according to 'group' you may, at the outset, be making an assumption that certain pupils can only achieve a certain level (the glass ceiling). Changing to an expectation mindset will raise your expectations of all pupils and apply the self-fulfilling prophecy positively; a key factor in pupil achievement.

 STRATEGIES FOR YOUR TEACHER TOOLKIT

Tomlinson (2001) identifies three elements of differentiation: *content*, *process* and *products*, which we can apply to how we tailor expectations within our classroom.

Expectation by content

The content, commonly defined by the curriculum, can be presented in a variety of ways and adjusted by degree of complexity to meet pupils' needs. For example:

* ensure you *know* your pupils so that ability, experience and interests can be planned to increase engagement;
* design and use *richness* of task to engage pupils collaboratively and meaningfully, and reinforce the growth mindset that effort underpins success, rather than specific activities for specific groups;
* *clarify* key concepts or big ideas to ensure that all pupils gain a deeper understanding and make connections that can be applied in future learning;
* use *varied* support through TAs and resources, making sure the lower ability or SEND pupils are not solely taught by the TA.

Write clear, visible learning objectives in *incremental steps* to create a continuum. This makes it easier for pupils to tackle the next step when entering at varying levels, avoids limiting certain groups and makes the learning pathway clear. Take a strand of the maths or English curriculum, for example fractions or punctuation, and write down the learning pathway for the year group you have worked with, referring to the expectations of the year groups above and below.

Expectation by process

Focus on flexible, dynamic grouping and the use of appropriate teaching strategies. For example:

* *vary* the lesson *structure*; use a three-part or five-part lesson with whole-class, group, pair or individual work;
* design a range of activities that *appeal* to differing needs or preferences; create pupil workstations, or pupil-selected tasks based on assessment information;
* *vary* the *input* based on assessment – if some pupils already know the information, engage them in an independent activity, followed up after the main input with the rest of the class, or offer a pre-learning lesson to specific pupils to prepare and sensitize them to the key concepts in the main activity;
* design tasks, activities and procedures that emphasize *collaborative* working and *critical* and *creative* thinking through the use of taxonomies (discussed in Chapter 6).

Expectation by products

Ensure you know each pupil's prior understanding and experience to plan for and respond to needs. For example:

* set the right *challenge* for all abilities to maximize learning potential – however, be aware of glass ceilings and personal factors affecting expectations and aspirations of certain groups/individuals;
* use *assessment* for learning as a teaching tool before, during and after a lesson to extend understanding rather than merely measuring performance;
* set different *outcomes*, whereby all pupils are given the same rich task, and the teacher evaluates the outcomes to support subsequent planning.

Make quality visible and model your expectations of excellence at key points in your lessons. Act as role model, use the pupils or, if appropriate, an outside expert (e.g. a professional or subject expert). Selecting high quality examples of pupils' work and carefully deconstructing these examples allows them to 'see' and understand the thought processes as well as the execution. This makes the task more real and therefore more 'doable' for the learner. Make appropriate, informed, high expectations a non-negotiable and consistent feature of your teaching.

 REFLECT

Select a lesson you have recently planned. Review the learning objective and your expectations for individuals or groups in your class. *Did pupils achieve and exceed or were limits placed on their learning and potential attainment?*

Now try rephrasing your learning objective using *quantitative* terms to determine how much is achieved in a given timescale; and *qualitative* terms to determine the depth of challenge. Use open language, such as 'at least', 'more than', 'a minimum of' for quantitative expectations; and set qualitative expectations along a continuum, making the previous and next steps apparent and accessible to pupils. For example: 'Write *at least* 3 sentences, 7 sentences, 10 sentences within a timeframe' (a *quantitative expectation)* 'using a range of compound or complex sentences and specific adjectives or adverbs' (a *qualitative expectation).*

Use phrases such as 'If you finish . . . then you need to . . .' to provide for clarity for the next step in learning. Challenge pupils to progress to more demanding tasks (dispelling glass ceilings), make learning decisions through the use of well-matched checklists and develop a culture of 'having a go' (growth mindset).

Target setting and getting

Targets for you and your pupils should be 'aspirational yet realistic' (i.e. informed and sufficiently challenging). Know your whole school's targets and how these relate to the school's performance data and national priorities. Build your knowledge of the developmental, social, economic or cultural factors that may affect the whole class, groups and individuals.

 STRATEGIES FOR YOUR TEACHER TOOLKIT

Target setting varies from pupil to pupil and is most effective when pupils are involved and take ownership of their learning. Try these two models when setting targets.

Be SMART: Specific, Measureable, Achievable, Realistic and Time-based (Doran 1981)

- Display the learning objective for the lesson/session/day/targets on the board.
- Make long- and medium-term targets visible and accessible so pupils refer to them regularly.
- Create individual, shorter-term targets, made visible and accessible to the pupils (e.g. use a different colour pen, target cards in their book, bookmarks or workmats).
- Demonstrate what success looks like and ask pupils to articulate to avoid misconceptions.
- Use accessible language so pupils understand and access their targets.
- 'Chunk up' learning into achievable parts, no matter how small, and plan for success and a feelgood factor.
- Regularly review and monitor learning and evaluate the effectiveness of targets.
- Involve pupils in their learning (e.g. the 'plan, do and review' approach used in the Early Years is a great example of involving pupils in their own target setting and getting.

Have POWER: Positive, Own role, What specifically? Evidence and Relationship (Day and Tosey 2011)

- State the target in the positive.
- Identify the pupil's role in achieving the target.
- What specifically? Pupils assess their own starting point and actions.
- What evidence will the pupil have to indicate progress towards their target and know when it is achieved?
- How does moving towards achieving their target affect the pupil's relationship with others, and their self-perception?

Lesson planning

Give me six hours to chop down a tree and I will spend the first four sharpening the axe.

Abraham Lincoln

Wise words indeed from Abraham Lincoln, because if we rush at something ill-prepared, without sufficient time given to both mental rehearsal and preparing the appropriate resources, we cannot expect to succeed. Appropriate content, process and products don't just happen, they need careful planning which requires time and thought. Planning, therefore, is the bedrock of a successful classroom. Ofsted differentiates between the existence of a lesson plan and evidence that a lesson *is* planned. This might sound like semantics but a lesson plan neatly (or not) presented on paper might bear no relation to what actually happens in the classroom. However, if a lesson *is* planned this comes from being able to see that the teacher knows the pupils and is meeting their needs in a structured, organized and well-managed manner. When the first round of Ofsted inspections occurred I was mortified to find I'd forgotten my lesson plan. I, of course apologized profusely to the 'I-will-show-no-emotions' inspector who replied 'Don't worry, I can see this is a well planned lesson with clear focus.' Phew! I wouldn't advocate throwing your lesson plans to the wind but for outstanding teachers less is sometimes more when it comes to planning. The less detailed the planning, the more flexible and responsive the teaching, and so the plan becomes more 'stage directions' than 'script'.

Detailed planning is entirely necessary when developing the multiple facets of your teaching, but once embedded the level of detail can be reduced. Recall a complex skill you have learnt, for example driving a car or learning to juggle. At first it seems complex and demands great cognitive and physical effort, but when each element is mastered it becomes more instinctive and almost effortless. Mastering teaching is the same – it takes time and effort.

Unfortunately the ultimate, failsafe recipe for an outstanding lesson plan doesn't really exist. Although many 'definitive' checklists and ready-made outstanding lesson plans can be downloaded to deliver that all-singing, all-dancing outstanding lesson, this 'off-the-shelf' approach may have contributed to the focus on teachers' performance rather than pupils' learning, and reduces the potential for creativity, spontaneity and innovation and responding to pupil's needs and interests.

Nevertheless, we can, and should, consider the many variables in planning, such as the pupils' learning and emotional needs; learning contexts; specific learning objectives; prior knowledge and experience; success criteria and assessment; lesson structure (beginning to end); plenaries; key questions; learning strategies; activities or tasks; resources; support and interventions; and use of space and time. A thorough knowledge of the whole curriculum is essential, as well as a clear understanding of the potential of ICT to support learning. If these variables are not fully planned, the result could easily be a poor learning experience and lack of motivation from the pupils and yourself.

An effective lesson plan requires clarity about what the intended learning is going to look like. Learning has to be planned with this outcome in mind, and knowledge of the pupils' prior learning experiences, interests and how they learn best is needed. A point worth noting is that lengthy planning tends to be done in advance. This is problematic if it is not informed through formative assessment (discussed in Chapter 6), and the lesson detail may inadvertently shift your focus from pupils' needs and interests to the content. Therefore, don't lose sight of what is important: the pupil. Be responsive, flexible, use assessment for learning and don't be afraid to stray from the lesson plan.

Models of lesson planning

There are a number of approaches to lesson planning, however a dominant model is Tyler (1949, cited in Richards and Renandya 2008), based on four steps:

- specify objectives (what are they going to be learning?);
- select learning activities;
- organize learning activities;
- specify methods of evaluation (how will they know if they have learnt it?).

However, teaching is rarely this linear. Your response to pupils' needs is paramount and particularly those that influence their motivation. Keller's ARCS model of motivation provides the basis for a systematic lesson planning process that supports creating motivational strategies that match pupils' needs (Keller 1987, 2000). The categories are: attention (A), relevance (R), confidence (C) and satisfaction (S).

 REFLECT

When planning or evaluating a lesson consider the following set of questions.

Attention: grab their attention through the use of, for example, a stimulating question, an artefact, role play, or a thought provoking reading or video clip.

- What can I do to capture their interest?
- How can I stimulate an attitude of enquiry?
- How can I use a variety of strategies to maintain attention?

Relevance: use language and examples that your pupils can relate or connect to (understand their cultural capital, their interests/activities within and outside school).

- How can I best meet my pupils' needs? (Do I know them?)
- How and when can I provide my pupils with appropriate choices, responsibilities and role models?
- How can I connect to the pupils' prior experiences?

Confidence: make sure the content is not too challenging through accurate use of assessment for learning. Plan for success through chunking tasks, modelling and support.

- How can I assist in building a positive expectation for success?
- How will the learning experience support or enhance the pupils' sense of self-efficacy?
- How will the pupils know their success is based upon their efforts?

Satisfaction: at the end of the learning experience pupils need a sense of achievement through acknowledging their effort and resilience to promote a growth mindset.

- How can I provide meaningful opportunities for pupils to use their newly acquired knowledge/skill?
- What will provide reinforcement to pupils' successes?
- How can I assist the pupil in anchoring a positive feeling about their accomplishments?

Learning objectives and outcomes

If our premise is creating *desirable change* in pupils the learning objective serves as an explicit way to describe the change expected. It describes the intended learning result or outcome, rather than the *process* of learning. Consider adding WIIFM (What's in it for me?), when sharing the WALT (we are learning to) and WILF (what I'm looking for), so that the pupils and their learning are at the very core of your planning and the objectives relate directly to them.

Learning objectives should be explicitly linked to a key skill and decontextualized so they do not include the context or activity. This has a positive impact on teaching and learning (Clarke 2008) and enables pupils to transfer the learning to another context. A trainee teacher commented: 'I have improved my learning objectives by decontextualizing them and then writing the context separately. If I continue to do this, it will improve the children's ability to transfer the skills they learn to other contexts.'

A learning objective should have a measurable or action verb that specifies what the pupil is able to do. These action verbs can be drawn from taxonomies, such as Bloom's, which provide focus for learning expectations (discussed in Chapter 6). Generally, closed learning objectives are often knowledge based, for example *To know that* . . .; *To identify* . . . and open learning objectives are often skill based, e.g. *To develop* . . ., *To reflect on* . . .

Be aware that a focus on achievable objectives and accountability can lead to learning objectives being formulated to be either observable or measurable. This can impede more constructivist or neo-constructivist approaches to teaching whereby collaboration and co-construction of knowledge is the focus. Such approaches will often produce less predictable outcomes and be perceived as risk-taking, but can be more valuable than the intended objective.

Success criteria

Pupils knowing what they are learning and how well they have learnt it can be achieved through the use of success criteria. A success criterion should be clearly linked to the learning objective and be in pupil-friendly language. Through modelling the success criteria you can raise expectations and inspire and empower your pupils by making the learning journey concrete and achievable. They act as building blocks for the steps toward achieving the learning objective – so aim high. Moreover, scaffold effective peer and self-assessment through the 'Can I . . .' or 'I can . . .' and 'Have I . . .?' or 'I have . . . ?' statements. The next step is for pupils to generate their own criteria and further personalize their learning and their ownership of it.

A guide to lesson planning

Outstanding lessons need careful planning and each element should be thought through with care. This following section offers a series of questions to guide you through planning great lessons from beginning to end.

Lesson 'starters' or 'dynamic starts'?

A lesson starter sets the expectations of not only the learning content but the pace, behaviour and tone of the lesson. Design starter activities to engage all pupils quickly, get them thinking and provide a purposeful atmosphere.

CHECKLIST for planning lesson starters

- Does it 'hook' the learner immediately and fully engage them? (If pupils are disinterested at the beginning, engagement and deeper learning is unlikely.)
- Does it incorporate the use of novelty, mystery, curiosity or particular relevance using visual, auditory and kinaesthetic elements?
- Do the pupils know what they are going to learn?
- Are the learning expectations clear and linked to the lesson objectives and success criteria?
- Do the pupils know why this learning is important to them?
- Does it connect with prior learning and experiences, building on previous lessons or assimilating a new concept or skill?
- Is it accessible for all learners through differentiating the level of challenge, questioning and resources, including use of a TA, to support the teaching points?
- What classroom layout or location is best suited for the starter activity?
- Is the time the pupils are sitting on the carpet/listening consistent with their concentration span? (Apply the formula of one minute for each year of age.)

If you can say 'YES' to most or all of the above questions you have planned a scintillating starter!

Further reading

Phillips, R. (2001) Making history curious: using initial stimulus material (ISM) to promote enquiry, thinking and literacy, *Teaching History*, 105 (December). Describes the use of varied *initial stimulus materials* (ISMs) such as visual sources, text and stories, and music to hook pupils into the lesson.

Plenaries and mini-plenaries

Plenaries can be carefully planned or spontaneous, informed through formative assessment. They help pupils appreciate not only what they learn but also how they have learned it (metacognition). Encourage pupils to explore and extend their learning through asking them to explain how they arrived at their answers and to uncover the skills and strategies used (Fisher 2002). In the process of explaining, support pupils to not only make connections but also use the appropriate vocabulary to explain their thinking.

 CHECKLIST for planning lesson plenaries

- Does the plenary link to the learning objectives and success criteria of the lesson? The flow of the lesson and connectedness needs to be clear.

- Is there a plenary at a strategic point in your teaching sequence?
- Does it summarize, assess, consolidate or extend learning? Make sure the plenary serves a specific purpose and know how you can evaluate its effectiveness.
- Will it give pupils a sense of achievement in the successful completion of tasks set or the learning steps? If the learning is chunked this will aide the feelgood factor.
- Does it enable pupils to crystallize their thoughts and see the 'big picture' by placing their learning in the context of past and future learning or steps to achieve the final outcome?
- Does it promote thinking and talking about the learning as well as the pupils' learning strategies and thinking processes?
- Will it stimulate interest, curiosity and excitement about the next phase of learning? Will it motivate the pupils (remember the formula V x E = M!).

If you can say 'YES' to most or all of the above questions you have planned a purposeful plenary!

Further reading

DfES (2004) *Key Stage 3 national strategy pedagogy and practice, Unit 5: starters and plenaries*. London: DfES. This study guide offers sound, practical strategies that can be implemented and adapted for your needs.

Pace

> *. . . like oxygen, too much and it gets you high, not enough and you die!!*

An outstanding lesson has a good pace, neither too fast nor too slow. This is one of the hardest teaching skills because it depends upon your judgement of each pupil's work rate (Beard 2014). Pace is often a target set for a trainee teacher to address, yet planning for pupils who progress at different learning rates while meeting both qualitative and quantitative expectations is demanding. Ideally the outstanding teacher is in tune with the dynamics of their classroom. They quickly notice when the pace of the lesson falters, when pupils become disengaged and the classroom 'buzz' changes, and respond accordingly.

The pupils' learning rather than the timings within your lesson plan should determine the pace of learning. However heartbreaking or worrying it might be to discard part of your carefully planned lesson and teach without this safety net, you must weigh up the cost of 'covering' the material and finishing the lesson on time or *actual learning*. Will you be left with a sea of blank faces or with the sparkle in the eyes that tells you their learning switch has been turned on?

 CHECKLIST for planning pace

- Have you made the learning goals clear through effectively sharing the learning objective and success criteria? Make expectations transparent to the pupils through modelling, explaining and consistently referring to and rein-forcing them.

- Is there a sense of urgency while still providing ample wait/think/take-up time? For example, try using sand timers, IWB timers, verbal countdown or auditory cues such as TV's *Countdown* music for the final moments of a task.
- Are explanations succinct, clear and focused? Avoid overly wordy instructions and explanations as this makes it difficult for pupils to identify what is import-ant information. Also avoid interrupting or adding further explanation once pupils start a task (refer to the WM sections in Chapter 4).
- Are instructions/guidelines displayed visually to support understanding, expectations and independence? Avoid repeating yourself – instead use the board or IWB to display relevant information. Ensure pupils can access, understand and apply the vocabulary you use. Use checklists, steps within the process, deconstructed final outcomes or an example of the final out-come as scaffolding.
- Are you using a range of teaching strategies to appeal to and engage all pupils? Reflect upon whether the planned activities promote independent learning. Select the most effective strategies from your teacher toolkit to promote that 'buzz' in the classroom. Use, for example, choral speaking or role play to enliven, draw together or develop learning if needed.
- Have you planned for smooth transition points? Identify the potential 'hot spots' in a lesson when engagement, noise, behaviour and time may be an issue. Aim to think two steps ahead and organize and prepare resources, pupils and so on, to minimize disruption to learning.
- Are all resources prepared, counted out, in working order and accessible? Please don't plan a cutting activity and find you have just 11 scissors left; brace yourself for the riot to happen!
- Have you embedded assessment for learning in your lesson plan? Well-formed, timely key questions and keen observations will inform you of the effectiveness of your teaching and resultant learning. Gauge this through, for example, the use of thumbs up, traffic lights, talk partners or learning thermometers during the lesson.
- Do you empower pupils to lead and monitor their learning? Assign roles to pupils who will take responsibility and help maintain pace and focus during tasks.
- Are you dynamic or do you limit yourself to a focus group? Have 360-degree awareness of what is going on in your classroom and act responsively.

If you can say 'YES' to most or all of the above questions you have planned for perfect pace!

Lesson 'enders' or lesson 'simply ends'?

All too often, teachers fail to reserve enough time to effectively close a lesson. Avoid feeling rushed or running out of time by rigorously setting aside time for the lesson ending.

CHECKLIST for planning lesson endings

- Does the lesson leave them wanting more? 'Sell' your subject as suggested in Chapter 3.
- Are the pupils aware of the significance of what they learned and connections to themselves and prior and future learning?
- Are you able to assess pupils' mastery of or progress toward the specific learning objective? Good subject knowledge and effective use of assessment for learning will support this.
- How will this inform your planning for the next lesson? Reflect on how your assessment will impact on the next steps for each pupil.

If you can say 'YES' to most or all of the above questions you have planned an excellent ending!

Homework

There are generally two purposes for homework – firstly to practise, and secondly for preparation or elaboration. With homework for practice, such as simple addition and subtraction problems, the pupils should already be able to solve them with confidence. Ensure that misconceptions or misunderstandings are dealt with prior to sending homework home and that parents have the necessary knowledge and skills to support their child. This will avoid the effort of undoing reinforced misconceptions and tackling the conversation 'That's how I did it in my day!' Homework for preparation or elaboration should be easily understood, modelled and differentiated if necessary. A homework policy should explain the role of homework, the amount expected, the consequences for not completing it, and the parental involvement required; refer to this when needed.

 CHECKLIST for planning homework

- Do pupils know the reason for the task? Apply the formula again: $V \times E = M$.
- Are the instructions clear and accessible to all pupils?
- Is there a realistic time expectation? Be aware of the time and level of abilities your parents have to support their child and don't set expectations that will induce anxiety.
- Are the expectations clear to pupils and parents? Know the language needs of your pupils and parents and provide bilingual instructions and support material if necessary.
- Is there a need or opportunity to offer parental workshops so they feel empowered and enabled to support their child? Knowing your parental body will enable you to more ably target specific needs through open sessions, drop-ins or workshops.

If you can say 'YES' to most or all of the above questions you have planned helpful homework!

Dialogic teaching

Dialogic teaching harnesses the power of talk to stimulate and extend pupils' thinking and advance their learning and understanding.

Robin Alexander, 2008

Dialogic teaching was developed by Robin Alexander in the early 2000s. He saw that engaging in productive, thoughtful and thought-provoking talk could develop pupils' learning and understanding. It is your role, as Alexander (2008) notes, to use dialogic teaching to harness this. As identified in the *School inspection handbook* (Ofsted 2015) 'teachers use questioning and discussion to assess the effectiveness of their teaching and promote pupils' learning'. Vygotsky's socio-constructivist theory is relevant to this approach as using language to communicate helps us learn and access higher-order thinking skills. Undeniably, we all want our pupils to be able to use a richness of language to express their thoughts, engage with others in building their understanding and develop reflective and more critical thinking skills. It is therefore important you explain and model this language and scaffold how they use it.

Dialogic talk enables pupils to gain from intermental experience, especially between a learner and more knowledgeable others, and intramental activity (discussed in Chapter 2) where the pupil uses metacognitive thinking. This nature of classroom talk helps teachers diagnose pupils' needs, frame their learning tasks and assess progress.

Developing a dialogic classroom

Dialogic teaching has an element of 'risk' as the direction of co-constructed talk between teacher and pupils is less predictable. If you seem to be doing most of the talking, think about how you could shift the balance toward the pupils. You might like to try the following strategies.

• •

 STRATEGIES FOR YOUR TEACHER TOOLKIT

Questioning

- Be mindful of the questions you ask and the range of responses you receive.
- Ask accessible, hypothetical or challenging open-ended questions which invite more than simple recall.
- Ensure you ask 'authentic' questions, to probe into pupils' understanding or views and not to see simply what they know and don't know.
- Select questions without predetermined answers (Nystrand and Gamoran 1991) to reinforce a genuine dialogue.
- Use checking and probing questions, such as, 'So, what I think you are saying is . . . is that right?'; 'Why do you think that?'; 'Who else agrees?' to clarify and

extend pupils' responses and understanding, but do avoid putting words into their mouths.

Teacher responses

- Your feedback should inform, encourage and extend thinking.
- Promote discussion, probe and challenge rather than unquestioningly accept.
- Be mindful of how you respond, show a genuine interest in thoughts and opinions and value the contributions from all pupils.

Approaches

- Classroom organization, climate and relationships influence dialogue.
- Encourage and model risk-taking to move classroom discourse beyond the safe and conventional.
- Apply a no-hands-up strategy (e.g. names on lolly sticks or top hat on SMART board) to volunteer answers.
- Provide opportunities to write answers on mini whiteboards from which you read a few.

Pupil responses

- Encourage a chain of exchanges to deepen lines of enquiry.
- Ask pupils to justify their answers, follow up and build upon their understanding.
- Offer a choice between several possible answers and then vote on or debate the options.
- Use think-pair-share: a cooperative learning strategy.
- Build in time for the pupils to think and respond.
- Apply POSE (pupils remain hands down and reflective); PAUSE . . . (think and think again to maintain reflection); BOUNCE (ask a pupil, identify support needed and allow for peer support); POUNCE! (ask opinion of first response individually or as a group focusing on 'why?' the pupil thinks this); EXPLORE (extend pupils' thinking rather than rushing on).
- Use wait time.

Further reading

Alexander, R.J. (2008) *Towards dialogic teaching: rethinking classroom talk*, 4th edn. York: Dialogos. Alexander's framework empowers the pupil for lifelong learning and active citizenship, as 'dialogic teaching is not just any talk'.

Hattie, J. (2011) *Visible learning for teachers: maximizing impact on learning*. London: Routledge. Provides a step-by-step guidance to the successful implementation of visible learning and teaching in the classroom.

Ritchhart, R., Church, M. and Morrison, K. (2011) *Making thinking visible*. San Francisco: Jossey-Bass. This illustrates numerous thinking routines in the 'Visible Thinking Program'.

Questioning and wait time 1 and 2

Good teaching is more a giving of right questions than a giving of right answers.

Josef Albers, 1963

Planning quality key questions, as Josef Albers (1963) notes, is essential to developing your teaching as it explores and challenges pupils' misunderstandings and promotes higher-order thinking skills as well as a dialogic approach. However, as studies show, teachers can unconsciously inhibit learning by getting trapped into initiation-response (I-R) or initiation-response-feedback (I-R-F) modes of questioning. The focus is wrongly placed on 'safe' coverage of material and deeper learning is inhibited, despite pupils apparently answering correctly. Effective questions require pupils to make connections and to challenge and reflect on their understanding as they respond to and articulate answers.

Mary Budd Rowe's extensive research (1974) found that increasing *wait time* (time between I and R) to a minimum of three to five seconds increased pupil recall, the quality of responses and, therefore, their learning. In other words, taking a deep breath and toughing out that awkward silence (and it will seem longer than three seconds) gives pupils an opportunity to manipulate information within their WM, draw upon LTM and articulate an answer. Increased wait time was also found to improve the number of pupils responding, their self-confidence and peer discussion.

Another type of wait time, wait time 2, is the time period after the pupil's initial response and before the teacher's reaction or feedback (I-R and F). Research, by Ian Gilbert (2014), showed that the average length of wait time 2 is less than one second and yet the optimum length is, again, a minimum of three seconds. By increasing this wait time teachers give pupils an opportunity to develop their answers and stimulate discussion. This does, of course, require the strong foundations of excellent subject knowledge and positive relationships with pupils. It also requires you to hold your nerve and maintain that silence.

The other benefit of increasing wait times is teacher related. Teachers listen more and engage pupils in discussions, asking a greater range of questions, including higher-order thinking ones. Their expectations also change, as they view less able or responsive pupils more positively.

Further reading

Rowe, M.B. (1974) Wait time and rewards as instructional variables, their influence on language, logic and fate control, *Journal of Research in Science Teaching*, 11: 81–94.

REFLECT – in the classroom

Monitor the amount and type of talking in your classroom using a digital recorder. Initially focus on one part of a lesson, such as a plenary or work with a colleague to observe each other's lessons.

Use Table 5.1 to analyse the use of wait times and the types of question, especially those promoting thinking skills and higher-order questions from Bloom's taxonomy (see Chapter 6).

Table 5.1 Style of questions.

Question type	No. of responses	Strategy used, e.g. lollysticks, no hands- up, tell a friend . . .	Wait time 1	Wait time 2
Closed questions (generally lower cognitive demand)				
Open questions (generally higher cognitive demand)				
Recall information (e.g. 'How many wives did Henry VIII have?')				
Probing				
Other				

Further reading

The Measures of Effective Teaching (MET) Project (2010), Bill and Melinda Gates Foundation (www.gatesfoundation.org/media-center/press-releases/2013/01/measures-of-effective-teaching-project-releases-final-research-report). Using Cambridge Education's Tripod Project survey, this focuses on the activities of the teacher referred to as the 'Seven Cs'.

Luthans, F. and Peterson, S.J. (2003) 360-degree feedback with systematic coaching, *Human Resource Management*, 42(3): 243–56. This approach suggests combining feedback with coaching focused on enhanced self-awareness and behavioural management.

A thought ... teacher expectations greatly influence whether or not desirable change happens for their learners. Your planning should make pupils think, make connections, use high quality discourse, understand the meaning of what is being taught and the value of their own learning. The litmus test is to ask yourself 'If there are no pupils in my classroom, could I still teach what I have planned?' If your answer is yes, don't do it!

An outstanding teacher creates a dynamic and challenging environment, yet affirming to pupils' self-worth and sense of self-efficacy. Resilience to failure is built and independence fostered. Your expectations will promote a mastery orientation and growth mindset and your attributions will encourage and reinforce either success or failure. Plan for success.

References

Albers, J. ([1963] 2006) *Interaction of color, revised and expanded edition*. New Haven, CT: Yale University Press.

Alexander, R.J. (2008) *Towards dialogic teaching: rethinking classroom talk*, 4th edn. York: Dialogos.

Alexander, R. J. (2010) *Children, their world, their education: final report and recommendations of the Cambridge Primary Review*. London: Routledge.

Alexander, R.J., Rose, J. and Woodhead, C. (1992) *Curriculum organisation and classroom practice in primary schools*. London: DfES.

Bandura, A. (1977) Self-efficacy: toward a unifying theory of behavioral change, *Psychological Review*, 84(2): 191–215.

Beard, R. (2014) *Outstanding lessons made simple*. United Kingdom: Author House.

Boaler, J. (2013) Ability and mathematics: the mindset revolution that is reshaping education, *Symposium Journals* 55(1): 143–52.

Clarke, S. (2008) *Active learning through formative assessment*. London: Hodder Education.

Coe, R., Aloisi, C., Higgins, S. and Major, L.E. (2014) *What makes great teaching? Review of the underpinning research*. Durham: Sutton Trust, Centre for Evaluation & Monitoring, Durham University.

Day, T. and Tosey, P. (2011) Beyond SMART? A new framework for goal setting, *The Curriculum Journal*, 22(4): 515–34.

DfE (2012) *Teachers' standards*, www.gov.uk/government/uploads/system/uploads/attachment_data/file/301107/Teachers__Standards.pdf.

Doran, G.T. (1981) There's a SMART way to write management's goals and objectives, *Management Review*, 70(11): 35–6.

Fisher, P. (2002) *Thinking through history*. Cambridge: Chris Kington Publishing.

Gilbert, I. (2014) *Why do I need a teacher when I've got Google?: The essential guide to the big issues for every teacher*, 2nd edn. London: Routledge.

Hattie, J. (2009) *Visible learning: a synthesis of over 800 meta-analyses relating to achievement*. London: Routledge.

Jobs, S. (2009) Apple CEO Steve Job's 12 rules of success, www.businessbrief.com/apple-ceo-steve-jobs-12-rules-of-success.

Keller, J. M. (1987) The systematic process of motivational design, *Performance & Instruction*, 26(9): 1–8.

Keller, J. (2000) *How to integrate learner motivation planning into lesson planning: the ARCS model approach*, Florida State University: paper presented at VII Semanario, Santiago, Cuba, February 2000.

Marks, R. (2013) 'The blue table means you don't have a clue': the persistence of fixed-ability thinking and practices in primary mathematics in English schools, *FORUM*, 55(1), 29–42.

Nystrand, M. and Gamoran, A. (1991) Instructional discourse, student engagement, and literature achievement, *Research in the Teaching of English*, 25: 261–90.

Ofsted (2015) *School inspection handbook*, www.gov.uk/government/ofsted.

Richards, J.C. and Renandya, W.A. (2008) *Methodology in language teaching: an anthology of current practice*. Cambridge: Cambridge University Press.

Rosenthal, R., and Jacobson, L. (1968) *Pygmalion in the classroom: teachers' expectations and pupils' intellectual development*. New York: Rinehart & Winston.

Rowe, M.B. (1974) Wait time and rewards as instructional variables, their influence on language, logic and fate control, *Journal of Research in Science Teaching*, 11: 81–94.

Stipek, D. (2010) *How do teachers' expectations affect student learning*, www.education.com/reference/article/teachers-expectations-affect-learning.

Tyler, R. (1949) *Basic principles of curriculum and instruction*. Chicago: University of Chicago Press.

Tomlinson, C.A. (2001) *How to differentiate instruction in mixed-ability classrooms*, 2nd edn. Alexandria, VA: ASCD.

Weiner, B. (1985) An attributional theory of achievement motivation and emotion, *Psychological Review*, 92(4): 548–73.

Williams, J. (2003) *Promoting independent learning in the primary classroom*. Buckingham: Open University Press.

6

Developing your understanding – assessment

Everybody is a genius. But if you judge a fish by its ability to climb a tree, it will live its whole life believing that it is stupid.

Attributed to Albert Einstein

Our coat hook! Your 'perfect jacket' now fits well and the pockets are full. And yet, just when you thought you had all the essential items, an unexpected situation arises and you are not prepared. You scrabble around trying to find something to meet this requirement, and sadly it's not there. It's time to fill your pockets more judiciously with just the right items and know exactly where to lay your hands on them.

This chapter discusses the what, the why and how of assessment, with a particular focus on formative assessment, and its contribution to outstandingness. If we create an assessment system that is rigid and unilateral we will be, as the above quote sagely notes, setting up some children to fail. If you view planning and assessment as integral by nature you are better equipped to assess for the good of the pupil and not to their detriment. Taxonomies are discussed to illustrate a way to support this.

The key themes in this chapter prompt you to:

- reflect upon how your *teacher identity and philosophy* influence your preference and use of assessment approaches;
- consider how your understanding of the *purpose of education* reflects in how you see and value the outcomes of assessment;
- appreciate how your focus on *well-being for you and your pupils* reflects in how you respond to the demands of pupil and the need to assess their progress;
- consider how your knowledge of assessment enables you to *meet the needs of the unique child*;

- reflect how your awareness of *creating an enabling and empowering environment* reflects in your assessment procedures and feedback for each individual pupil;
- appreciate how your own *self-awareness* and *critical self-reflection* enhances how you plan, assess and feed back to each pupil to develop their potential;
- consider how your understanding of the range of assessments and the use of taxonomies identifies needs for *continuous development as a lifelong learner*.

This chapter addresses the following *Teachers' standards* (DfE 2012):

2 Promote good progress and outcomes by pupils.
6 Make accurate and productive use of assessment.

The purpose of assessment

If we refer back to the origins of the word pedagogy, *paidagogus*, meaning 'to tend to the child', and the Latin origins of assessment being *assidere*, meaning to 'sit by', the role of a teacher is very clearly defined – namely one whose central focus is on the child. Of course an outstanding teacher constantly monitors the learning of their pupils and uses assessment as the tool to inform them. Effective assessment leads the pupil, and working or 'sitting' with them identifies what a pupil has and has not understood. Assessment is a tool to evaluate teaching methods and strategies. It provides a valid and reliable measure of desirable change we make for our pupils, ourselves, the school, both nationally and internationally. The focus needs to be on how assessment relates to outstanding teaching and effective learning. Therefore all assessment practices should improve learning; if this is not the case, stop and change what you are doing.

Over the past 20 years, summative, high-stake testing and demanding tracking documents have strongly influenced attitudes towards assessment. Mention assessment in the staffroom and you may receive an exasperated sigh and a slump of the shoulders, the sign that assessment is a burden. Perhaps if the purpose of assessment is really understood and the potential data elicited are seen to enhance and scaffold practice rather than weighing it down, colleagues' responses to assessment would be positive.

The removal of levels in 2014 to reports on attainment (except end of key stage) requires schools to develop their own approaches to monitor and formatively assess progress and attainment. A culture shift to move the preoccupation away from assigning levels and sublevels to pupils to a more informed and informative approach, with an emphasis on actual progress, has been slow to realize. Perhaps over time 'life without levels' may see embedded assessment *for* learning (AfL), enhanced pupil engagement in their learning and the resultant positive impact on progress as pupils are no longer assigned a number.

However, the end of Key Stage 2 tests remain and so accountability will still be a driving force behind assessment practice. There are four purposes of assessment, as follows.

1   Assessment for accountability

A summative assessment that informs others! Since the introduction of the National Curriculum this form of assessment has taken greater prominence. Comparing school examination results in the form of 'league tables' and increased parental awareness, online information (*go compare* your school!!) and freedom of choice all add to the pressure on the school and individual teachers to get the requisite percentage of Level 4 or above at the end of Key Stage 2. Although Ofsted (2015) state inspectors should use a range of data to judge a school's performance, (including RAISE online, the school data dashboard, examination or key stage results and internal assessments), the effects of 'high stakes' testing, increased accountability on pupils' progress and judgements made against teacher performance have been significant. This pressure has resulted in teachers more readily adopting the seemingly safe 'transmission' model of teaching rather than potentially more effective strategies which promote deeper learning.

The pressure of accountability starts so young (in Key Stage 1) and this inevitably results in some pupils' early disengagement with learning – compounded, in some cases, with the main aim in Year 6 being *success* in end of Key Stage 2 tests (Hall et al. 2004). This need for *success*, as Waugh and Jolliffe (2008) note, has resulted in some children leaving primary education with a feeling of failure. If we reframed the term 'success' to mean success for each individual pupil and not for the teacher, the school or nation, we would avoid this harmful feeling of failure.

2   Assessment of learning

A summative assessment that sums up the learning! Assessment *of* learning (AoL) checks if individual pupils have reached certain learning goals. It is criterion referenced so, for example, comparisons between pupils can be made, and it provides information for transition between classes, years, key stages or schools. AoL can have limited impact on pupils' learning. However, if the analysis of summative assessment is used for formative purposes it will benefit the pupil (Scriven 1967). Reflecting on the nature of deep learning, discussed in Chapter 4, there is a clear case of using testing to enhance the learning process. Nevertheless, the focus on accountability and amassing performance data has undermined Scriven's more synergistic assessment practices – an unfortunate case of 'weighing the pig doesn't make it fatter'.

Popham (1998) uses the terms *fixing* (using formative assessment to improve practice) and *firing* (using summative assessment associated with accountability as described above, such as performance-related pay – PRP – or performance management), which seems to sum up current feelings toward assessment. 'Fixing', however cannot happen without an enabling environment, otherwise teachers with potential to improve could feel at risk and fear will inhibit their development and that of their pupils. A shift of focus from an external (firing) to an internal (fixing) analysis of summative assessment would allow pupils, teachers and stakeholders to see that the core aim of assessment is to improve the learning and success of each unique pupil, and not simply a method by with which to measure and report to others.

3   Assessment for learning

A formative assessment that informs you of the learning! The achievement gains associated with assessment *for* learning (AfL) have been described as among the largest ever reported for educational interventions (EEF 2015), especially for low attaining or SEN pupils. The 10 principles identified by the Assessment Reform Group (ARG 2002) remain an invaluable reference point:

- part of effective planning;
- how pupils learn;
- central to classroom practice;
- key professional skill;
- sensitive and constructive;
- importance of learners' motivation;
- promote commitment to learning goals and shared understanding of the criteria;
- constructive guidance about how to improve;
- develops learners' capacity for self-assessment;
- recognizes the full range of achievement of all learners.

AfL necessitates the need to create a culture which promotes learning and achievement for all pupils. Promoting a growth mindset which feeds success and celebrates mistakes and effort rather than making comparisons and limiting expectations is needed. Teachers, therefore need to not only develop their toolkit of *teaching strategies*, but of *assessment strategies* too, so pupils can be assessed in the most effective ways to help facilitate their success. Moreover, the teacher needs to work with the pupil as a *reflective* and *active agent* who makes accurate judgements, provides appropriate inputs, scaffolds understanding and empowers them as learners.

4   Assessment as learning

A formative assessment that informs the learner! Assessment *as* learning (AaL) regards assessment as an instrument in its own right to develop the learner. Through this process learners become aware of how they learn – essentially the *metacognitive* element of learning – and of strategies they can further employ; or, as Guy Claxton (1997) aptly says, pupils 'know what to do when they don't know what to do'. The Gilbert Review (DfES 2006) concurred, and considered that pupils should reflect on their learning by reviewing *what* they have learnt and *how* they have learnt. By involving them in determining their level of achievement, pupils become owners of their own learning, thus paving the way towards independent learning, as discussed in Chapter 5.

AaL encourages greater pupil autonomy and therefore more responsibility for their own learning and progress towards learning goals. Within this mode of assessment teachers also model assessment skills, empowering pupils to monitor and assess themselves.

Table 6.1 Summary of modes of assessment in school.

	Assessment of learning	Assessment for learning	Assessment as learning
What?	e.g. Measures pupil attainment	e.g. Informs learning and teaching	e.g. Informs learner
Why?	e.g. Track pupil progress	e.g. Improve learning	e.g. Learner autonomy
When?	e.g. End of key stage	e.g. Within lessons	e.g. Within lessons
Who?	e.g. Teacher-led	e.g. Pupils involved	e.g. Pupil-led
How?	e.g. Unit tests, SATs	e.g. Traffic lights to gauge understanding	e.g. Self-assessment using criteria
Where?	e.g. externally, at a desk	e.g. externally, wherever they are taught	e.g. internally, whenever learning

 REFLECT

Categorize assessment procedures in your school using Table 6.1 to help you. Identify your core beliefs, values of education and professionalism (discussed in Chapter 1) and reflect to what extent the modes of assessment fulfil these. For example:

- Are they child-centred?
- Do they engage and motivate pupils?
- Do they consider the pupil's well-being?
- Do they promote independent learning?
- Which have enabled pupil voice, independent learning or growth mindset?
- Do they promote metacognitive skills?
- Which mode of assessment do you consider has greatest impact on the learner?

Using taxonomies to support outstanding assessment

For effective learning and teaching to take place the pupils and teacher need to know exactly where they are going and when they've arrived. Teachers often have a 'picture' of the learning outcome in their head. However, a challenge of teaching is to develop, refine and define these 'pictures' so that the learner also has the picture in *their* head, making the learning process clear, defined and connected with prior learning and experiences. Through making the teaching and learning 'visible' there is clarity of what is taught and learnt. It helps if you can *see* learning through the eyes of your pupil and that your pupils *see* themselves as their own teachers (Hattie 2009). The use of shared, precise language supports making the thinking and learning visible (Ritchhart et al. 2011).

Taxonomies, a form of classification, categorize cognitive processes and order these categories. The precise language used, such as *predict, compare* or *classify* can form both the learning objectives and activities, and link directly to how these might be assessed. For example, '*Predict* what will happen to . . .' rather than simply asking 'What do you think will happen . . .' would elicit specific understanding the pupil possesses which can be effectively assessed either through a verbal or written response. Taxonomies add clarity to the cognitive processes involved in learning by providing a hierarchy or continuum. For example, analysis and evaluation are higher-order thinking skills, which require knowledge and understanding in order to access and achieve them. As such it gives us greater confidence that the teaching is at the correct level for a particular pupil and enables us to identify next steps to ensure progression.

Four taxonomies will now be discussed:

- Bloom et al.'s cognitive taxonomy (1956);
- Anderson et al.'s taxonomy (2001) (Bloom revised);
- Churches' digital taxonomy (2007);
- Structure of the observed learning outcome (SOLO) (Biggs and Collis 1982).

Bloom's taxonomy: original and revised

Bloom's taxonomy divides learning into three domains: cognitive, affective (attitudes and behaviour, e.g. acceptance, cooperation) and psychomotor (e.g. be attentive to, perform with skill). Bloom believed it could:

- *serve as a common language* about learning goals to promote communication;
- *determine the specific meaning* of broad learning goals;
- *determine congruence* between learning objectives, activities and assessments;
- *provide a spectrum for the range of educational possibilities* against which breadth and depth of educational material could be evaluated.

The cognitive domain has six categories (shown in Figure 6.1), with each category including the previous one and increasing in complexity. For example, in order to *analyse* you need the relevant *knowledge* and *comprehension* and the ability to *apply* it.

Figure 6.1 Bloom's taxonomy.

 ACTIVITY

Let's have a go . . .

We'll take something we should all know a little about.

- Knowledge: who painted the *Mona Lisa*?
- Comprehension: describe the specific characteristics of the *Mona Lisa*.
- Application: how has portrait art changed over the years?
- Analysis: contrast its compositional principles and specific techniques to today's portraits.
- Synthesis: based on the painting, hypothesize how life was then.
- Evaluation: evaluate the *Mona Lisa*, stating your opinion.

Consider your response. Was there a clear lower- and higher-order response? Bear in mind the hierarchy may not be as clear cut, as a pupil may respond with a very deep response to the supposedly lower-order question, such as 'describe'. Similarly, a pupil may provide a superficial response to 'evaluate'.

When writing learning objectives identify which cognitive level to target, for example:

- (who?) the learner . . .;
- (what?) . . . will be able to *identify* (*comprehension*) the parts of a plant . . .;
- (how?) . . . labelling a diagram correctly (Bloom's taxonomy staircase is useful to support this).

Anderson et al.'s taxonomy

Anderson et al. revised Bloom's taxonomy, extending it into two dimensions, namely: *the cognitive process dimension and the knowledge dimension*. The use of two dimensions in a taxonomy table (shown in Table 6.2) provides a clear analysis

Table 6.2 The two dimensions of Anderson et al.'s taxonomy.

Knowledge dimension	Cognitive process dimension					
	Remember	Understand	Apply	Analyse	Evaluate	Create
Factual						
Conceptual						
Procedural						
Metacognitive						

of both dimensions as well as the relationship between the knowledge and cognitive processes inherent in learning objectives (Krathwohl 2002). The use of the second dimension enables us to check whether, for example, a lesson is simply requiring lower-order thinking skills when asking a pupil to *remember factual* knowledge or higher-order demands to *evaluate* and reflect on how and why learning occurred through *metacognitive* skills.

This taxonomy uses verbs rather than nouns, as in Bloom's original version, to provide clearer and more precise language with which to form the learning objective and assessment activity.

When writing learning objectives, identify which cognitive level you are targeting within the two dimensions – cognitive and knowledge:

- (who?) the learner will . . .;
- (what? in two dimensions) predict (cognitive process: *understand*) what will happen in the story based on the details and events so far (type of knowledge: *conceptual*).

For example: *What happened in 1066?* This requires the pupil to *remember* the *factual* knowledge learnt, whereas *What led up to the significant event of 1066 and what implications did it have for England?* requires pupils to *analyse* and use *procedural* knowledge to respond.

Churches' digital taxonomy

Andrew Churches (2007) revised Bloom's original taxonomy by matching the cognitive dimension to twenty-first-century digital activities and literacy skills. For example, when *analysing* the learner may carry out a scenario using a virtual environment, or when *creating* learners might construct an ebook or develop a podcast or presentation, such as Prezi. The emphasis is on giving learners greater opportunity to create their own knowledge and use digital tools to shift the learning responsibility from teacher to learner and so promote independence.

Structure of observed learning outcome (SOLO)

The SOLO taxonomy, developed by Biggs and Collis (1982), is based on a system of *constructive alignment* between the teaching content and the pupil's level of understanding. Using the taxonomy enables pupils and teachers to understand and evaluate learning experiences and outcomes in terms of cognitive complexity across five levels. This makes the SOLO taxonomy similar to Piaget's stages of development (from pre-operational to formal operation).

The first three levels are mainly quantitative and the last two are qualitative, as follows:

- *Prestructural*: the pupil is confused, which means that the learning has failed. The responses will be negative, i.e. 'I dunno'.
- *Unistructural*: the pupil can generalize but only in terms of one aspect; they may jump to conclusions but generally they are correct. Biggs and Collis (1982) liken this to a blind man describing an elephant – a rope, a wall, a snake, a tree trunk – all are correct but not connected.
- *Multistructural*: the pupil can generalize in terms of a few limited and independent aspects and comes to different conclusions about the same information. At this stage, generally, surface learning is still taking place.
- *Relational*: pupils can generalize within their own concrete experience or knowledge and can see how these aspects relate. Unlike the previous levels deeper learning now occurs as connections are made.
- *Extended abstract*: the pupil uses deduction and is able to generalize to situations outside their experience. They are also open to other possibilities.

To help exemplify this taxonomy consider a 'laundry' analogy. Start with a jumbled basket of clothes (prestructural), which are simply ordered into rails and items, such as shirts or trousers, placed together (unistructural and multistructural) so they can be retrieved more easily. With greater understanding, skill and awareness the rails are then organized, for example into colour coordinated or seasonal outfits, and selected with ease and purpose (relational and extended abstract). These rails are now coherently organized and connected to pre-existing schematas.

This structure provides teachers with a common understanding of the learning process, a developmental base and criteria to identify increasing complexity when pupils are mastering new learning (Biggs 1999). It is content independent and so useful as a generic measure of understanding across many subjects.

ACTIVITY

Let's try out the *Mona Lisa* again. This time consider whether the questions could be rewritten to elicit a higher level of response or how the pupils' responses could be classified. Ideally the level of question should match the level expected from the pupil.

- Prestructural: *Mona who*?
- Unistructural: who painted the *Mona Lisa*?
- Multistructural: describe at least two features present in the painting.

- Relational: contrast its compositional principles and specific techniques to today's portraits.
- Extended abstract: evaluate the painting and theorize what Da Vinci wished to convey.

 REFLECT

Consider your possible responses and classify them accordingly.

- Were your responses structural, based on the basic knowledge and facts required (surface learning)?
- Were they relational and extended abstract using information and knowledge that were related to each other (deeper learning)?

 ACTIVITY

Plan a lesson and ask the pupils to define the SOLO level of the activity. For example, will they be using and applying *factual knowledge* or *predicting* an outcome based on *applying* or *generalizing* previous understanding? Then challenge them to change the activity to a higher level, which they complete – for example, instead of simply describing something use an analogy to explain it.

Aim to spend a third/quarter of the time on surface learning (basic knowledge and understanding) and the rest on deeper learning (relational and extended thinking), which is mirrored in the taxonomies discussed.

Assessment *for* learning in the classroom

If you can both listen to children and accept their answers not as things to just be judged right or wrong but as pieces of information which may reveal what the child is thinking, you will have taken a giant step toward becoming a master teacher, rather than merely a disseminator of information.

Easley and Zwoyer, 1975

AfL should be responsive and revealing and provide both you and the pupils with information about how well they are doing, and guide their next steps so they can improve (ARG 1999). Too often we get swept away with our need to cover the content and, as Easley and Zwoyer (1975) note, disseminate the information and fail to 'hear' and process the answers and responses pupils give. AfL emphasizes collecting information on what pupils know, partly know and don't know, and using this information to inform teaching. So you need to take time to understand the depth of understanding your pupils have. It is most important that this process is not seen as an additional demand placed upon you but integral to your teaching and most effective if it is seen as a two-way process between both teacher-to-pupil and pupil-to-teacher. Without pupil involvement assessment can become judgemental, relying on the teacher's concept of success, expectation and desired next steps, therefore disempowering the pupil.

Let's put those marking pens down for a second and consider how to gather this necessary assessment information. Data is essentially gathered in three ways: what pupils *know*; what they *do* and what they *produce*. Immediately you can tick off the first two as you are exposed to a continuous stream of assessment data about what each pupil in your class knows and can do as you observe, listen and question.

 CHECKLIST for gathering data

Consider the following questions to ensure a good depth of data regarding pupil's learning:

- Can the pupil explain something in their own words?
- Are they asking questions?
- Are they making connections?
- Are they re-creating and extending their ideas?
- Can they make their own decisions about their learning?
- Can they justify their decisions?
- Are they selecting their own strategies?
- Are they collaboratively talking?
- Can they reflect and explain how they are learning?
- Can they offer analogies and metaphors of their own – 'It's like . . .'?
- Can they evaluate their own progress?

Begin to integrate such questions into your planning as prompts or use them as part of a mini-plenary or plenary. In addition, develop strategies to *capture* the data so it can be used to best effect to inform your next steps. Post-its, note taking (by TA or other adult), journal writing, head count for positive responses, digital recording and so on can be used.

Assessment *for* learning and feedback

> *Feedback is one of the most powerful influences on learning and achievement, but this impact can be either positive or negative.*
>
> Hattie and Timperley, 2007

Providing pupils with feedback about their learning, orally and in writing, is central to effective assessment. However, the quality of feedback, as Hattie and Timperley (2007) conclude, will affect how effectively the gap between what is understood and the intended understanding is closed. When feedback is poor or lacking pupils can lose interest and develop a sense of uncertainty as they move through the learning process unaided and unfocused (Wragg 2003).

To be equipped to give effective feedback, have the *foundations* in place, i.e. knowing each unique child and having positive teacher-pupil relationships (Chapter 1); understanding of theory (Chapter 2); and strong subject knowledge (Chapter 3).

●●

STRATEGIES FOR YOUR TEACHER TOOLKIT

Know your pupils

Assessment has a profound influence on the motivation and self-esteem of pupils. It is therefore essential to know the social and emotional needs of your pupils, as well as the cognitive (remember emotions and cognition are entwined). Providing the right feedback helps learning, fosters pupils' beliefs in their own abilities, increases resilience and reduces the fear of failure. It is particularly effective with low-achieving pupils and gives higher achievers the confidence to attempt more challenging tasks. Knowing your pupils also facilitates an ipsative approach, whereby assessments are made with self and not compared to or involving others – for example, a pupil trying to beat their own time and accuracy in a maths quiz or obstacle race. This approach is highly encouraging as it assesses all learners' progress at an individual level, placing a lens onto each learning step, no matter how small, rather than striving to meet standards, comparing with others and external criteria.

CHECKLIST to know your pupils

- Create a good *rapport*, e.g. when speaking one-to-one with a pupil use the same physical level, appropriate language, tone and pace.
- Ensure your responses are *positive* and you are aware of the social and emotional needs of the pupil.
- Aim to enable pupils to take *responsibility* for their own learning through skilful scaffolding, support and an expectation of independence.

Know your theory

The feedback should lead to improvement in learning for each pupil. However, for teachers to be able to develop the most effective AfL approaches there is a need to draw upon an understanding of the theory and reflect on pedagogy as science, discussed in Chapter 4. An understanding of constructivism and socio-constructivism, for example Vygotsky's ZPD, adds clarity to how assessment and feedback scaffolds the learner and closes the gap between current and desired knowledge. Also recognize how, for example, the theories of Gardner (multiple intelligences), Mary Rowe (wait time), Bandura (role models), Bjork (desirable difficulties) or Dweck (growth mindset), impact on how you develop and implement assessment in your classroom.

CHECKLIST to know your theory

- Focus on the *learning goals* and effort/process-related comments, which support a growth mindset; 'celebrate' mistakes as learning opportunities. Be aware that pupils may avoid tasks after initial success, because it signifies that they have already reached an adequate level of performance, and further effort may run the risk of disproving this (Hattie and Timperley 2007).
- Aim to *challenge thinking* and be aware of the effect of your attributions.
- Give *scaffolded responses* so that thinking skills are promoted, as 'minimal teacher intervention' promotes deeper learning (don't respond/think for them).
- Consider how you *communicate* your feedback using vocal cues (changing the volume of your voice; either suddenly go softer or louder), visual cues (such as underlining or using different colours on the board), signal phrases ('The key point is . . .'), and body language (eye-contact, smiling and nodding, hand gestures or position in the classroom).
- Allocate *thinking time* for pupils to consolidate and act upon feedback.

Know your subject

For successful assessment it is essential that the teacher has depth of subject knowledge. Substantive subject knowledge allows feedback to be specific and matched to learning needs – the next steps in learning understood and misconceptions identified and addressed. Torrance and Pryor (2001) found that teachers gave more general feedback comments, such as 'good' or 'satisfactory', in subject areas in which they were less confident, and in which they were not able to concentrate on subject-specific detail.

CHECKLIST to know your subject

- Establish *shared learning goals* and the expectations of quality.
- Keep *expectations consistently high*, taking into account pupils' needs and starting points.
- Ensure your feedback is *learning goal related and specific*; referring to success criteria supports this.
- Communicate your *expectations* through modelling answers or outcomes.
- Try using an *'ABC' process*: other pupils could add, build upon or challenge the comments made. As a result, feedback is deeper and more detailed.

Oral feedback

Oral feedback provides an instant response to a pupil. This feedback should be thoughtful, reflective and focused to explore pupils' understanding and provide opportunities to think and express their ideas (Black and Wiliam 1998). In addition, the teacher can gauge and develop understanding through a more dialogic approach, as discussed in Chapter 5.

It is, however, impossible for a teacher to respond to every observation, piece of dialogue or comment in a single lesson. This highlights the importance of planning time and opportunities for effective feedback and formative interactions, for example a mini-plenary. Also be aware that feedback may often slip away from the learning focus and may instead address behavioural or other needs.

 REFLECT

With a colleague or friend describe a lesson or activity that you have recently taught. Ask your colleague to respond with pure praise. Now ask them to criticize the lesson. Perhaps they focus on your relationship with pupils, your understanding of theory or your subject knowledge.

- How did each of the interactions feel?
- What impact could this have on your future engagement with the class or subject?
- Consider the pupils you teach: what has been their emotional response to feedback? Have you been fully aware of the impact your feedback has or had?

Written feedback

Marking is an essential part of the continuing learning dialogue between the teacher and the learner. The quality of marking is a clear demonstration of the value the teacher places on learner efforts. Too little and the learner can lack guidance. Too much can demotivate. It is a case of getting the marking 'just right' for each pupil. Ofsted's focus has shifted to evidence within pupils' books as the primary source and considers this the best and most reliable evidence base. However, it is recognized that this attention has resulted in a proliferation of marking which does not necessarily lead to improvements in achievement, but has certainly increased teacher workload!

Marking must promote further learning. When work is marked with a pupil the next step for learning can be discussed and misconceptions addressed at the time. A trainee teacher stated: 'I was advised to mark at least one question for every pupil during their mental warm-up. I went around during the lesson marking children's work so that they knew how they were doing. Any work that was incorrect, the children had the chance to look at again and I was able to model and support when necessary. This is much more effective than marking after the lesson as the children will not gain as much when adapting their answers the next day.'

If the marking is not followed-up and focused on progressing a pupil's learning, it may not be of value. Therefore plan time for pupils to respond to your written comments, so increasing not only the learning but the value both they and you place on your marking.

In addition, a teacher may unintentionally restrict a pupil from moving forward by focusing on *surface characteristics*, such as handwriting, neatness or task completion rather than providing specific feedback to close a particular learning gap. Research also indicates that giving quantitative marks, or a grade, alongside qualitative comments devalues the learning impact of the comments; the pupil simply does not see them.

CHECKLIST for written feedback

- Feedback should be a learning *dialogue* which is informed, focused and supportive.
- Use *checklists* that can enable the same points to be made to a number of pupils.
- Allow *space* for pupils' comments, responses and questions.
- Write *legibly* in the appropriate handwriting style, at the correct reading and developmental age so that comments can be read and *understood*.
- Ensure feedback is *child-friendly* in language style, size, form and quantity (some schools do not use red pen as it is deemed negative).
- Design more challenging activities to provide opportunities for broader *ranges of comments*.
- The marked work should be returned promptly so *misconceptions* can be swiftly addressed.
- During the next lesson allow time for the pupils to *respond to the marking*, then *feed forward* to form the next steps in learning.
- Be *diagnostic* when marking so that pupils can identify exactly what should be addressed.
- Use colour highlighting, or similar, *during lessons* rather than afterwards. For example, pink to highlight work that needs improving and green for work that is good. Pupils will then know how they are doing, reflect upon this during the lesson, and see if they can improve it themselves.
- Use, for example, *three stars and a wish* to ensure positive comments are made. The 'wish' should be a specific and prioritized area for improvement.
- Likewise 'EBI' (even better if), feedback adds a point for development, or can be an alternate to the above.

REFLECT

Analyse your current marking practice. Try to identify two or three different patterns that could be enhanced or changed. Consider how you are moving pupils' understanding forward, as well as the emotional impact on them, their motivation and sense of self-efficacy.

Assessment *as* learning

Self-assessment is at the heart of the matter.

Earl, 2003

Pupils' active engagement in the learning process is a key feature of formative assessment. AaL focuses on pupils being able to assess themselves and others, as well as understanding the learning process and how they learn. Ideally to achieve our educational goal, namely a motivated, independent learner, with a mastery orientation commensurate with a growth mindset, we should shift the assessment focus from teacher-based assessment to peer- and self-assessment.

CHECKLST for peer- and self-assessment

- Possess a growth mindset, accept failure and criticism as platforms for learning.
- Feel comfortable, safe and secure within the learning environment.
- Possess a clear understanding of the expectations you are aiming for.
- Be able to compare and articulate pupils' actual (or current) abilities with the set expectations.
- Be engaged in actions, especially those within metacognition, which can begin to close their gap in learning.
- Engage in a dialogic approach.

Remember, if you want your pupils to be engaged and clear about their learning you also need to engender a classroom environment which is supportive, constructive and open.

Peer- and self-assessment

Peer assessment, aligned with the socio-constructivist model, improves pupils' motivation and communication as learning occurs collaboratively with peers who use the same or similar language. This can provide models of achievement that the teacher alone could not produce and through this social interaction enables greater independence and access to higher-order thinking skills.

In addition, pupils generally accept criticisms more readily from their peers, although do be aware that pupils' perceptions of peer feedback can be more negative, possibly due to their lack of expertise or experience. There is a need to teach and encourage pupils how to assess constructively and for the teacher to model and scaffold the process of peer- and self-assessment explicitly using success criteria. Clarke (2003) advocates establishing response partner rules, which can be displayed and referred to.

Frequent peer assessment will build pupils' skill in critically evaluating a peer's work against specific criteria and justifying reasons for their decisions. This supports pupils to think more objectively and they start to move along the continuum toward self-assessment more confidently. The next step is for pupils to generate their own success criteria and by doing so personalize their learning further and enhance ownership.

Self-assessment enables pupils to understand themselves as learners, and access increasingly complex tasks and learning goals, as they are equipped with the knowledge of how they can improve. However, pupil self-assessment can be a challenge for many. Pupils can view feedback as the responsibility of the teacher, whose job it is to 'tell' them how well they are doing, what the goals are and what to do next time (Hattie and Timperley 2007). Self-assessment requires the teacher to hand over an element of control to the pupils and empower them. As a trainee or new teacher this can be seen as risk-taking and daunting as the outcomes cannot be predicted or controlled. It is like most things developmental – it is a gradual process, built through clarity of expectation and trust, value and respect from your pupils and yourself.

To support this shift to effective self-assessment it is also useful to refer to 'expectancy-value theory' and 'attribution theory' discussed in Chapters 4 and 5. Pupils need to see value and potential success in their learning, and form attributions about their potential success based on internal and controllable factors. To develop this, pupils should be prompted to answer: *Where am I going?* (What are the goals?); *How am I doing?* (What progress is being made toward the goal?); and *Where to next?* (What activities need to be undertaken to make better progress?). These questions will underpin effective self-assessment and correspond to notions of *feed up*, *feed back* and *feed forward* (Fisher and Frey 2009) which together strongly promote the use of metacognitive skills. Pupils evaluate their understanding, effort and strategies used and regular self-assessment promotes richer and more informed self-assessment.

If pupils are to become competent at self-assessment they need sustained experience and support in ways of questioning and improving the quality of their work, in addition to understanding the expectations and criteria on which they will be assessed.

Further reading

Clarke, S. (2003) *Enriching feedback in the primary classroom*. London: Hodder Education.

Clarke, S. (2014) *Outstanding formative assessment*. London: Hodder Education.

Both books provide a wealth of ideas, as well as practical strategies to support how to implement and enhance formative assessment.

 ## CHECKLIST for promoting assessment as learning

- Use well-formed learning objectives and success criteria, which enable pupils to exercise power over their own learning (Clarke 2008).
- Involve your pupils in 360-degree feedback and ask them what they find most helpful in developing their understanding.
- Make sure the ratio of pupil-teacher thinking is pupil-weighted.
- Provide prompt sheets/checklists to aid reflection.

- Provide appropriate language through word banks, placemats or aides memoires.
- Use a whole class assessment tool such as confidence rating in the form of a wall chart (thermometer) where pupils add their names at points in a lesson.
- 'Thumbs' or 'traffic lights' can be used after exposition, at the end or at different points in the lesson to assess whether pupils understand the task; this will facilitate clarification of misconceptions and encourages pupils to reflect on what and how they are learning.
- 'Stretch, stress and comfort zones', for example, can be used in the classroom for pupils to go to during a lesson or at the end.
- One-minute/two-sentence summary or 'exit tickets' (e.g. What have I learnt? What do I already know? What might I need extra help with? How have I progressed in the lesson?) can be used in the plenary or after a specific task completion to assess what pupils have learnt or what they don't understand.
- Smiley faces drawn in the margin or on the whiteboard at different stages of the lesson help gauge understanding.
- Plenary pals, class debates or teacher/pupil conferences and interviews develop a more dialogic classroom.

 REFLECT

We need to match the assessment method to the desired learning outcome. Careful and well-considered assessment methods will enable you to be more tactical and efficient in assessing pupils' learning (remember fish can't climb trees!) and so have greater impact on their achievement. If, for example, we were measuring knowledge acquisition the tool could be a test or test conditions. Alternatively, we may choose an unaided practical activity for assessing a pupil's acquisition of specific skills (thinking and practical), or a concept map to identify certain concepts or ideas they may have.

Referring to the points made in this chapter and your own assessment practices in school, describe how you assess your pupils. Create a table with three columns as follows

What needs to be assessed	Best assessment method	Impact on learning
Knowledge of phonetics	*e.g. 1-1 reading conference*	*Able to identify specific sounds that are unknown*

Reflect on whether the assessment tool you currently use or have seen used is the most effective for what you wish to assess. If not, reflect upon alternatives and why they might enhance learning (e.g. elicit more specific information or uncover root causes of misconceptions).

A thought . . . effective assessment for learning enables pupils to continue to gain knowledge, understanding and skills and develop a strong sense of self worth. It is essential that you and your pupils have a clear 'picture' of your expectations and learning goals. In your outstanding classroom your pupils don't give up in frustration and have a fear of failure; instead they develop greater independence, resilience, a mastery orientation and a growth mindset. You now have the teacher toolkit equipped to plan, deliver and assess to make desirable change happen and achieve success.

References

Anderson, L.W., Krathwohl, D.R. et al. (2001) *A taxonomy for learning, teaching and assessing: a revision of Bloom's taxonomy of educational objectives.* New York: Longman.

ARG (Assessment Reform Group) (1999) *Assessment for learning: beyond the black box.* Cambridge: University of Cambridge.

ARG (Assessment Reform Group) (2002) *Assessment for learning: 10 principles,* http://webarchive.nationalarchives.gov.uk.

Biggs, J. (1999) *Teaching for quality learning at university.* Buckingham: Society for Research into Higher Education/Open University Press.

Biggs, J. and Collis, K. (1982) *Evaluating the quality of learning: the SOLO taxonomy.* New York: Academic Press.

Black, P. and Wiliam, D. (1998) *Inside the black box: raising standards through classroom assessment.* London: School of Education, King's College.

Bloom, B.S., Engelhart, M.D., Furst, E.J., Hill, W.H. and Krathwohl, D.R. (1956) *Taxonomy of educational objectives: the classification of educational goals* (Handbook I: cognitive domain). New York: David McKay.

Churches, A. (2007) *Bloom's digital taxonomy,* http://edorigami.wikispaces.com/file/view/bloom%27s+Digital+taxonomy+v3.01.pdf.

Clarke, S. (2003) *Enriching feedback in the primary classroom.* London: Hodder Education.

Clarke, S. (2008) What makes effective learning objectives? in *Active learning through formative assessment.* London: Hodder Education.

Claxton, G.L. (1997) *Hare brain, tortoise mind: why intelligence increases when you think less.* London: Fourth Estate.

DfE (2012) *Teachers' standards,* www.gov.uk/government/uploads/system/uploads/attachment_data/file/301107/Teachers__Standards.pdf.

DfES (2006) *2020 vision: report of the Teaching and Learning in 2020 Review Group* (the Gilbert Review). Nottingham: DfES.

Earl, L. (2003) *Assessment as learning: using classroom assessment to maximize student learning,* Experts in Assessment series. Thousand Oacks, CA: Corwin Press.

Easley, J. and Zwoyer, R. (1975) The impact of classroom evaluation practices on students, *Review of Educational Research,* 58(4): 469.

EEF (2015) *The Education Endowment Foundation,* https://educationendowmentfoundation.org.uk.

Fisher, D. and Frey, N. (2009) feed up, back, forward, educational leadership, *Multiple Measures,* 67(3): 20–5.

Hall, K., Collins, J., Benjamin, S., Nind, M. and Sheehy, K. (2004) SATurated models of pupildom: assessment and inclusion/exclusion, *British Educational Research Journal,* 30(6): 801–17.

Hattie, J. (2009) *Visible learning: a synthesis of over 800 meta-analyses relating to achievement.* London: Routledge.

Hattie, J. and Timperley, H. (2007) The power of feedback, *Review of Educational Research,* 77(1): 81–112.

Krathwohl, D.R. (2002) Theory into practice, *College of Education,* 41(4).

Ofsted (2015) *School inspection handbook,* www.gov.uk/government/ofsted.

Popham, W.J. (1998) The dysfunctional marriage of formative and summative teacher evaluation, *Journal of Personnel Evaluation in Education,* 1: 269-73.

Ritchhart, R., Church, M. and Morrison, K. (2011) *Making thinking visible.* San Francisco: Jossey-Bass.

Scriven, M. (1967) The methodology of evaluation, in R.W. Tyler, R.M. Gagne and M. Scriven (eds) *Perspectives of curriculum evaluation,* pp. 39–83. Chicago: Rand McNally.

Torrance, H. and Pryor, J. (2001) Developing formative assessment in the classroom: using action research to explore and modify theory, *British Educational Research Journal,* 27(5): 615–31, http://web.ebscohost.com.

Waugh, D. and Jolliffe, W. (2008) *English 3–11: a guide for teachers.* London: Routledge.

Wragg, E.C. (2003) *Assessment and learning in the primary school.* London: Taylor & Francis.

Summary of the personalization level

Your perfect jacket

Your 'perfect jacket' fits well, feels more equipped with items you both need and want, and hopefully it has become an essential belonging through its increasing versatility. You can wear this jacket with confidence throughout the day, every day, so you feel enabled and empowered to tackle a range of challenges and changes that you encounter.

Your professional knowledge

This level focused on pedagogy as science, craft and art, as well as links with motivation, growth mindset and neuroscience, looking at memory and deeper learning. It explored the learning experience with regards to teacher expectations and the effects of teacher attributions, modelling and grouping. The roles of effective dialogic talk and formative assessment were explored, which has hopefully raised your awareness of the need to equip yourself with an extensive teacher toolkit to plan, deliver and assess outstanding learning experiences.

Your professional development and action plan

Identify areas of strength and development and connect the content of this level to the key themes. Reflect upon the extent to which you have achieved each statement. To support your journey to outstandingness, rate each key theme statement 1–5 (1 not confident to 5 most confident) to form actions points.

Table 6.3 Key themes confidence rating – the personalization level has prompted you to . . . .

Key theme	Confidence level
Reflect and appreciate how your *teacher identity and philosophy* influences: your pedagogy and how you promote deeper learning; your expectations and how you plan, use teaching strategies and talk within the classroom; your approach to assessment	1 2 3 4 5
Consider how your understanding of the *purpose of education* reflects: your pedagogy and your teacher toolkit; your expectations of all pupils and how you plan; how you implement classroom assessment	1 2 3 4 5
Appreciate how your focus on *well-being for you and your pupils* reflects in: how you respond to the needs of each pupil; how you plan and deliver the curriculum; how you assess and feedback to each pupil	1 2 3 4 5
Consider how you *meet the needs of the unique child* through: your knowledge of pedagogy and the breadth and depth of your toolkit; your teaching strategies and effective lesson planning; effective assessment and feedback	1 2 3 4 5
Reflect how your awareness of *creating an enabling and empowering environment* reflects in: how you plan for the needs of each individual pupil; how you set expectation and plan your lessons; your use of self- and peer assessment.	1 2 3 4 5
Appreciate how your own *self-awareness* and *critical self-reflection* enhances: the strategies and approaches you choose; your expectations and responses to an individual pupil or group; how you assess and feedback to each pupil to develop their potential	1 2 3 4 5
Consider the need for *continuous development as a lifelong learner* in relation to: your understanding of pedagogy and deeper learning; your understanding of independent learning, effective lesson planning and dialogic teaching; the range of assessments strategies you use	1 2 3 4 5
Total score	

Reflecting upon the above, identify key areas to address. This activity will serve as an action plan (Table 6.4) to bring about a desirable change in your teaching, with a particular focus on personalizing learning.

Table 6.4 Action plan.

Desirable change	Perceived barrier/risk	Time/support/training required	Timescale
This could be focused on *developing a growth mindset culture; dialogic teaching; enhancing strategies; developing expectations; independent learning or assessment for learning*	List these and consider whether they are significant or insignificant	Identify support that might help you to address these barriers/risks, e.g. *'I need further support in . . . to develop my strategies to. . .' or ' To use of peer-and self-assessment more effectively . . .'*	These may be immediate, e.g. *'By the end of the day I will . . .'* or longer term, e.g. *'By the end of the unit of work I will . . .'*

I would like to finish this Level with a quote to make you consider that getting the necessary elements in place will not only light each pupil's fire but, as Einstein reflects, create the right conditions to allow it to burn brightly (remember fires do need watching, feeding and occasionally poking!).

I never teach my pupils, I only attempt to provide the conditions in which they can learn.

Albert Einstein

PART 3

Motivation level – inspiring!

7

Inspiring, defining and developing creativity

Logic will get you from A to B. Imagination will take you everywhere.
Albert Einstein

Our coat hook! Your 'perfect jacket' fits perfectly, its pockets are filled fruitfully, so now you begin the process of personalizing it; perhaps you may want to add a splash of colour, a badge, sew on some beading, sequins to dazzle. It will become original, individual. It communicates, very explicitly, who *you* are, *your* personality and professionalism. The jacket has now transcended beyond its original conception and function and has become a symbol of *you*.

This chapter defines creativity within the curriculum and the conflicts therein. It provides a rationale as to why it should be embraced when striving toward outstandingness. Logical, safe and tried-and-tested approaches will make sure you are a good teacher but imagination, a key element for creativity, sees beyond fixed parameters and established norms and will, as Einstein states, 'take you everywhere'. The creative teacher and creative teaching are explored, as is how to overcome barriers to creativity and develop your and your pupils' creative skills.

The key themes in this chapter prompt you to:

- consider how your *teacher identity and philosophy* influences your own creativity;
- reflect upon how your understanding of the *purpose of education* reflects how you perceive creativity in the curriculum;
- consider how your focus on *well-being for you and your pupils* reflects how you respond to the demands of the curriculum and the essence of creativity;
- evaluate how your understanding and skill in creativity enables you to *meet the needs of the unique child*;
- appreciate how your awareness of *creating an enabling and empowering environment* reflects in how you support the development of creativity and risk-taking;

- reflect how your own *self-awareness* and *critical self-reflection* enhances how you develop your own creativity and that of your pupils;
- identify how your understanding of creative teaching and teaching creatively focus your needs for *continuous development as a lifelong learner.*

This chapter addresses the following *Teachers' standards* (DfE 2012):

1 Set high expectations which inspire, motivate and challenge pupils
4 Plan and teach well structured lessons

Global need for creativity

Creativity is part of a universalized discourse in the western world and reflects global markets and competition (Craft 2005). It is imagination that leads to creativity; creativity to innovation; innovation to opportunities; and opportunities to employment. Think of the success of, for example, Richard Branson and the Virgin Group or the late Steve Jobs and Apple. Would they have achieved so much without being creative?

Our world economy needs increased levels of entrepreneurship, but also, increasingly, 'intrapreneneurship' where employees have the skill set and aptitude to improve organizational performance from within. Children who start school this year will potentially enter the world of work around 2035 and be working until at least the year 2080. How can anyone predict how the world will look then? If creativity is promoted in schools our children may develop into more adaptable, flexible and inventive adults who cope with our rapidly changing environments, feel empowered to challenge the status quo constructively and generate ideas for innovation and improvement.

Defining creativity

REFLECT

- What image does the word 'creativity' conjure up?
- How would you define creativity?

Perhaps your initial thoughts regarding creativity are 'I'm not a creative person!'; 'I wish I was more creative'; 'Creativity can't be taught'; or 'I haven't got the time to be as creative as I could be!' Your definition of creativity would almost certainly include imagination. Nevertheless, imagination is often underused as an educational tool as emphasis is placed on facts, recall, description or thinly veiled activities labelled as creative. If influential people, such as Einstein and Dewey, felt strongly about imagination almost a century ago, why have we not embedded imagination and creativity in schools?

Perhaps the notion that creativity is 'ethereal and elusive' or confined to 'special people' has contributed to this. The matter of defining creativity is considered troublesome and dissuades many from pursuing it in practice. Having clarity of definition is the first step in being able to understand and implement creativity within your pedagogy.

For the purposes of this chapter creativity will be defined as an 'imaginative activity fashioned as to produce outcomes that are both original and of value' (NACCCE 1999: 30). Creativity can therefore be characterized by these four main components – imagination, purpose, originality and value – which benefit a pupil's education and engage them with their learning. In addition, Education Scotland (2013) defines creativity as looking at familiar things with a fresh eye, examining problems with an open mind, making connections, learning from mistakes and using imagination to explore new possibilities. This wholly complements how you are developing your teacher identity and philosophy and your toolkit to realize this. Moreover, creativity promotes desirable aspects so far extolled within this book and very much embedded in effective pedagogy (Chapters 4 and 5), such as growth mindset, deeper learning, risk-taking, resilience and metacognition. It also enables us to connect with ourselves as well as others and be more mindful and self-aware (as discussed in Chapter 1).

Make creativity part of you and your teaching

1   To enable this, our first premise must be that creativity *is* accessible to all. NACCCE coined the phrase 'democratic creativity', to mean the creativity of the ordinary person. It is useful to consider creativity as a continuum, with 'democratic' creativity anywhere between the extraordinary (Einstein or Picasso) and ordinary (me) creativity. Craft (2001) uses the terms Big C and Little c to describe this continuum. Our goal is to understand and aspire to the Big C and impart the Little c in our day-to-day teaching.

2   Our second premise is that creativity can be taught. If you offer mastery to your pupils across the curriculum they then have the skills and deeper understanding to explore other avenues of thinking. Moreover, if these original ideas are of value this implies certain criteria are needed in order to assign value. These criteria become the learning focus and form the learning objectives. Your secure subject knowledge, highlighted in *The importance of teaching* (DfE 2010) and Chapter 3, is also fundamental in delivering the curriculum creatively. Use this knowledge to plan lessons which are more open-ended, require higher-order thinking and are within different learning environments to further support the teaching of creativity.

3   Our third premise is that creativity can both release and realize a pupil's learning potential. Creative teaching depends upon a pupil's emotional engagement and sense of excitement or, as Egan (1991, cited in Pound and Lee 2011) refers

to it, an *ecstatic response* (which releases 'teacher's pet': dopamine!). Intrinsic motivation is a catalyst for creativity (Torrance 1962; Amabile 1983; Fryer 1996) and has the power to open up doors for pupils where other approaches have failed.

As a newly-qualified teacher I taught a boy called Jamie, a Year 5 pupil who had never really liked school, was a very reluctant writer and appeared disengaged for a large proportion of the time. Then, when working on a D&T project we both had our *eureka* moment. The day was busily spent making pneumatic ghost houses – skeletons and ghouls were popping up all over his shoebox house, his project was near completion and the end of the day arrived. He came in the next morning proudly clutching two sheets of paper. He presented them to me with a beaming smile. For the first time Jamie had been motivated to write, and carefully illustrate, his own story about a ghost house. It was a turning point for him – he now knew he could enjoy learning and achieve success. I just needed to know which button (or pneumatic system) to press! From that point creativity became deeply embedded in my own pedagogy and practice.

Creativity is without a doubt a multifaceted concept that allows freedom, choice and fun within activities designed specifically for pupils to engage and enjoy their lessons (Desailly 2012; Starko 2013). Being creative is neither easy nor straightforward and it would be wrong to assume it is needed in every aspect of teaching, yet it is wholly desirable and without it progress within societies would cease.

Further reading

Witkin, W.R. (1974) *The intelligence of feeling*. London: Heinemann. This book, along with works by Malcolm Ross (various publications) emphasizes the importance of engaging children's feelings and emotional resources, particularly via arts-based activities (though not exclusively) as a means of accessing creative skills and general disposition.

 REFLECT

- Take a moment to reflect on your definition of creativity and identify how this relates to your teaching philosophy.
- In what ways, if any, do you think of yourself as creative? List three to five key words.
- Reflect on who you consider to be a creative teacher – list the characteristics you identify.
- Discuss your list with a colleague or friend. What does your discussion tell you about how you currently perceive creative teachers?

Creativity, the curriculum and conflict

Creativity in the curriculum is not a new phenomenon – the work of ancient philosophers, such a Socrates and Plato, explored the world creatively and encouraged fellow scholars to do the same. However, it was the late twentieth century when Plowden (1967) explicitly put creativity on the curriculum map with her highly influential theory of child-centred learning. We then wait, and wait, and finally in 1999, nearly a decade after the introduction of the National Curriculum, Sir Ken Robinson published *All our futures* (NACCCE 1999). This report has been significant in informing the way that creativity has been developed, especially in the Foundation Stage, and was the catalyst for further policy initiatives, such as *Excellence and Improvement* (DfES 2003), Creative Partnerships (2002–11), 'personalized learning' (DfES 2004) and *Creativity: Find it! Promote it!* (QCA 2005).

The Early Years curriculum 2000 and 2007 made 'creative development' explicit through focusing learning on imaginative role play, exploration and problem solving. The updated 2012 version retained the essence of the previous version but replaced 'creative development' with 'expressive arts and design'. This has meshed the Early Years Foundation Stage more tightly with the primary National Curriculum, which specifically, albeit briefly, mentions creativity in connection with a range of subjects and cites one of its central aims as 'to engender an appreciation of human creativity and achievement' (DfE 2016: para. 3.1).

Although creativity is an aim in the current National Curriculum, for many the notion of the creative curriculum means the arts subjects: music, art, drama and dance. The Robinson Report (NACCCE 1999) argues that, while there are strong links between the expressive arts and creativity, viewing creativity as solely or mainly the province of the arts is unhelpful because it can lead to a denial of the role of creativity in other areas, such as science and mathematics.

This restricted view of creativity is further fuelled by the notion of the purpose of education. As Chapter 2 discusses, the role and purpose of education can be viewed as meeting economic, cultural, personal or social needs. If the view is solely economic, subjects will be regarded as either useful or not. Pupils are encouraged to focus on subjects that are of economic use and 'steered' away from 'less' valuable ones. This preoccupation with the more 'valuable' subjects, or the 'basics' (our core curriculum), the current performativity culture to 'raise' standards in schools and the nation's global status are all in direct competition with the nature of creativity.

At times, enlightened experts, such as Professor Robin Alexander (2009) or Paul Roberts (2006) have proposed more creative approaches to the curriculum, but these have often been discarded. The difficulty with this is that the 'basics' determines what is to be tested and is therefore high stakes and high focus. This view of the perceived hierarchy of subjects is made explicit in our daily timetable. How often is dance or art taught Monday morning, or drama and music for an hour a day? We are communicating to our pupils which subjects they should value at a very early age, which poses a challenge to stimulating creativity (Craft 2011).

Our conundrum is to resolve whether creativity can be fostered at the same time as developing the necessary knowledge and skills in our pupils. Weisberg (2006) describes this as a *tension view* paradigm that sees creativity ('thinking outside the box' referred to in Chapter 3) and knowledge in conflict – the less knowledge or expertise the better conditions are for creativity. So if we are cultivating knowledge and skills within a traditionalist perspective, are we actively suppressing creativity and educating it out of our children? However, if we refer back to the definition of creativity as 'an imaginative activity producing an outcome of originality, purpose and value', this implies that certain knowledge is required to spark imagination and identify whether the outcome is of value and purpose or not (our second premise). Therefore, developing knowledge and skills is fundamental to creativity. This may be, for example, a poetry style, a law of physics or mathematics or the properties of materials from which creative outcomes can be generated. Creativity also naturally sits within a constructivist pedagogical approach (referred to in Chapter 2) whereby exploration and discovery within a learning environment based on a co-constructed curriculum is fostered.

Nevertheless, a challenge to creativity remains, as it would seem there is an inherent need for education to be conformist and those within it to meet the needs centrally imposed. For example, the national literacy and numeracy hour (DfEE 1998) demonstrated how readily some schools adopted a conformist, formulaic approach to teaching these subjects, despite these frameworks being contrary to effective teaching and learning. A fear culture (I need to be doing it right!), exacerbated by performativity and PRP incentives, has led teachers to require their pupils to also conform. Pressurized timetables have resulted in reproducing knowledge, responding correctly within certain timeframes rather than embracing creativity, engaging learners and going with the 'flow'. When a pupil doesn't 'conform' there are even drugs to help this! (Ritalin being prescribed readily for ADHD, with a shortage in the USA in 2011 due to overmedication).

A young child's natural creativity and vast appetite for learning cannot, and should not, be ignored. My 2-year-old's favourite question is 'Why?' and, like others, he is highly inquisitive and will construct his own knowledge while engaging with his environment. Torrance (1981) found that a child's creative ability flourishes at around 4 years old; their imagination is greater, even their grasp of language is more creative. As a family we were amused and impressed that my then toddler named his trainers 'Runnervators' – so obvious: you run in them, why would you call them anything else? He was, as young children do, making sense of his world through invention and connections. I do wonder if at 10 years of age he would feel so comfortable or able to 'play' with language and make creative connections. Meador (1992) also presents evidence from the USA that creativity (as measured by divergent thinking tests) declines when children enter kindergarten, at the age of 5 or 6.

Could it be that once in the school system they quickly learn that it is not all right to make mistakes? As a society mistakes have been stigmatized and the result is *fear to fail*; fear to question the 'norm' and let go of certainty; afraid to risk individual and the sometimes flawed or challenging thinking that could lead to creativity.

Contrary to Edward de Bono's (1992) notion that creativity is a human resource to be developed, many schools frequently and uncritically offer a variation of what has gone before. Teachers actively share or download resources year on year. Arguably, the wheel should not be reinvented but we should question if the material has simply been repackaged and repeated. Without reflection and critical evaluation how can we guarantee it will meet the needs of potentially creative learners, leading to innovation and invention?

Teaching creatively

For us, to learn is to construct, to reconstruct, to observe with a view to changing – none of which can be done without being open to risk, to the adventure of the spirit.

Paulo Freire, 1998

Our first point of change is with ourselves, and secondly in how we see learning and the learner. Teachers who, as Freire (1998) observes, embrace risk-taking and challenges, and have a firm understanding of creativity and creative strategies, are those who can best inspire creativity in their pupils. Teaching and learning should be an adventure.

Creativity: teacher and learner orientation

Creativity can be further defined as follows.

Teacher orientated

Creative teaching focuses on teachers using their creative skills and diverse repertoire to make ideas and content more interesting and connecting this to pupil interests, making learning both fun and effective. Certain qualities found in creative teachers include: confidence; enthusiasm; independence; dominance; introversion; openness; self-acceptance; intuitiveness; flexibility; social poise; commitment; curiosity; originality; and sense of self-efficacy with regard to their own creativity (Sternberg 1997; Jones and Wyse 2004). Reassuringly, teaching creatively does not have to involve teachers being 'flamboyant or extrovert' (Grigg 2010).

The creative teacher will draw upon the pedagogy of constructivism and socio-constructivism, and combine this with a strong humanist approach. Learning is therefore scaffolded and connected, individuals are valued and nurtured (Woods and Jeffrey 1996), their ideas developed and they are encouraged to fulfil their potential, taking into account their personal, social and cultural interests. Above all a creative teacher will engage pupils, which may result in coming away from the 'script' to inspire a love of learning.

Use Tables 7.1 and 7.2 to self-assess your own approaches to teaching creatively and teaching for creativity.

ACTIVITY

Table 7.1 Teacher-orientated creativity.

Teachers who teach creatively will	1 most confident and comfortable to 5 least
Be comfortable with risk-taking (Craft 2001; Ofsted 2010) and perceive failure as a learning opportunity	1 2 3 4 5
Demonstrate their creativity through their passion and breadth of interests and openness to ambiguity and uncertainty (Csikszentmihalyi 1996)	1 2 3 4 5
Use their creative capacity in their planning and teaching	1 2 3 4 5
Combine childlike play and exploration with adult-like self-awareness and discipline (QCA 2005; Starko 2010)	1 2 3 4 5
Be aware of the emotions and feelings of those around them	1 2 3 4 5
Model creativity through experimenting with resources, engaging in problem-solving and generating and evaluating their ideas (Wilson 2015) as well as using self-talk	1 2 3 4 5
Be innovative, spontaneous and responsive to pupils and consider the lesson plan a working, organic document that is both flexible and adaptable	1 2 3 4 5

Learner orientated

Teaching for creativity involves teachers identifying pupils' creative strengths and fostering them. Here the focus is on the learner developing their own belief in their creative potential; their sense of possibility and confidence to try (NACCCE 1999). This approach draws upon Plowden's child-centred learning, which enables greater pupil ownership, control, experimentation, innovation and opportunities to apply their skills and knowledge to question and explore new possibilities.

ACTIVITY

Table 7.2 Learner-orientated creativity.

Teachers who teach for creativity will	1 most confident and comfortable to 5 least
Be able to exert their own professional autonomy	1 2 3 4 5
Be flexible and responsive	1 2 3 4 5
Focus on purposeful outcomes across the curriculum	1 2 3 4 5
Foster an in-depth understanding and subject knowledge	1 2 3 4 5
Offer clarity and time to develop, process and execute ideas	1 2 3 4 5
Develop an environment that promotes and stimulates imagination and embraces difference and novelty	1 2 3 4 5

REFLECT

In addition to your self-assessment above recall a recent lesson that you believe led to creativity.

- Did the pupils offer unusual or innovative ideas, make connections, ask questions or generate possibilities?
- How relevant was the task to your pupils personally and/or emotionally?
- How much control or ownership did your pupils have over the activity?
- Was time and space offered for open exploration?

Consider your personal roadblocks to creativity and use the next section to help address these.

Roadblocks to creativity

There is no doubt that creativity is the most important human resource of all. Without creativity, there would be no progress, and we would be forever repeating the same patterns.

Edward de Bono, 1992

Without creativity, thinking would be limited and we would be literally stuck, as de Bono (1992) concludes, with the same way of thinking and doing. However effective at the outset it will inevitably lead to complacency and then decline. The teachers and schools I worry about the most are those who are in such a trap. These schools, despite the recognition that creative approaches to learning can motivate pupils and raise their standards, may feel a sense of conflict and confusion with their established norms as well as the co-existence of creativity and accountability policies. This confusion has been further compounded by previous National Curriculum guidance, which instead of being a 'guiding light' was 'weighing teachers down and squeezing out room for innovation, creativity, deep learning and intellectual exploration' (DfE 2010: 40).

However, by identifying and removing mental blocks (Stenberg 1999) and disproving or challenging myths or patterns of behaviour, either internally or externally imposed, you can develop creativity and all that it offers.

Internal roadblocks

Self-belief: *Face your fears and do it anyway!*

The fear of what others think can cause you to censor what you think, feel and do. Just contemplate the progress in science if the astrologer and scientist Copernicus (1530) had not circulated his theory that the Earth was not the centre of the universe. It was a very unpopular view for philosophical and religious reasons and required his confidence and strength of commitment. Or the implications for the Reverend Martin

Luther King's belief in the civil rights for African-Americans if he was deterred by the setbacks and considerable political and societal pressure to conform.

Control: *Plan to let go and create flow!*

Fear of too much freedom and lack of control is systematic of a behaviourist classroom where teacher control is high but pupil autonomy low. Misplaced thinking that creativity is about letting yourself go, running around the room or going a bit crazy does not help us to embrace creativity. Therefore, define a creative classroom as one in which pupils construct and co-construct their learning with the teacher acting as guide.

Values: *Without creativity, there would be no progress!*

If you do not see the value in creativity and creative endeavour this will impact on how you develop your teacher-self, your planning and delivery of the curriculum; therefore, interrogate your values and beliefs.

Habit: *Change your habits; change your life!*

Some people may have the tendency to approach problems in a rigid, habitual manner or persistent pattern – known as a *response set*. If you always respond to a problem the same way, creativity will be very limited. Likewise *functional fixedness* is the tendency for people to use objects or tools in a certain, specific way. If you only think about something in just one way, its creative potential is limited. Try to view things from another perspective and shake things up.

External roadblocks

Time and space: *Make time and find space!*

The sheer quantity of ready-to-go lesson plans that can be downloaded from the DfE website is an indication of our readiness to accept being directed how to teach. Many teachers would have considered this unthinkable a few years ago as it can suppress their creativity and flair, yet it has become endemic due to the pressures placed upon teachers. Reflect upon the discussion in Chapter 1 regarding professionalism and sense of control in being able to define yourself. Reflect upon whether there are creative limits placed on pupils through whole-school policy, practice and ethos.

Do you give yourself and your pupils time and space to ponder, to wonder, to fully download the information of the day? Is there a place or space within the classroom or school that is empowering, enabling and facilitates the 'flow' of creative thought?

Accountability and performativity: *Focus on a deep and lasting love of learning!*

Identify whether you are promoting mastery orientation and growth mindset in your pupils through an inspiring and creative learning experience. If you feel inspired, the chances are your pupils will too.

Peer pressure: *Find your core philosophy and identity and hold on to it!*

The need to conform can hinder both you and your pupils' creativity. Chapter 1 discussed how dissonance can occur and the resultant stress if expectations and philosophy are mismatched. Therefore be aware of the ethos of your school, key stage or year group and how this can impact on your personal creativity.

Reward: *Nurture intrinsic motivation through pleasure and success!*

External motivation or assessment can undermine creativity. An artist friend refers to a sense of excitement when heading off on a journey of discovery. He expressed this as follows: 'unhindered by too much self-doubt or the expectations of others, nor unduly influenced by the achievements of others the heart, mind and soul freely inform the direction of travel.' Engage your pupils with the curriculum so that they find pleasure and fulfilment in creative endeavour.

Expectations: *Create an 'I can and will do' culture!*

Sometimes colleagues, friends, teachers and parents unintentionally limit what others can do by sending messages that express or imply limits on their potential achievement and attainment – the Pygmalion effect or self-fulfilling prophecy, described in Chapter 5. Expectations are communicated verbally and nonverbally and within the explicit (taught) and implicit (hidden) curriculum. Be mindful of ensuring that your communication – verbal, nonverbal and self-talk – does not impose glass ceilings on your pupils or yourself.

• •

STRATEGIES FOR YOUR TEACHER TOOLKIT – creative environment

Play

Fundamental to a creative environment is the encouragement of play. Play is strongly featured in the Early Years curriculum. Indeed, older children and adults are often encouraged to be 'playful' in order to facilitate creative thinking and to use the whole personality (Winnicott 1971). Some of the most successful companies such as Google. com and Apple actively design playful, unconventional working environments with bright colours, textures and spaces to play and 'think'.

The benefits of play go beyond curriculum boundaries and form the building blocks for subsequent learning and for a love of learning. Play promotes creative and lifelong skills, such as planning, organization, taking risks, creating challenges, problem-creating and -solving, concentration, persistence, engagement, involvement, participation and metacognitive abilities (Wood 2012). Play is a process, an end in itself, but all too quickly, as a child moves through school, the focus moves toward the tangible end-product. The, often stark, transition from play-based, informal learning to structured, formal learning can be too much for some pupils, resulting in a sense of loss: loss of freedom, choice, motivation, enjoyment, which can hinder a pupil's engagement with learning.

Children are naturally playful and, as teachers, tapping into this will only benefit teaching. Consider Piaget's theory – the child as a lone scientist – and seek opportunities for pupils to explore, play and construct meaning without being prescriptive or didactic and focusing on the outcome alone. Identify how play can be developed within your pedagogy and learning environment. The Reggio Emilia approach is a good place to start, and although it focuses on young children, the principles are sound throughout subsequent key stages.

The physical environment

A key aspect of a Reggio Emilia setting is the use of spaces, or *ateliers*, to promote collaboration using stimulating resources. This includes the layout of the classroom, use of outdoor space and the quality and richness of the equipment and materials.

Talk

Within Reggio Emilia the *ateliers* are designed to encourage verbal and nonverbal communication, which is observed collaboratively with the teachers and other adults. The pupils' thinking is made visible through making them feel valued and 'listened to'. Digital recording and visual representations in 2- or 3D or through movement or music also make thought processes tangible.

Time

Sustained time, physically and emotionally, is needed for immersion in an activity in order to realize creative outcomes (Burnard et al. 2006).

Resources

A wide range of appropriate, authentic materials, tools and other resources stimulates creativity – from newspapers and modelling clay to digital resources. Often free-formed, non-specific resources promote more imagination. As an example, my boys will prefer the cardboard box to most contents as it is their imagination they use to create ships, forts, rockets and dens.

Outdoor environment

Use the space outside of the classroom to foster creative development. My boys adore their woodland days and when asked how their day was the response is always 'amazing', and they will recount activities with great enthusiasm. Use 'anchors' to promote a positive and secure environment. These can be physical, visual or auditory, for example specific music as a signal or cue to tidy, talk, reflect, line up or praise, and instructions given in a predictable way. This is discussed in more detail in Chapters 8 and 9.

Further reading

Malaguzzi, L. (1993) History, ideas, and basic philosophy: an interview with Lella Gandini, in C. Edwards, L. Gandini and G. Forman (eds) *The hundred languages of children: the Reggio Emilia Approach – advanced reflections*, 2nd edn. Greenwich, CT: Ablex Publishing. This book fully describes the above approach.

REFLECT

- How do you use the physical space within and outside your classroom?
- Does your use of space promote collaboration and opportunities for quality dialogue?
- Are the resources adaptable and flexible and do they tap into the pupils' imagination?
- Do you find time to value pupils' conversation and feelings and develop their ideas by consciously slowing down to listen to them?

Developing your creativity

If you want to be creative, stay in part a child, with the creativity and invention that characterizes children before they are deformed by adult society.

Jean Piaget, 1952

Take a moment to reflect on the above quote from Piaget and consider whether we actively nurture and stimulate our children and ourselves to be creative. As a teacher you need to create an environment to promote such creative skills as originality, divergent thinking, connection-making and self-confidence. Remember you are the role model for you pupils so like unused muscles, your creativity will improve with exercise. So let's warm up those potentially underused creative muscles. Improvisation is a great way to enliven your imagination and creativity. I loved watching the TV show *Who's line is it anyway?* and I still play around with random objects my boys find and think of as many interesting ways to use, wear or fashion them.

ACTIVITY

Collect three random objects and on a large sheet of paper use them to plan a 'creative' lesson. Consider subject coverage, cross-curricular links, use of indoor/outdoor space, use of senses, organization/grouping of pupils, other resources and key questions. Refer back to Table 7.1 (p. 148) which lists creative qualities.

- How many of the creative qualities shown in the table did you use?
- What connections did you make with your own personal interests and within the curriculum?
- When planning your lesson, how did you feel?
- Was this uncomfortable for you or did you feel a sense of autonomy and excitement?
- How do you think your pupils would respond to this lesson?

There is no failsafe recipe or routine, however some strategies may help to promote creative thinking and in turn develop your pedagogy. This gains momentum as greater personal creativity helps to overcome or manage constraints and barriers as you begin to think beyond what has gone before and aspire to more.

 ## CHECKLIST to develop creativity

Autonomy and risk-taking

Plan a way to harness and enrich your creative professional autonomy and demonstrate flexibility and confidence. Challenge yourself to think about things and do things differently. This means being open-minded and accepting critical feedback. Take on board the following:

- *risk-taking*: don't be afraid to risk failure and to be challenged in the face of ambiguity and uncertainty;
- *observation*: take time to see what is really there and think up new and unexpected patterns to change approaches and mindsets;
- *perseverance and resilience*: acknowledge that creativity may not just 'happen' – it requires effort, time and openness.

Repertoire and subject knowledge

Central to your personal development will be your ability to use a full and varied repertoire and secure subject knowledge to promote creativity within your classroom. As the hierarchy explains in the Introduction, the foundations must be in place before 'higher order' skills can be developed. The concept of *mastery* means that to 'think outside the box' you still require the 'box' which is your secure subject knowledge that enables ideas to grow and flourish.

Empathy and playfulness

Reflect upon your 'creative lesson' and put yourself in your pupils' shoes. Consider what they will experience in terms of creativity and how this could be enhanced. If you embed a sense of empathy in your day-to-day teaching this will enable you to move both your thinking and practice forward as it will provide a context for reflection.

Make sure you get the pupil-teacher relationship right, as discussed in Chapter 1, as it is imperative in creating a classroom ethos which promotes creativity. A positive, trusting, emotionally secure and safe environment is required, with a focus on the well-being of your pupils. Just as you and your creative autonomy are affected by the whole school ethos and policy, you will affect the pupils within your classroom. The concept of *playfulness* means reflecting on your teaching style: is there a sense of playfulness? Do you use humour and embrace fun?

Planning for play

Within the Key Stage 1 and 2 curriculum, see the potential for play in history and drama with the pupils acting out events or taking on roles; or in science, playing with toys to investigate how they move and how mechanisms work, or playing with materials to find out their properties.

Having worked on the above now consider how secure you are with creativity. You will hopefully echo Billy Connolly when he says, 'I think my securities far outweigh my insecurities. I am not nearly as afraid of myself and my imagination as I used to be.'

Developing learner creativity

Engaging the learner and equipping them with learning *how* to learn is vital (metacognition); however, engendering a culture of positive, productive learning in all pupils can be challenging. Learning and teaching creatively can be frustrating for pupil and teacher alike but developing these skills is necessary in effective and ultimately outstanding teaching. Think about *how* they learn as well as *what* they learn.

• •

 STRATEGIES FOR YOUR TEACHER TOOLKIT

Questioning

* How often do you use closed/rhetorical questions?
* How often do you have the answers you seek predetermined?

Use large framing questions or speculative, thought-provoking starting points regardless of the subject or the age of the pupil. This will generate possibilities and promote conditional or abductive reasoning, especially through 'What if . . . ?' questions and reframing problems.

Focus on open-ended and enquiry-based questions or those with more than one correct answer. For example, instead of asking what's 5 + 5 = ? ask ? + ? = 10 and explore possibilities: decimals, negative numbers as well as the bonds to 10, dependent upon ability. Help your pupils to evaluate their questions by discouraging the idea that you ask questions and they simply answer them (I-R and I-R-F discussed in Chapter 5). Develop speculation and possibilities and employ reverse questioning making the pupil responsible for resolving problems – for example, What can you do to solve this? Why do you think this problem occurred? These questions more readily promote key qualities such as persistence, resilience and resourcefulness.

Pupil ownership

* Do you use the language of choice and ensure a sense of pupil autonomy?
* How do you see yourself as a facilitator or oracle?

Creativity by nature is personal, so let personalization and choice be given more freely and allow pupils to take responsibility for their learning approaches. Redefine your role from teacher to facilitator or coach. Consider a more socio-constructivist approach, whereby collaboration between learners and teachers and, where appropriate, among learners, gives them autonomy and ownership.

Applying and connecting

- How do you facilitate or encourage your pupils to make connections?
- Do you readily use analogies to scaffold connections?

A creative teacher will use metaphors, anecdotes and analogies to promote connection-making and imagination. They recognize how this creative experience applies across subjects and they integrate a strong dialogic element. This requires careful planning and sufficient time and space for reflection to help pupils make connections independently and collaboratively.

Verbalizing and modelling

- Do you actively encourage and model self-talk and a dialogic approach?
- How do you model or scaffold a task or project so creativity and success can be achieved?

The most powerful way to develop creativity in your pupils is to be a role model, therefore be cognizant of your responses, actions and attitudes as these influence your pupils. A creative approach to teaching may be daunting for some pupils, especially those who either prefer or have experienced more formal and structured approaches or those whose skills are not developed. Be aware that a blank page or too many options, resources or space may leave pupils unsure and unable to engage. Identify how to reduce the fear factor in each case (my secondary art teacher used to ask us to add a squiggle in the corner of the sheet of paper so it wasn't a scary blank sheet). Through your modelling and thinking-out-loud you will promote greater creativity as you unpack a trial and error approach, show resilience and so support a pupil's 'I can do' attitude and growth mindset.

● ●

Planning for creativity

Planning for creativity is not an easy, quick option, especially set against the back-drop of influences in terms of how you should plan over the last few decades. The national strategies, for example, and their prescriptive, three-part lesson, can affect our willingness to push boundaries and consider more creative approaches. You may ask yourself 'Should I be doing it like this?' And, 'Am I doing this right?'. It is important you give yourself permission to take risks and try something new (ask yourself, 'What's the worst that can happen?').

 REFLECT

Take a few minutes to identify how you currently plan and structure your lessons. Note what resources you draw upon; who you collaborate with; how the structure may vary from subject to subject; and if you have delivered the same lesson or similar, how it affects your planning. It is also important to bear in mind that any learning experience may offer the opportunity to develop skills that you did not plan.

Now consider if your core focus is creative engagement. What is superfluous to achieving this? Sir Ken Robinson would question whether the creative process requires worksheets, books, tables, chairs, the IWB, even the classroom. Take these away and you are left with the pupils, the teacher and their enthusiasm, imagination and skills, which will inspire creativity.

Here are some questions to support your planning for creativity.

Does your pedagogy draw on the skills and abilities of your pupils? Do you 'tap' into your pupils' interests and cultural capital? One of the key ideas in encouraging creativity in pupils is to make sure their learning and play involves a multisensory approach using touch, smell, hearing, taste and sight. If pupils are having trouble understanding or engaging with a subject or concept, ask questions related to their interests or home life or their community centre and culture. The context may spur creative ideas because the pupil finds the topic more enjoyable – it has tapped into their 'cultural capital', and it may counteract some of the anxiety caused by the concept.

Does your planning identify key skills to develop and how the learner will/can apply them? What is the value of these skills within and beyond this experience or activity? Avoid being restricted by subject boundaries by applying learning, knowledge and skills across the curriculum. Seek to integrate subjects and make connections within and between subjects and beyond the classroom. Revisit prior knowledge and offer opportunities for pupils to work collaboratively in order to widen their perspectives. This cross-fertilization motivates pupils who lack interest in subjects taught discretely or abstractly; through using higher-order thinking skills, pupils are learning at a deeper level.

Do you emphasize product over process and accept all ideas from pupils, seeing mistakes as inherent in the learning process? Goal-orientated, performativity-focused learning will not enable or empower all pupils, so ensure your focus is on the learning journey you take with your pupils and not the outcome and performance you expect. This learning process is problematic and mistakes should be celebrated not feared, as Edison (1847–1931) ably illuminated (as he tried many thousands of times to get his lightbulb working): 'I have not failed. I have just found 10,000 things that do not work.'

Praise pupils for their imagination in generating ideas, regardless of whether some are silly or unrelated, while encouraging them to identify and develop their best ideas or suggestions into high-quality outcomes (Sternberg and Williams 1996). Try 'I wonder if . . .', or pose questions that are challenging or impossible to answer: 'What does God look like?'

Ask children thought-provoking questions to help them to think creatively, for example:

- *What* would happen if the country stopped producing power?
- *How* would it change how we lived?

- *Who* would or would not benefit?
- *Where* would you build a new home?
- *Why* would you do this?
- *When* would you change?

Ask 'How many different ways . . . ?' questions. For example, 'How many ways can a lump of plasticine be used?' Then hand round the object to help the pupils generate ideas. The purpose of this style of questioning is to break away from, firstly, I-R/I-R-F questions and, secondly, because there is not a correct answer to a singular question.

Does it 'feel' good to be in your classroom and do pupils love their learning? The classroom ethos should reflect respect for pupils' emotional comfort and engagement, enabling them to perceive themselves as individuals. Make connections to their personal lives as well as their learning (discussed more fully in Chapter 8). View classroom environments as the pupils' space and share responsibility; use pupil voice when decisions are made. Make teaching and learning relevant and encourage ownership of learning by passing back control to the learner.

Do you give your pupils time and space to think, talk, explore? Does your own awareness of time affect pupil creativity? Fast foods, fast connection speeds, fast track . . . quickness is valued and aspired to. Our emphasis, as well as our enemy, is time. Allow time in your planning which is sufficient and sustained for pupils to respond and to wonder and ponder. I would dread asking a certain pupil a question, as I know his answer would be long-winded and almost painfully slow. I had to stop myself from leaping in either to close him down or put the words into his mouth just to speed the lesson up. If I had planned 'thinking and responding time' I wouldn't have been so impatient.

Think of those pupils looking out of the window and daydreaming (which I did quite a lot of at school), who may be just about to come up with a tremendous idea and your need for speed has broken the thread. Daydreaming is now being explored through neuroscience and scientists are discovering that the brain is very active while daydreaming, using parts which are not used for focused work (if only my teachers knew that when I was 9 years old). If you give pupils time to be reflective, to think and articulate their ideas, their thinking is likely to be significantly deeper than a snappy answer in response. How often are different brain states facilitated?

- Beta state: 13–25 cycles per second (cps) of electrical impulses. The brain is in conscious alertness.
- Alpha state: 8–12 cps. Aware of the outside world, own thoughts and 'meaning making'; a state of relaxed alertness and so more receptive.
- Theta state: 4–7 cps. Processing information within the subconscious part of brain; deep reflection/reverie occurs.

Our preoccupation with curriculum coverage and 'pace' results in pupils remaining within a beta state for the school day. I often refer to a metaphoric dot-to-dot, or low-demand activity, as downtime to enable pupils to process and make sense of the day without continuous information bombardment. Build these times into your day or week and monitor your pupils' responses and well-being. In addition, reflect upon the theory of Maslow, for example, and how your desire for self-actualization and higher-order thinking may be quite taxing if those 30 tummies are rumbling before lunch.

Assessing creativity

The focus on the high stakes, tested curriculum, coupled with the lack of need or clarity as to how to test creativity, has perpetuated its low curriculum status. Nevertheless, the removing of levels in 2014 and a strong focus on formative assessment, as discussed in Chapter 6, might facilitate greater creativity within the curriculum. The suggested further reading below provides useful information and tools to assess creativity within your schools.

Further reading

Redmond, C. (2009) *The creativity wheel: assessing creative development teacher resource*. Durham: Creative Partnerships. This framework is based on imagination with a purpose, originality and value, in line with the NACCCE definition.

Spencer, E., Lucas, B. and Claxton, G. (2012) *Progression in creativity: developing new forms of assessment, final research report*. Newcastle: CCE. The CCE commissioned the Centre for Real-World Learning (CRL) which created an assessment tool comprised of five habits and 15 sub-habits designed to cultivate creativity in pupils.

REFLECT

How might you make creativity more explicit in your pedagogy and classroom ethos? Draw pictures or take another approach you seldom use (concept map, video, diagram, cartoon . . .) to express these challenges/barriers to embracing and embedding creativity. Inwardly observe how you respond differently when approaching this task.

Now *select one barrier* to action and analyse why this barrier is there. Think of many, varied, and unusual ways of solving this problem.

List all the possibilities regardless of how silly you think they are. *Remember*, creative thinking must have a positive, accepting environment in order to flourish.

Filter out the solutions that do not appeal and develop those that do. Develop your action plan and add a timescale. For example, *by next week I will plan and deliver a creative lesson that promotes creative skills*.

A thought . . . the *litmus test* for creativity and great teaching is to ask yourself and your pupils what were the *memorable moments* of the day, week, term and year. I wonder if they will say, 'That amazing literacy session we sat on the carpet and listened, wrote for 20 minutes, then sat on the carpet and listened' or 'When the classroom was an alien spaceship and our teacher was abducted and we had to set her free (or not)!'

References

Alexander, R.J. (2009) *Children, their world, their education: final report of the Cambridge Primary Review*. London: Routledge.

Amabile, T.M. (1983) *The social psychology of creativity*. New York: Springer Verlag.

Burnard, P., Craft, A. and Cremin, T. (2006) Documenting 'possibility thinking': a journey of collaborative enquiry, *International Journal of Early Years Education*, 14(3): 243–62.

Craft, A. (2001) Little c creativity, in A. Craft, B. Jeffery and M. Leibling (eds) *Creativity in education*. London: Continuum.

Craft, A. (2005) *Creativity in schools: tensions and dilemmas*. London: Routledge.

Craft, A. (2011) *Creativity and education futures: learning in the digital age*. London: Routledge.

Csikszentmihalyi, M. (1996) *Creativity, flow and the psychology of discovery and invention*. New York: Harper Collins.

de Bono, E. (1992) *Serious creativity: using the power of lateral thinking to create new ideas*. London: Harper Collins.

DfE (2010) *The importance of teaching: the schools white paper*. London: DfE.

DfE (2012) *Teachers' standards*, www.gov.uk/government/uploads/system/uploads/attachment_data/file/301107/Teachers__Standards.pdf.

DfEE (1998) *The National Literacy Strategy framework for teaching*. London: DfEE.

DfES (2003) *Excellence and improvement*. London: DfES.

DfES (2005) Personalised learning: building a new relationship with schools.

Desailly, J. (2012) *Creativity in the primary classroom*. London: SAGE.

Education Scotland (2013) *Creativity across learning 3–18*, www.educationscotland.gov.uk/Images/Creativity3to18_tcm4-814361.pdf.

Freire, P. (1998) *Pedagogy of Freedom*, Lanham (MA): Rowman & Littlefield Publishers, Inc

Fryer, M. (1996) *Creative teaching and learning*. London: Paul Chapman Publishing.

Grigg, R. (2010) *Becoming an outstanding primary school teacher*. Upper Saddle River, NJ: Pearson Education.

Jones, R. and Wyse, D. (eds) (2004) *Creativity in the primary curriculum*. London: David Fulton.

Meador, K.S. (1992) Emerging rainbows: a review of the literature on creativity, *Journal for the Education of the Gifted*, 15(2): 163–81.

NACCCE (1999) *All our futures: creativity, culture and education*. London: DfEE.

Ofsted (2010) *Learning: creative approaches that raise standards*, www.ofsted.gov.uk/publications/080266.

Piaget, J. (1952) *The origins of intelligence in children*. New York: International University Press.

Plowden, B. (1967) *Children and their primary schools* (the Plowden Report). London: HMSO.

Pound, L. and Lee, T. (2011) *Teaching mathematics creatively*. Abingdon: Routledge.

QCA (Qualifications and Curriculum Authority) (2005) *Creativity: Find it! Promote it!* London: QCA.

Roberts, P. (2006) *Nurturing creativity in young people: a report to government to inform future policy* (the Roberts Review). London: DCMS/DfES.

Starko, A.J. (2010) *Creativity in the classroom*, 4th edn. Abingdon: Routledge.

Starko, A.J. (2013) Creativity on the brink, *Educational Leadership*, 70(5): 54–6.

Sternberg, R.J. (1997) *Thinking styles*. Cambridge: Cambridge University Press.

Sternberg, R.J. (1999) *Handbook of creativity*. Cambridge: Cambridge University Press.

Sternberg, R.J. and Williams, W.M. (1996) *How to develop student creativity*. Alexandria, VA: ASCD.

Torrance, E.P. (1962) *Guiding creative talent*. Englewood Cliffs, NJ: Prentice-Hall.

Torrance, E.P. (1981) Predicting the creativity of elementary school children (1958–1980) – and the teacher who 'made a difference', *Gifted Child Quarterly*, 25: 55–62.

Weisberg, R.W. (2006) *Creativity: understanding innovation in problem solving, science, invention, and the arts*. Chichester: Wiley.

Wilson, A. (2015) *Creativity in primary education*, 3rd edn. London: Sage.

Winnicott, D.W. (1971) *Playing and reality*. Abingdon: Routledge.

Wood, E. (2012) *Play, learning and the early childhood curriculum*, 3rd edn. London: Sage.

Woods, P. and Jeffrey, B. (1996) *Teachable moments: the art of creative teaching in primary schools*. Buckingham: Open University Press.

8

Inspiring environments – the learning environment

In brief, the environment consists of those conditions that promote or hinder, stimulate or inhibit, the characteristic activities of a living being.

John Dewey, 2001

Our coat hook! Your 'perfect jacket' expresses who you are and is comfortable throughout the whole day. Your jacket is now becoming an invaluable and trusted resource; friend even. It reflects your personality and individuality. Your jacket must now make you feel good in any environment you are in and whomever you are with.

This chapter addresses the learning environment and how the physical, social and emotional aspects, as Dewey (2001) points out, promote and stimulate pupils' learning. It also discusses effective TA deployment and parental involvement.

The key themes in this chapter prompt you to:

- consider how your *teacher identity and philosophy* influences your organization and ethos of your classroom;
- reflect whether your understanding of the *purpose of education* is evident in how you have established your learning environment;
- identify how your focus on *well-being for you and your pupils* is reflected in how you organize classroom systems, routines and learning support;
- evaluate how *meeting the needs of the unique child* is demonstrated in your classroom organization, level of support and level of parent involvement;
- identify how your awareness of *creating an enabling and empowering environment* is reflected in how you organize and manage your classroom;
- consider how your own *self-awareness* and *critical self-reflection* enhances how you empower and enable each pupil to develop their potential regarding classroom organization, approaches, support and interactions;
- identify how your understanding of the physical, social and emotional aspects of the learning environment and those involved therein focuses your need for *continuous development as a lifelong learner*.

This chapter addresses the following *Teacherspter addres* (DfE 2012):

1 Set high expectations which inspire, motivate and challenge pupils
7 Manage behaviour effectively to ensure a good and safe learning environment
8 Fulfil wider professional responsibilities.

Outstanding learning environments

A learning environment is one in which social, physical, emotional and all things pedagogical occur. The design and management of learning spaces is fundamental to the achievement of positive learning outcomes as well as to the health and well-being of your pupils. Your role is pivotal to all that happens in the classroom, therefore getting the strategies right to ensure a positive learning environment, which promotes your core goals in education, is key. Dewey (2001) further remarks that water is an environment for a fish – it is sustaining, necessary. We would not dream of placing a fish in any other environment and yet, as UNESCO (2012) concludes, the importance of creating optimal conditions to enable and sustain learning has sometimes been overlooked as a 'peripheral' factor in the provision of quality education. A pupil's psychological attitude to school should be of importance to educational practitioners, as without the motivation to work and without feeling comfortable in the learning environment pupils are unlikely to progress efficiently towards higher academic achievements (Knowles 2011). We therefore need a full understanding of the importance of environment and pupil learning.

The theories of Dewey, Piaget, Plowden, Skinner, Reggio Emilia, and recent advances in neuroscience and digital technology have all influenced modern classrooms. Learning is a complex process influenced by how your pupils not only interact with the curriculum and your pedagogical and assessment approaches but their learning environment. The quality of these interactions depends not only on how well the environmental elements support learning but on the skill of the teacher in motivating, managing, building self-efficacy and scaffolding the learning sequences (UNESCO 2012). It is here your teacher philosophy and beliefs serve as the guiding force behind the decisions you make to shape your 'ideal' learning environment.

Classrooms are complex working environments with vast amounts of information and interacting factors continuously generated by your pupils. The skill is being able to process this information quickly and accurately. A better understanding of the learning environment enables you to closely connect your knowledge of theory, curriculum and pedagogy in order to increase learner motivation and abilities.

As a starting point, Fisher (2005) suggests the following when focusing on how an effective environment can be developed:

- What pupil abilities do you want to achieve (Chapter 2)?
- What pedagogies should be used to achieve the desired learning outcomes (Chapters 4 and 5)?
- How can we assess these abilities (Chapter 6)?
- What learning environment should be developed for these pedagogies (Chapter 8)?

UNESCO (2012) very succinctly states 'good learning environments foster quality learning, and bad learning environments do not'. An outstanding teacher strives to make a good classroom environment both enabling and empowering to equip their pupils with the attitudes, attributes, skills, knowledge and understanding for their futures.

Empowerment

The Merriam-Webster dictionary defines 'to empower' as a means 'to enable; to promote the influence or self-actualisation of'. Empowerment is dynamic and can be viewed as a continuum, as individuals may feel more or less empowered in different environments and at different times. The factors affecting the level of feeling empowered are either *internal* (e.g. self-efficacy, knowledge and skills) or *external* (e.g. social group, parents, teachers) (Zimmerman 1995).

 REFLECT

Take a moment to reflect upon times you have felt very empowered or disempowered.

- What were the factors that caused this feeling?
- What were the effects or outcomes from that feeling?

Refer back to Maslow's hierarchy of needs and how the environment and those in it were influential.

Empowerment can be seen as a *process*, which Chamberlain (1997) defines as having 15 qualities (examples are shown in Table 8.1), though not all are necessary to be considered empowered. In essence, empowerment necessitates a sense of ownership, personal control or *agency* (Blackmore et al. 2011), including the belief that one's actions are related to desired outcomes and a sense of self-efficacy.

 REFLECT

To create an environment that empowers your pupils consider to what extent Chamberlain's qualities are reflected in and facilitated within your classroom.

Table 8.1 Qualities of empowerment.

Qualities for empowerment	1 not at all to 5 considerably
Having decision-making power	1 2 3 4 5
Having access to information and resources	1 2 3 4 5

Table 8.1 (continued)

Having a range of options from which to make choices	1 2 3 4 5
A feeling an individual can make a difference	1 2 3 4 5
Learning to think critically and seeing things differently	1 2 3 4 5
Learning skills that the individual defines as important	1 2 3 4 5
Growth and change that is never ending and self-initiated	1 2 3 4 5

Enabling

The dictionary defines 'to enable' as 'to provide with the means, knowledge, or opportunity'. Outstanding teachers aim to create an environment that enables every pupil to excel through developing mastery, providing opportunities for pupil voice and the sense of security and safety to develop it. Therefore 'enabling' must be considered a key word within your developing philosophy and made explicit in your planning. Reflect again upon the theory of, for example Gardner's multiple intelligences, Maslow's hierarchy of needs, Bowlby's attachment theory or Kolb's divergent or convergent learners, and how the classroom environment you create is enabling emotionally and socially, as well as physically and cognitively.

The social and emotional environment

> *Sometimes a simple, almost insignificant gesture on the part of a teacher can have a profound formative effect on the life of a student.*
>
> Paulo Freire, 1998

Raising your awareness of your actions and how you influence your environment, as Freire (1998) poignantly notes, will affect your pupils. Building and maintaining positive pupil-teacher relationships underscores a healthy and emotionally supportive environment. Pupils who perceive the social climate as cohesive and with little friction do well and the recognition and respect of pupils' voice improves motivation and positive feelings about school and their teacher (Rudduck and McIntyre 2007).

Pupil voice is about genuine participation, which has an actual impact on the pupils' learning environment. Ensure they see change happen as a result of their participation and decision-making in their learning environment. It is important to plan for opportunities for pupils to express their views, but do be careful not to let the pupils and yourself defer to the most articulate or popular pupils for the class views. Using circle time, anonymous suggestion boxes, joining focus groups, surveys and questionnaires, diaries, class noticeboards, group reps and the school council are ways to offer a voice to all your pupils. There may already be pupil-oriented initiatives in place in the school, such as the UNICEF RRR (rights respect responsibility) programme, which can be used as a platform to continue to develop pupil participation.

The teacher and the pupils play a determining role in creating the classroom environment. However, it is the teacher who largely establishes social rules, arbitrates the pupils' experiences, determines expectations and sets tasks, time, space and resources. They shape the group dynamics, the level of pupil talk and decide upon rewards and sanctions. Some of these teacher behaviours, if over- or underdirected or mismatched to learners' needs, can affect the pupil and the effectiveness of the learning environment. It is necessary for you to raise your own self-awareness and be mindful of how you affect those within your environment.

 REFLECT

Would you want to be a pupil in your class? List your reasons. Consider how *empowering* and *enabling* your classroom environment is.

- Do the pupils feel confident and secure both socially and emotionally? How is this exhibited?
- Do you offer them regular opportunities to express their feelings about their work, the classroom or school?
- Are pupils active agents in determining and directing their own learning?
- How do you encourage pupils to take charge of their learning and make their own decisions?

Further reading

Fielding, M. (2004) Transformative approaches to student voice: theoretical underpinnings, recalcitrant realities, *British Educational Research Journal*, 30(2): 295–311. This article examines the notion of voice and offers frameworks to move towards real pupil participation.

Hart, R. (1992) *Children's participation: from tokenism to citizenship*. Florence: UNICEF International Child Development Centre. Hart provides a useful ladder to assess the level of pupil participation.

The physical environment

One of the lessons that children learn from a very young age is that space is both enabling and constraining.

John Morgan, 2000

Primary school pupils relate strongly to their classrooms, as this is where they spend the great majority of their time and very quickly, as Morgan (2000) concludes, they understand how to respond to that space. There is growing evidence that 'the design of schools and classrooms directly influences what goes on inside them, and can sometimes be a critical factor in how well pupils succeed in school' (UNESCO 2012: 41). The HEAD Project (Holistic Evidence and Design) (Barrett et al. 2015) concluded that the individual classroom is most influential and could boost pupils' academic performance in reading, writing and maths (Barrett et al. 2015), and indicated that moving an 'average' pupil from a least effective to the most effective classroom saw considerable gains (around 1.3 sub-levels).

Physical aspects, such as layout, density, displays, furniture, lighting, temperature, resource area and workstations, all affect the effectiveness of a classroom. Each physical aspect can influence learning and communicates the teacher's approach to learning. Pedagogy influences how learning spaces are organized. Desks arranged into groups demonstrates the teacher values collaboration or interactive workstations or an emphasis on outdoor space indicates that the teacher believes in active enquiry and pupil-centred learning. There is substantial evidence that learning environments, such as school gardens and small learning communities, engage pupils through giving them a joy of learning (UNESCO 2012).

What is clear is that the learning environment needs to be flexible and reflect the needs of your pupils; it should emphasize the multiple uses of a space and personalized or independent learning. Therefore it is up to you, the teacher, to throw light on how the social, emotional and physical contexts of your classroom are being used.

Maximizing physical space

STRATEGIES FOR YOUR TEACHER TOOLKIT

Based on the HEAD findings (2015) the physical aspects of your classroom should consider the following.

Naturalness

This aspect was found to be the most significant, with air quality, light and temperature also significant in affecting pupils' learning.

- Make sure there is enough light; supplement natural light with artificial light and avoid displays on windows as this blocks out natural light.
- Reduce glare from daylight, lighting and IWBs or projectors.
- Ventilate the room to reduce excessive levels of carbon dioxide and pollutants. HEAD found just 30 minutes in an average sized classroom with 30 pupils reduced the air quality if there was no ventilation. Install a CO^2 meter.
- Keep temperatures cool as heat and humidity impair performance.
- Ensure auditory perception is clear and background noise minimized. Soft textures, such as drapes, rugs or posters absorb acoustics.
- Use the access to outdoor spaces if available or have plants in the classroom.

Individualization

This aspect develops the sense of classroom belonging and community. It develops the sense of connectedness the pupils have with you and their classroom.

- Use classrooms flexibly; provide breakout spaces and different learning zones (e.g. carpet area, reading corner, role-play area or writing station).
- Make your classroom distinctive (unique to you and your pupils) so pupils instantly identify with it.
- Display pupils' work on boards and tables to create a sense of ownership.
- Personalize drawers, pegs, etc.
- Ensure furniture, equipment and storage is child-centred and age- and size-related.

Stimulation

This aspect ensures that the use of colour and display enhances and doesn't detract from learning.

- Balance the use of space between too boring/bland and too complex/confusing.
- Younger pupils prefer brighter colours; ideally light-coloured walls with a brighter feature wall, chairs or blinds used as an accent colour. The overall stimulation of colour should be pitched at a mid-range – neither too neutral nor too bright.

Displays

Displays serve a variety of purposes within a school classroom. The displaying of work should be an integral part of planning, not an add-on at some future date when you have time. A good display can enhance the well-being, independence and support mechanisms happening within the classroom. Moreover, your and your pupils' sense of ownership and aspirations can be communicated through thoughtful, well-designed displays. Displays should be an integral part of the planning process as this elevates them to an effective tool for teaching and learning.

However, you should be aware that a display could potentially form an off-task behaviour option as pupils can be 'looking' at the walls and be distracted. A study showed that pupils in low visual distraction or sparse condition classrooms spent less time off-task (28.4 per cent compared to 38.6 per cent in high visual distraction or highly decorated classrooms) and showed better attainment (Fisher et al. 2014). Considerable amounts of wall displays can appear cluttered and disorganized, making it more difficult for pupils to recognize and find pertinent information. In addition, content-specific material may not be useful in many situations. The conclusions from the HEAD study suggested 20-50 per cent of available wall space should be kept clear. Less can sometimes be more.

Displays for instruction

- Evolve and change wall displays to keep pupils connected with current learning and to help them develop coherency between ideas, tasks and lessons.
- Create a general 'word wall': key vocabulary for that lesson or topic and ensure ease of access and reference.

- Establish an interactive or working wall, based on a current topic, with some essential starter images and questions, ongoing mind/concept maps, or post-it notes.
- Display charts/checklists for memory jogging and aides memoires for specific learning goals or to reinforce your expectations (discussed in Chapter 5).
- Use displays to model and make explicit expectations, for example the writing style, presentation, use of vocabulary or next steps.

Displays for essential information

- 'Stuck walls': a resource in the form of a poster or criteria that is displayed in classrooms. If a pupil is stuck, establish systems to find the answer using other sources (e.g. try a display, book, peer, resource or notes – before you ask for help). This promotes resilience and independent learning.
- Classroom management (e.g. list of response partners, reading buddies).
- Roles and responsibilities (e.g. monitor jobs, school council).
- Daily and weekly timetable; visual timetables.
- Code of conduct and school ethos/class rules.
- Rewards and sanctions.

Displays for motivation and ownership

- Birthdays.
- Star of the day.
- Whole-class goals.
- Individual targets.
- Class news.

Displays for celebration

- Value effort (reflect upon promoting a growth mindset) Most pupils enjoy having something displayed publicly. In the words of the Peter Dixon (poet, performer, educationalist and artist) single mount = I like this piece of work, double = I really like this piece of work, triple = I like this piece of work, but I have time on my hands!
- Make sure there is always work displayed that reflects the efforts of everyone in the class.
- Train pupils to mount their own work.
- Encourage visits by family and the community to reinforce the value placed on the pupils' work.

Displays for modelling expectations and mastery

- Share and evaluate work displayed. Deconstruct and display the process, with the steps and the final product, to add clarity of what is expected at each stage and the 'look' of the final outcome.

- Promote interaction and engagement with the display, for example post-it note comments.
- Use teacher modelling, with hand-written rather than digitally produced headings and key questions to make expectations clear.
- Use mind/concept maps of ideas and carefully selected visual images to scaffold learning.

Measuring the learning environment

The DfES measured the financial and pedagogical value of school learning environments through a study carried out by PriceWaterhouseCoopers (2000). This study focused on the relationship between schools' capital investment and pupil performance and found that headteachers viewed capital investment as having a strong positive impact on pupil behaviour and motivation (Fisher 2005). There are tools, as suggested below, which can be used to support the evaluation of your school and learning environment.

Further reading

Moos, R. and Trickett, E.J. (1974) *Classroom environment scale manual*. Palo Alto, CA: Consulting Psychologists Press. This instrument has become the prototype for other tools developed and/or adapted by school climate researchers over the past three decades.

Other measures: the What is Happening in this Class? (WHIC) questionnaire is a popular instrument; 'My Class Inventory' (MCI) is suitable for pupils aged 8–12 years; or the Learning Environment Inventory (LEI).

REFLECT

Return to Fisher's (2005) questions at the beginning of the chapter and identify a change you could make in your pedagogy, which requires a change in learning environment.

ACTIVITY

Explore how the pupils 'see' their classroom using the following suggestions.

- Ask the pupils to draw a plan of it as this can 'reveal' what they see as important, how they perceive space and key areas, such as a reading corner or resource area.

- Use a concept mapping technique with key words such as routines, monitors, space, resources, displays to see how the pupils view and connect concepts within their environment (more suited to pupils in Key Stage 2).
- Video-record a session to capture the full picture of the learning environment and how you and your pupils operate within it.
- Analyse the classroom interactions of your pupils with others and the elements within the classroom. For example, classroom routines, organization and systems, use of resources and equipment, pupil-pupil, teacher-pupil and pupil-TA relationships.

Effective TA deployment

In the late 1980s and 1990s there was an increase in the number of TAs in schools in England, as an outcome of the 'inclusion agenda' and the resulting education of pupils with SEN and disabilities in mainstream schools. Some research indicates TAs add value to pupils' learning experience and enhance the learning environment (UNISON 2013). Moreover, teachers generally feel that the presence of a TA in their classroom increases their job satisfaction and effectiveness (Blatchford et al. 2009) and improves the motivation and attention of those pupils being supported. Pupils also viewed the presence of TAs positively, as they offer them support, a place to turn (Bland and Sleightholme 2012) and helped improve their work confidence (Webster et al. 2013).

The importance of the teacher deploying the TA effectively is key. To ensure their effectiveness the teacher and the TA must work closely together, especially when planning, and have the necessary knowledge and skills to carry out the tasks assigned to them (Blatchford et al. 2009). It is therefore important that the teacher is active in building team spirit and the 'feelgood' factor. I have found that embracing the use of two Cs, *communication* and *collaboration*, supports team-building. If people are communicated with positively, honestly and openly and this communication is a genuine collaboration, where they feel they have a voice, and it is of value, teams work effectively.

• •

MODELS TO ENHANCE YOUR TEACHER TOOLKIT

Cremin et al. (2003), suggest that teachers and TAs work flexibly as a team to improve teaching efficiency, and offer the following models to support this.

The **'room management model'** requires the adults in the classroom to take on different roles: 1) the 'individual helper' works with individuals or small groups on a teaching activity while 2) the 'activity manager' works with the rest of the class keeping them on task and focused. This model has been shown to provide the greatest improvements in pupil engagement as TA and teacher assume both roles.

In the **'zoning model'**, the teacher and TA are allocated *zones* and in their zone they are responsible for the teaching and organizing. If used dynamically it can prevent certain pupils frequently avoiding attention and others receiving too much and potentially leading to learned helplessness.

The **'reflective teamwork model'** is based on a humanist approach and involves the teacher and TA using reflective practice and communication to review the previous lessons together and plan the next session. The model, although the most time-consuming, improves the relationship and teamwork between teachers and TAs, enabling greater TA empowerment as they contribute their skills and insights to this process.

In addition the TA can assume a **'roaming role'** whereby specific pupils requiring attention are identified and prompt interventions are made before moving on. This approach could reduce the likelihood of pupil dependency on adult support and the risk of learned helplessness. It also enables the TA to support a greater number of pupils during a lesson.

However, findings indicate that although TAs can have a positive impact on pupil achievement this is not universal. It is suggested that TAs have little impact on pupil progress and may even hinder learning. Unsatisfactory deployment and inadequate supervision has led to pupils putting too much reliance on the TAs and becoming dependent on the TA to complete their work or provide all the ideas (learned helplessness).

Barriers to effective deployment

Internal factors

- A teacher may feel threatened by the TA's presence and anxious over the possibility of their competency being questioned.
- There are complexities in managing extra staff. The DISS Project (Blatchford et al. 2009) found that the majority of teachers who line managed TAs had not received sufficient training to help them with this responsibility.
- TAs may lack the necessary knowledge, skills and experience to develop independence and deeper learning. Many TAs do not receive effective training or information to fully support pupils resulting in underperformance of the TA as well as the pupils (DfES 2011; Russell et al. 2012).
- TAs may inadvertently create 'learned helplessness' (discussed in Chapter 5). It should be emphasized they should *facilitate not do* pupils' work and discuss effective strategies that promote a growth mindset and facilitate metacognitive and higher-order thinking.

External factors

- Insufficient time for the teachers and TAs to discuss plans and evaluate lessons (Blatchford et al. 2009).
- Inadequate training for the role of TAs results in them failing to offer pupils maximum potential support (Webster et al. 2013).

 REFLECT

Consider effective TA deployment as two aspects: training and time (as indicated below), and work with your TA to undertake each as a cycle.

Training and professional development of TAs and teachers

- Discuss and facilitate the TA undertaking a reflection/self-assessment exercise.
- Identify the activities/pupils where TAs can support learning most effectively.
- Pinpoint area(s) for development and discuss programmes, courses, in-house, training or mentoring/peer shadowing.
- Observe the TA support in lessons; have a clear focus and offer feedback.
- Discuss the impact on pupils' learning and how you know whether strategies used are effective.
- Keep notes/data to evidence pupil impact and feed this feedback into the development cycle.

Time for joint planning and feedback between TAs and teachers

- Discuss strategies for communication and collaboration between you and your TAs and ensure these are negotiated and agreed.
- Discuss the most effective way to share the planning for a lesson/session, for example, one-to-one time, via email or phone.
- Discuss the most effective way to ensure pupil information and assessments are shared, for example, TA record book, post-its, email feedback or one-to-one time.
- Identify the methods and data needed to evaluate the effectiveness of the deployment of your TAs.
- Analyse the effectiveness of the methods and data collected in terms of refining TA deployment and feed back into the cycle, refining strategies.

I feel I ought to add 'there is no such thing as a bad cup of tea!' So, before you review your TA deployment do make those all-important cuppas.

Further reading

The DISS Project conducted by Blatchford, P., Bassett, P., Brown, P., Martin, C., Russell, A. and Webster, R. (2009) is a comprehensive report on the effectiveness of TA deployment. Research and publications into effective deployment of TAs (EDTA Project) is available at: http://maximisingtas.co.uk/research/the-edta-project.php.

Parents and the wider community

If pupils are to maximise their potential from schooling they will need the full support of their parents.

Deforges and Abouchaar, 2003

Parental involvement, as Deforges and Abouchaar's (2003) extensive review concludes, significantly influences a child's educational achievement (and social behaviour), and continues to do so into adolescence and adulthood (DCSF 2008). Desforges and Abouchaar regard parental involvement in the form of 'at-home' good parenting as most significant even after all other factors affecting attainment have been removed. The combined knowledge and skills of parent and teacher should be shared and understood to create richer and more connected home-school learning environments.

Parental involvement generally occurs through three modes (Hoover-Dempsey and Sandler 1995):

- *modelling*: the parent can demonstrate that school-related activities are worthy or not;

- *reinforcement*: attention, praise and reward relating to their child's success in school will often encourage the child to engage in the rewarded behaviour again and so be more likely to do well;

- *open-ended instruction*: for example, asking their child how they worked out the problem or how they might approach something, developing their cognitive thinking.

A parent will communicate skills, attitudes, values and behaviour dependent upon how they communicate between home and school, their willingness to volunteer and attend parents' evenings or collaborate with the community and families (Goodall et al. 2011). Both *The importance of teaching* (DfE 2010) and the *Field Review* (Field 2010) reinforce the need to involve parents in education, and to create a good home learning environment.

Despite Ofsted judging how effectively schools engage with parents since 2009, and a government focus, there still seem to be some barriers preventing the desired level of involvement. In the USA the *Strong families, strong schools* report (US Department of Education 1994) reflected 30 years of research into family involvement in education and similarly found the sad fact that many parents didn't feel welcome in school.

Internal factors

- A '*disconnect*' between the school and the families, which may be a result of their own negative school experience or cultural, social and language issues.

- The parents' *understanding* of their child's abilities and beliefs about their child.

- A parent's *ability* and sense of *self-efficacy* to support their child with developmentally appropriate activities and strategies, particularly as children's natural willingness and enthusiasm wanes around the transition to secondary school (Hoover-Dempsey and Sandler 1995). A parent must therefore believe that he or she has the necessary skills to be involved.

External factors

- *Demands* of work, costs, time and transport.
- The parents' differing perception and/or lack of understanding regarding the school's *expectations*.
- *Unclear* or inconsistent strategies for parental involvement.

Aim to identify those potential barriers your parents have and use the next section to help address them.

Building bridges

Schools and teachers need to recognize the extent of disconnection parents may feel as a precondition for involving them in their children's education. Desforges and Abouchaar (2003) suggest a programme of parental involvement taking the form of multidimensional intervention programmes. It is therefore imperative to identify the barriers and implement effective interventions that support parental involvement, particularly for those 'hard-to-reach' parents who lack engagement with the school. In other words, aim to empower and involve parents in as many ways as possible.

 STRATEGIES FOR YOUR TEACHER TOOLKIT

Connectedness

Where schools build positive relationships with parents and work actively to embrace racial, religious and ethnic and language differences, evidence of sustained school improvement can be found (Goodall et al. 2011).

- Have an open-door policy and encourage parents to come into your classroom (at appropriate times) and 'chat'.
- Be proactive rather than reactive and make sure the first contact with parents is positive; don't let 'niggles' fester and become larger issues.
- If required, meet parents in the community instead of the expectation that they will come into the school.
- Effective communication requires a two-way flow of information, for example newsletters, home-school books, school websites or emails. Any strategy must be tailored to the school population in order for communication to be successful.
- Communicate (verbally and in written form) in ways a range of parents can relate to and understand; avoid using educational 'jargon'.
- Regularly ask parents to share their concerns and opinions about the school, and then be seen to address those concerns.
- Be sensitive and understanding to the circumstances of all families.

- Accommodate parents' work schedules; offer flexible arrangements for parents' evenings (Estyn 2009) or family workshops.
- Provide translators for parents who do not speak English (Estyn 2009) and accommodate all language and cultural differences.
- Reach out to the community for resources to strengthen schools. The Cambridge Primary Review (Alexander 2009) recommended that 30 per cent of teaching time should be framed by a community curriculum drawing on local organizations, resources and environments.
- Ensure teachers have the knowledge and confidence to meet the needs of a range of parents, especially cultural, language or social differences and particularly parents from deprived communities (Dyson et al. 2007).

Understanding

Providing parents with an honest and transparent profile of their child will better enable them to work with the school to benefit their child. Build trust and openness and invite families to share hopes for and concerns about their children and work together to set educational goals.

- Share assessment and, if required, behaviour and attitude information in a positive and factual manner.
- Ask for the parents' input and openly discuss differences.
- Provide sufficient information on homework to support and guide the parent (Estyn 2009).
- Choose homework where parents can easily help (Estyn 2009).

Self-efficacy

Create a school and classroom climate that actively supports family involvement and learning. The evidence of the impact of family literacy, language and numeracy programmes on pupils' achievement is extensive, particularly in the case of literacy, numeracy and related outcomes such as motivation and achievement (Goodall et al. 2011).

- Be supportive and non-judgemental when involving parents in support programmes.
- Offer academic outcomes and training in parenting skills as programmes.
- Ensure guidance and that parents' expected involvement is clear and detailed.
- Provide opportunities for parents to observe successful involvement activities and programmes, especially from other similar parents.
- Provide families with a list of core 'mastery skills' for each year group; these will be transferable skills based on English and maths, and embed higher-order thinking skills.
- Be explicit and respectful in acknowledging the contributions all parents make.

● ●

A thought ... in some ways, detangling the relationship between highly productive learning environments and highly effective classroom management is a chicken-and-egg scenario. Which comes first? Are highly effective teachers better able to organize and manage classroom resources, routines and systems and therefore enable more effective teaching and learning? Or do highly effective teachers who effectively use their repertoire and teacher toolkit have fewer classroom and behaviour problems to manage? The next chapter will hopefully lead you to answering whether indeed it is the chicken or the egg.

References

Alexander, R.J. (2009) *Children, their world, their education: final report of the Cambridge Primary Review*. London: Routledge.

Barrett, P., Zhang, Y., Davies, F. and Barrett, L. (2015) *Clever classrooms, summary report of the HEAD Project*. Manchester: University of Salford.

Blackmore, J., Bateman, D., Cloonan, A., Dixon, M., Loughlin, J., O'Mara, J. and Senior, K. (2011) *Innovative Learning Environments Research Study*, Victoria, Australia: Deakin University.

Blatchford, P., Bassett, P., Brown, P., Martin, C., Russell, A. and Webster, R. (2009) *Deployment and impact of support staff (DISS) Project*. London: DCSF.

Chamberlain, J. (1997) A working definition of empowerment, *Psychiatric Rehabilitation Journal*, 20(4).

Cremin, H., Thomas, G. and Vincett, K. (2003) Learning zones: an evaluation of three models for improving learning through teacher/teaching assistant teamwork, *Support for Learning*, 18(4): 154–61.

DCSF (2008) *The impact of parental involvement on children's education*. London: DCSF Publications.

Desforges, C. and Abouchaar, A. (2003) *The impact of parental involvement, parental support and family education on pupil achievement and adjustment: a review of literature*, DfES Research Report 433. London: DfES.

Dewey, J. (2001) *Democracy and education*, Chapter 2. A Penn State Electronic Classics Series Publication (ebook).

DfE (2010) *The importance of teaching: the schools White Paper 2010*, CM 7980. Norwich: The Stationery Office, www.education.gov.uk/publications/eOrderingDownload/CM-7980.pdf.

DfE (2012) *Teachers' standards*, www.gov.uk/government/uploads/system/uploads/attachment_data/file/301107/Teachers__Standards.pdf.

DfES (2011) *Working with teaching assistants: a good practice guide*. London: DfES.

Dyson, A. et al. (2007) *The Manchester Transition Project: 108 implications for the development of parental involvement in primary schools*. London: DfES.

Estyn (2009) *Good practice in parental involvement in primary schools*. Her Majesty's Inspectorate for Education and Training in Wales, www.estyn.gov.wales/thematic-reports/good-practice-parental-involvement-primary-schools-april-2009.

Field, F. (2010) *The Foundation Years: preventing poor children becoming poor adults, the report of the Independent Review on Poverty and Life Chances*. London: HM Government.

Fisher, K. (2005) '*Linking pedagogy and space*', www.sofweb.vic.edu.au/knowledgebank/pdfs/linking_pedagogy_and_space.pdf.

Fisher, A., Godwin, K., Seltman, H. (2014) Visual environment, attention allocation, and learning in young children: when too much of a good thing may be bad, *Psychological Science*, May.

Freire, P. (1998) *Pedagogy of Freedom*. Lanham, MD: Rowman & Littlefield Publishers, Inc.

Goodall, J., Vorhaus, J., Carpentieri, J.D., Brooks, G., Akerman, R. and Harris, A. (2011) *Review of best practice in parental engagement: practitioners summary*. London: DfE.

Hoover-Dempsey, K.V. and Sandler, H.M. (1995) Parental involvement in children's education: why does it make a difference? *Teachers College Record*, 97(2).

Knowles, G. (2011) *Supporting inclusive practice*, 2nd edn. London: Routledge.

Morgan, J. (2000) Critical pedagogy: the spaces that make the difference, *Pedagogy, Culture and Society*, 8(3): 273–89.

PriceWaterHouseCoopers (2000) *Building performance: an empirical assessment of the relationship between schools capital investment and pupil performance.* London: DfES.

Rudduck J. and Macintyre, D. (2007) *Improving learning through consulting pupils.* London: Routledge.

Russell, A., Webster, R. and Blatchford, P. (2012) *Maximising the impact of teaching assistants: guidance for school leaders and teachers.* Abingdon: Routledge.

UNESCO (2012) *A place to learn: lessons from research on learning environments.* Paris: UNESCO, Institute for Statistics.

UNISON (2013) www.unison.org.uk/news/article/2013/04/teaching-assistants-play-vital-role-in-schools/.

US Department of Education (1994) *Strong families, strong schools: building community partnerships for learning.* Washington, DC: US Department for Education.

Webster, R., Russell, A. and Blatchford, P. (2013) *Teaching Assistants. A guide to good practice.* Oxford: Oxford School Improvement.

Zimmerman, M.A. (1995). Psychological empowerment: issues and illustrations, *American Journal of Community Psychology*, 23: 581–99.

9

Inspiring learning behaviour – behaviour and attitudes to learning

Behaviour in the human being is sometimes a defense, a way of conceal-ing motives and thoughts, as language can be a way of hiding your thoughts and preventing communication.

Abraham Maslow, 1966

Our coat hook! At this point your 'perfect jacket' looks great and fits like a glove, but may need an extra waterproof layer or bigger shoulder pads . . . teaching can be a bit like living in the UK with April showers taking us by surprise or a sudden unseasonable snowstorm or heatwave causing equal havoc. With a greater understanding your jacket will become ready to protect you in the most challenging environments.

This chapter prompts you to move beyond a 'quick-fix', reactive approach to a deeper, proactive approach to behaviour. It discusses nonverbal communication and the impact upon the learner, and a collaborative approach to behaviour man-agement. Understanding how you and your pedagogy influences pupils' responses and behaviour is essential. It will enable you to see the unique child and understand why they may behave as they do. It is important to recognize that behaviour fulfils a need and, as Maslow (1966) concludes, can act as a defence to potentially hide a developmental gap – be it cognitive, physical, emotional, social, moral, sexual, cul-tural or spiritual.

The key themes in this chapter prompt you to:

- reflect upon how your *teacher identity and philosophy* influence your approach to behaviour;
- consider how your understanding of the *purpose of education* reflects how you address behaviour issues;
- consider how your focus on *well-being for you and your pupils* is demon-strated in your classroom management and responses to behavioural needs;

- evaluate the extent your knowledge of behaviour theory and approaches enables you to meet the *needs of the unique child*;
- analyse how your awareness of creating an *enabling and empowering environment* reflects in your classroom management of pupils and their behaviour;
- reflect upon how your *self-awareness* and *critical self-reflection* enhances your understanding and response to the class and individuals;
- identify how your understanding of behaviour, learning theory, classroom management and communication focuses your need for *continuous development as a lifelong learner*.

This chapter addresses the following *Teacherse Standards* (DfE 2012):

1 Set high expectations which inspire, motivate and challenge pupils
2 Promote good progress and outcomes by pupils
7 Manage behaviour effectively to ensure a good and safe learning environment.

Behaviour in schools

As a beginner teacher getting behaviour right in your classroom is paramount and rightly so. According to Hattie (2011), classroom behaviour is the sixth (out of 130) most important contributors to a pupil's academic success. However, behaviour is an area of concern and stress for many teachers. For instance, a YouGov poll in 2014 found over half of primary school teachers and just under half of secondary teachers reported worsening behaviour and as a consequence more than a third had considered leaving the profession.

Behaviour is high on the government's agenda, reflected in the Elton Report (1989), The Steer Report (2009) the White Paper, *The importance of teaching* (DfE 2010) and, more recently, in *Behaviour and discipline in schools* (DfE 2014). Notably, this guidance has moved away from the term 'behaviour management' to 'discipline'. Take a moment to contemplate what a list of actions or attitudes for each term would look like. Behaviour management may be associated with modification strategies and rewards. On the other hand, discipline may evoke past images of corporal punishment with a punitive and unilateral approach, and words such as compliance, training, obedience and consequence may also come to mind. Both approaches reflect behaviourist theory whereby certain behaviours are rewarded and others punished.

Perhaps this shift in emphasis, coupled with the influence of media, has led many teachers to perceive 'behaviour' as establishing control over disruptive or non-compliant pupils. As a result quick-fixes, in the form of more and more strategies to manage behaviour, are sought with the hope that pupils will comply and be successfully managed. However, given this perception, to be totally prepared is unrealistic as it is impossible to accurately anticipate and prepare for the behaviours of the entire range of pupils within a classroom.

To get behaviour right in your classroom it is essential to establish those positive relationships, understand the whole child, use effective pedagogy and create the right learning environment. Sayeski and Brown (2011) suggest a useful three-tiered model to behaviour management, which highlights the need for prevention, in terms of creating a learning environment that responds to the particular needs of all pupils. They use the terms 'preventative classroom management', 'first line interventions' and 'intensive individualized interventions'. Prevention rather than cure! If the prevention of unacceptable behaviour is built through positive relationships, high expectations set within routines, rules and systems, and non-evasive strategies, such as nonverbal communication or praise, the learning in the classroom is not disrupted. So, at the outset, let's consider *prevention as intervention* through your engagement with pupils, which starts, not with a lesson plan or a list of behaviour strategies, but with who you are and how you connect with your pupils.

Teacher presence and behaviour

Your teacher presence affects the feel and function of your classroom, the relationships with pupils and how well you 'sell' the curriculum. Experience suggests teacher presence should be assertive without aggression, calm without being laid back, warm without fluffiness, passionate without being gushing. You get the picture. It is your presence that embodies your professionalism, however you may face nerves and unforeseen challenges that can broadside or simply paralyse you. Your professionalism may slip and suddenly you feel lost or floundering. Developing some simple techniques can help prevent this.

● ●

 STRATEGIES FOR YOUR TEACHER TOOLKIT

Life is like the stage . . .

I think teaching is akin to acting with a teacher's interpersonal skills comparable to those associated with the performing arts (Seymour Sarason 1999, cited in Griggs 2001). You develop skills in communication, voice control, body language and movement, facial expression (especially Early Years to Year 3), attention grabbers, catch phrases, and so much more. I frequently suggest that my trainee teachers watch stand-up comedy for 'homework' (another suggestion of mine is to listen to great dictators, but this is a less popular choice!), not so they can reel off a series of one-liners in their lessons but to observe how a lone comedian engages the whole audience, makes them want to listen and feel part of the 'show'. Note how the voice changes in pace and pitch, where silence is used for effect, how the eyes draw the audience in and every movement is used with intent to emphasize, invite, enliven or punctuate content.

Your classroom is your stage . . .

Use space with purpose and to best effect. Consider how you move around the room. Do your arms, hands and eyes direct pupils attention? Where do you deliver your expositions, reprimands or reminders? Avoid giving expositions from various places around the class-room, which can result in 'guess where the teacher is?' as pupils swivel and turn to find you. Your returning to or standing in your 'exposition spot' is a visual cue for the pupils; likewise you may create a reprimand spot (perhaps next to the classroom rules) or a reward spot in arms-reach to the points chart or the like.

If you don't feel it, act it . . .

Keep calm and carry on, or as I often say, think the 'swan effect'. On the surface serene and graceful, gliding effortlessly along, but all the while you are paddling like mad under the surface, but no one can see this! To calm yourself, apply the mindfulness technique discussed in Chapter 1. Focus on the breath and be aware of your own senses and tensions. Breathe calm energy in and, when exhaling, send the wave of energy out to every pupil that says 'I'm the teacher, I'm in control'. Have in your repertoire a suitable technique to refocus the class and yourself on the learning.

Three things to remember on a bad day: 'Head up, shoulders back, and SMILE!' (Tomorrow is another day . . .).

● ●

Verbal communication

Effective verbal communication is necessary for effective teaching. A teacher's skill is to match the vocabulary, form and structure of language to different contexts. For example, communicating with friends will differ from when you're communicat-ing with the headteacher or parents. Likewise, teaching an Early Years group will require substantially different communication structures from Year 6 pupils.

 CHECKLIST for verbal communication

- *Articulation*: speak clearly and crisply (think crisps not marshmallows).
- *Clarity*: organize your thoughts in a logical and coherent manner that is rele-vant to pupils' learning and interests.
- *Talking* to *not* at: make eye contact and scan the room.
- *Actively listen*: show you are listening before you appropriately respond.
- *Understand pupils' needs*: use developmentally appropriate vocabulary so all pupils can understand what you're saying.
- *Value what is being said*: show genuine interest and authenticity when listening.
- *Use visual and oral feedback*: check the effectiveness of your communication through observing the pupils' body language and responses.
- *Vocal qualities*: develop your use of voice so it engages and interests pupils.
- *Give the right attention*: focus on positive, desired behaviours and catch 'em being good.

Attention and verbal praise

Praise is an immediate tool every teacher can use, however be aware attention intended to correct certain behaviour, for example 'telling off', can reward and reinforce that behaviour (the behaviourist theory of Skinner discussed in Chapter 2). When this occurs the pupil may either be resistant to positive praise or negative attention-seeking may become habitual. Another possible explanation is that the pupil learns and takes on the role implied (for example, 'You are naughty, the rest of the class behave', resulting in the pupil taking on the role of the 'naughtiest child in class', which is in turn reinforced by further negative attention). If the focus is on sanctions and reprimands the behaviour may not only be reinforced but may lead to longer-term and more complex behaviours.

 REFLECT

Consider this scenario with a sanction-based approach:

A pupil is persistently calling out during a lesson. The teacher responds by sending the pupil out of the classroom (inadvertent reward). In subsequent lessons this pupil exhibits further behaviours such as scribbling over work, annoying a neighbour and asking to leave the room. Over time the pupil 'opts out' of working more frequently and the learning gap widens, resulting in further and more extreme work avoidance behaviours.

Now consider the scenario with a reward-based approach:

A pupil is persistently calling out during a lesson. The teacher strategically ignores the calling out and the moment the pupil is complying with the class rules is specifically praised. The teacher then addresses the cause of the unwanted behaviour in a one-to-one, as all behaviours fulfil a need. He finds the pupil is anxious about his work and struggling. Class-based interventions are then considered and implemented which begin to close the pupil's learning gap and the pupil feels more engaged with the learning.

Shift the attentional balance from unwanted behaviour to wanted behaviour. If you target behaviours that underpin mastery orientation and a growth mindset, as discussed in Chapter 4, with praise related to effort, resilience and perseverance, it is reinforced. There are many approaches to praise, such as parallel praise, but the most useful to consider is the notion of 'three part praise' (Williams 2012), which can be used to guide your attributions:

- *positive* (e.g. 'fabulous', 'well done');
- *name* the pupil;
- *specify* the behaviour, for example, 'for sitting up straight', 'concentration on work and effort' (e.g. 'Excellent, Lucas, you have worked incredibly hard on . . .').

Most notably the praise you choose may undermine, enhance or have no effect on a pupil's motivation. Therefore raise your self-awareness to ensure you are sincere and focus on how to boost a pupil's self-efficacy and intrinsic motivation.

Further reading

Williams, H. (2012) Fair pairs and three part praise – developing the sustained use of differential reinforcement of alternative behaviour, *Educational Psychology in Practice*, 28(3): 299–313. This technique stems from operant conditioning (behaviourist theory, Chapter 2) and applied behavioural analysis (ABA) to reinforce desirable behaviour.

Nonverbal communication

The main job of the teacher is to communicate effectively, which requires an understanding of verbal and, crucially, nonverbal communication as between 55–93 per cent of communication is nonverbal (Mehrabian 1971; Hogan and Stubbs 2003). Nonverbal communication includes facial expressions, gestures and posture, which stem, in part, from our culture and are intertwined with our language. From handshakes to hairstyles, nonverbal details reveal who we are and impact on how we relate to others.

Developing an understanding in this area will help you communicate more effectively with pupils and others involved in their education. The well-worn phrase 'It's not what you say, it's how you say it' sums up the importance of this area and affects how you convey your own enthusiasm and passion for teaching and learning; enthusiasm begets enthusiasm.

In many instances, facial movement, body posture and other nonverbal signals are enough to correct inappropriate, off-task behaviour (perfect the 'teacher look'. Such communication is often a combination of features, for example, a frown with crossed arms and unblinking gaze to indicate disapproval. In addition, postural congruence, or mirroring a pupils' body language (discussed in Chapter 2), will increase rapport and can address undesirable behaviours.

Aim to consciously make your whole self part of the pupils' learning experience and most importantly make sure there is congruence between verbal and nonverbal communication (what you say matches what your pupils see, hear and feel). Consider how you can use the components described below to enhance your pupils' learning.

STRATEGIES FOR YOUR TEACHER TOOLKIT

Facial expression

Our face conveys messages to our pupils – for example, we can show interest, disapproval, affection or surprise. As you read in Chapter 1, pupils respond and achieve better if their teacher is likeable, warm, caring and positive. Smiling is important – it tells the pupils that you are interested and happy to have them in your classroom, and builds that all important pupil-teacher relationship. It can be effectively employed during wait times to say 'I'm attentive and expecting some great responses' and it will relax you during those potentially torturous few seconds of silence.

The use of voice (paralinguistics)

Paralinguistics is an element of vocal communication that is distinct from actual language. It includes tone of voice, volume, pace, inflection, pauses and pitch. You have your own unique voice so don't try to 'put on' a voice, be yourself but work on its effectiveness. Tone of voice has a powerful effect on the meaning of a sentence. Use a strong tone and pupils may be more attentive, yet speak hesitantly and pupils may disengage as it may convey a lack of interest or confidence. Aim to have a certain lilt and melody to your voice and ensure it is not monotone or flat. Also consider the use of 'conversational oil' (Williams 1997), such as 'uh huh'; 'mm, mmm', 'I see', 'that's right' or 'good', as these serve as a vocal 'head nod' to encourage and affirm the speaker.

Practise modulation (e.g. changing from highs to lows), working out the facial muscles, tongue and soft palette. Work on your vowels (aay, eee, aah, ohh, aww) and take time to hone and tone your voice through practising tongue twisters. Your modulation will vary dependent upon the age of the pupil; would you use the same voice for an Early Years pupil and a Year 6?

Charismatic dictators and leaders have used paralinguistics to great effect. Hitler's speeches contained great intensity, building in pitch, speed and volume to whip his followers into a frenzy. Churchill, on the other hand, used a deep, gruff tone and slow pace to convey his authority and control. I am not advocating a megalomaniac spree to fight them on the beaches but simply point to the power and influence voice alone can have.

Remember, it is important to look after your voice and don't stress it (a day in school with a lost voice is a tad challenging). Breathe from the diaphragm, avoid raising your voice to a high pitch (a tendency when we are stressed or over-excited; think *low* and *slow* when this happens!). Remain hydrated throughout the day (and the odd spoonful of honey does help).

The use of gestures and posture (kinesics)

Posture and movement communicates a wealth of information. To convey your teacher presence, practise standing in a confident posture. Consider the angle of your torso, the position of your shoulders, the tilt and movement of your head, the position of your feet, and the use of your arms and hands. Make deliberate movements and signals to communicate confidence and meaning without words. For example, open palm gestures invite pupils to join in; palms down settle and quieten; raising both hands can increase motivation or participation; or a statue-like posture, with hands on hips, can signal impatience and disapproval.

Open versus closed body positions invite different responses. For example, leaning forward slightly, smiling and nodding will encourage and reinforce positive pupil responses. Conversely, folded limbs, an unanimated face and set shoulders will communicate that the pupils should stop. Adopt certain poses to signal certain expectations: a 'thinking pose'; a 'quiet pose'; a 'hurry up' pose; and your 'swan pose' when you need to remain calm and in control.

REFLECT

Try this: say 'Jemima please sit down' in as many ways as you can (ideally in front of a mirror or colleague).

Note changes in volume, speed, pitch, inflection, intensity and pauses. Connect with the subtle changes in your body language: hand movements, tilt of head, facial expressions, shoulder position, chest, and direction of feet and hips. Now imagine a large balloon tied to the crown of your head, and two smaller ones on your shoulders. Feel the pull of the balloons and say the phrase again. Can you feel a difference?

The skill is to know how to use your voice and body to command, control and cajole pupils. So, now you can add your whole body to your toolkit!

The use of space (proxemics)

The amount of personal space is influenced by a number of factors, including social norms, situational factors, personality characteristics and level of familiarity. For example, our intimate zone is up to 45cm; when communicating with friends or family members it is usually between 45cm and 122cm (friend zone), while an acquaintance or professional interaction (social zone) requires from 122cm to 370cm.

Deliberate use of proxemics affects change in pupils' behaviour. For example, when pupils enter the class, reduce the space in the doorway. Your moving into their intimate zone will firstly ensure they enter in single file and secondly it will affirm your teacher presence as they have to take notice of you. Another use of proxemics is to 'approach' a pupil exhibiting some low-level behaviour you wish to stop. Instead of breaking the flow of the lesson, subtly move into their space and notice how quickly they refocus on the learning.

The use of eye contact (oculesics)

The use of eye contact and communication enables deeper person-to-person contact. We say the eyes are the mirrors of the soul and this is because the brain stems connect upon eye-to-eye contact and this indicates openness to one another. When we encounter people or things that we like, the rate of blinking increases and the pupils dilate. Using eye contact will rekindle interest in pupils' learning as it invites engagement and shows respect when listening to them. Invite pupils to participate through maintaining eye contact. Connect with as many pupils as possible when you are talking (but do avoid staring and seeming to be intimidating). Eye contact will also provide you with a considerable understanding of how well pupils understand the lesson: identifying the glazed-puzzled look of the non-plussed; the fire behind the eyes of the enthusiastic learner; or the far-away look of the day-dreamer provides assessment for learning information.

The use of touch (haptics)

Communication through touch can be used to convey affection, familiarity, sympathy and other emotions. Haptics in the classroom can be used strategically to divert or distract a pupil from an unwanted behaviour as they know you are physically 'there' and aware of what is happening. Some would say never touch a child: of course being professional and applying common sense should prevail, but a simple shoulder squeeze can change a child's day or prevent a behaviour escalating – it communicates more than words can say (actions do speak louder than words).

The use of dress and appearance (objectics)

Choice of clothes, hairstyle and other factors affecting appearance are all means of nonverbal communication. Appearance can alter the physiological reactions, judgements and interpretations we have and make of others. First impressions are important, which is why experts suggest that job seekers dress appropriately for interviews with potential employers. Let's revisit the perfect jacket and picture yourself as your perfect teacher. How does your appearance influence how you feel? If you had a non-school uniform day at school and you wore jeans, would you feel that same sense of control, presence and 'teacherness'? A focus on your teacher identity encompasses your philosophy, but how you externally communicate this to others is through how you look.

● ●

Assessing the effectiveness of verbal and nonverbal communication requires a keen sense of self-awareness. To support your development, watching a video-recording of yourself is incredibly enlightening. I remember in my first year of teaching I asked a friend to video a lesson. As I watched it I was surprised to see how many times I assumed the posture of a 'tree' (standing still, arms stretched out) and my irritating use of 'okay'. I quickly addressed my use of the 'okay trees'.

Ensure there is congruence between verbal and nonverbal communication, for example expressing interest in a pupil's response, then glancing at the time or turning to write on the board gives a contradictory message. This will almost immediately shut them down and potentially reduce their future participation (refer to Chapter 5 and dialogic teaching).

Further reading

Tuaber, R.T. and Sargent Mester, C. (2007) *Acting lessons for teachers, using performance skills in the classroom*, 2nd edn. Westport, CT: Praeger. This book provides an insight into how teachers can recognize and develop performance strategies to enhance enthusiastic teaching.

Classroom rules and routines

Prevention as intervention should be established at the outset by defining the exact behaviours you desire in your classroom through collaborative, whole-class discussion. If pupils are engaged in the process it will increase their sense of ownership and belonging, creating a more effective learning environment. Be clear about how these rules or codes of conduct should look and feel and establish an expectation of how to uphold them. Ensure pupils know what will happen if they are not followed.

CHECKLIST for rules and routines

Ensure rules are:

- *fair* and support an inclusive ethos (e.g. we help and support one another);
- phrased in the *positive* (e.g. 'Listen when others are talking' rather than 'Don't shout out and interrupt'), not only to maintain an upbeat classroom but to avoid the 'recency effect' (discussed in Chapter 5) whereby the pupil will hear 'run' instead of 'don't run';
- clear, *concise* and age-appropriate (e.g. 'We use the right voice at the right time').

Successful teachers know that even a one-time deviation from the established rules or code of conduct can undermine time spent creating them (Lemov 2010). However, despite the best intentions, as you get tired or overloaded, class rules and routines can slip. Consistency is fundamental, so create a checklist, display rules clearly and use visual cues as reminders to the pupils – for example, aides memoires to illustrate expectations in terms of setting out work, how to interact with talk-partners or tidy up. Reinforcement of classroom rules can also be made through the selective use of praise and this avoids your reminding pupils of the rules becoming 'background noise' or 'nagging'.

Routines must work for both you and your pupils. My advice is to spend time thinking very carefully about the routines you establish and ensuring they can be maintained with ease. Routines should enhance the learning environment and promote independence, self-efficacy, mastery and self-confidence. Thoughtful routines will also ensure you are not working harder than your pupils in the lesson (I use a simple economic equation to remind me: *teacher input < pupil output*). Routines may be, for example, to set-up for a lesson, check work, solve queries, tidy away, read with a partner, peer-assess or present work.

Further reading

Charlie Taylor's (2011) harlie Taylor's (2011) with ease. checklist is a valuable reference point. See www.gov.uk/government/uploads/system/uploads/attachment_data/file/283997/charlie_taylor_checklist.pdf. This checklist serves as a starting point for you to adopt and adapt to meet your own needs.

STRATEGIES FOR YOUR TEACHER TOOLKIT

It is illuminating to dissect the *anatomy* of a lesson on a timeline. Identifying what you and your pupils are doing with clear expectations (discussed in Chapter 5) adds clarity to lesson planning. Consider the following strategies:

Meet and greet

Think about how you set the 'tone' for the day or lesson. Establish routines in how you greet pupils, whether in the playground or classroom. This adds to your teacher presence and will set out your expectations. In addition, it enables you to continue to build those all-important teacher-pupil relationships.

Go to tasks

Establish a routine to immediately engage and warm pupils up. Use start-up tasks or small initial targets to gain a sense of achievement. I love skiing, so every morning, on the board, my 'go to task' was green, blue, red and black run problems to answer. Pupils could start and finish at any point and if they wanted to go off-piste that was an option as well (just mind the rocks!).

The main activity

Establish routines and systems to scaffold learning to avoid the six-deep queue, with pupils asking basic questions that could be answered through other means. For example, do the pupils understand the learning ahead? Are the expectations regarding layout, quantity and quality clear and modelled? Are there routines for asking for help, thinking or assessment? Do the pupils know where to find the resources to help them? Do the pupils have motivation to find out for themselves? Are they able to show perseverance and resilience when faced with challenge or failure?

Transitions and end points

Clarity of expectations is needed and visual or auditory cues will support transition points. You may have a count-down, music or visual signal to alert pupils to change and reinforce how you wish this to be carried out.

• •

 ACTIVITY

Focus on key routines or the classroom rules. Observe colleagues and identify how their classroom is managed.

How do they address, for example, increases in noise level, low-level behaviour or transition points; how do the pupils enter and leave the classroom or set up and collect resources?

 REFLECT

Reflect on your classroom practice and identify specific times when you are 'nagging' pupils or feeling you have to be more assertive. Recognize when you repeat certain names. Are there patterns emerging? For example, is this during transition points, just before lunch, or during specific tasks?

> Decide on one or two points for change, for example increasing clarity of expectations when moving from the carpet to tables; providing a visual aide-memoire to scaffold specific learners; or increasing the use of praise.
>
> Have you moved beyond aiming to control behaviour to a focus on the inextricable link between learning and behaviour?

Pedagogy and behaviour

The final aspect of *prevention as intervention* is through your pedagogy. Turn your attention toward your pupils having a 'thirst for knowledge and understanding and a love of learning', as highlighted by Ofsted (2015). Considering pedagogy and behaviour together links an understanding of *cognitive theories*, such as Chomsky's and Piaget's (understanding how mental processes are developed through interactions with the environment and subject matter), and *social constructivist* theories, such as Vygotsky's and Bruner's (understanding how knowledge is built through making connections and interactions with others), and *humanists theories*, such as Maslow's and Rogers' (understanding how pupils develop their potential), to inform how you create the best learning environment. Would a 'serial low-leveller' continue with their behaviour if their needs were met and they were fully engaged in their learning?

According to Stipek (2002), children enter school full of enthusiasm and curiosity. They will often refer to themselves as clever and point to evidence, such as tying shoelaces. However, by age 7 or 8 they begin to compare themselves to peers and those they see as the 'best'. Perhaps, for the first time, the child starts to experience a sense of failure and becomes anxious. The focus moves from learning to performance. This can lead to a self-fulfilling prophecy: 'I am not very clever. I don't want others to know how stupid I am. Therefore I will develop a complex array of strategies to avoid looking dumb' ('the dog ate my homework' or my personal favourite, 'my goldfish leapt out of the tank, grabbed my homework and ate it!' Thank you Craig!). By this stage the concept of engendering the 'love of learning' can sadly be lost.

The Steer Report (DCSF 2009) concludes that if the learning experiences provided are stimulating and incorporate pupils' interests, and the teaching quality is good, this motivates pupils to learn, raises standards and reduces disruption. This is dependent on the breadth and depth of your pedagogy and toolkit. The work of Stipek (2002) succinctly echoes key messages from previous chapters, and is a useful reference point to plan for learning behaviour.

• •

 STRATEGIES FOR YOUR TEACHER TOOLKIT

Choice as a motivator

In your own school experience it is likely that you did not enjoy being forced to do something, such as reading a particular book. Offering choice and greater independence may be difficult for teachers as it inevitably means the teacher will have to relinquish a degree of control. However, controlling the choices on offer makes this doable, so decide the options and guide pupils knowingly.

Tasks meaningful to pupils

Giving tasks relevance and purpose is achieved through knowing your pupils and giving them the flexibility to learn in their own way. This is motivating and promotes metacognition.

Intellectually engaging tasks

A dialogic approach makes learning engaging. The span of attention is variously estimated between 10 and 40 minutes with intrinsically interesting information attended to for longer.

'Just the right challenge' (baby bear's porridge)

A task which is too easy or too difficult may lead to frustration, lack of motivation or a sense of failure. Getting this right can be a trial and error approach and necessitates understanding your pupils' abilities.

Learning versus performance

Communicate the message that the purpose is to learn and not perform. The goal for the teacher is to foster a classroom culture of celebrating achievement where mistakes and errors are seen as a natural part of the learning process.

● ●

Further reading

Powell, S. and Tod, J. (2004) *EPPI review. A systematic review of how theories explain learning behaviour in school contexts*. London: University of London EPPI-Centre. This model uses the term 'learning behaviour' to describe the relationship with self and the curriculum.

When prevention as intervention is not enough

Generic strategies, teacher presence, communication skills and effective pedagogy may work for most pupils most of the time, but that's not good or outstanding enough for us. Ideally we want all pupils all of the time to have the right behaviour to learn. Consider a shift in perception and culture beyond trying to control and manage pupils, with a focus on *discipline* (teacher-led, unilateral, reactive and punitive) and *behaviour management* (teacher-led/managed, extrinsic, compliant, based on rewards and sanctions with some collaboration), to *understanding behaviour collaboratively* (pupil-focused, intrinsic, individualized, proactive and collaborative).

If we adopt an *understanding behaviour collaboratively* (UBC) approach, the focus is firmly on the pupil as unique, and like onions, we have to sensitively peel back layers (the exhibited behaviours) to see what is underneath. If the pupil and their behaviour are viewed superficially, with attempts at controlling and simply managing them (that crunchy outer layer), this may misdirect well-intentioned efforts and interventions, rendering them ineffective, and perpetuate or even escalate inappropriate behaviour. Therefore, time spent gaining that deeper understanding of the pupil and finding the root cause of the issue is needed before desirable change can occur.

Now, here's the challenge or conundrum. To be successful in addressing the root cause of the 'problem' requires time and effort with individual pupils, while at the same time meeting the complexity of demands of the whole class. Undeniably quite a feat and not something that will happen in a week or even a term – it takes time and conviction. However, attention to individual pupils has a longer-term, synergistic consequence as it benefits the child, the whole class and you as the teacher.

Understanding behaviour collaboratively

Gaining an understanding

Jamil is a kind, quiet girl with a small group of friends in Year 3. She likes science and art and will often want to stay in at breaktime to help or work. Her work is always neat and she quietly enjoys praise. She joins in reluctantly in whole-class work and needs nurturing and support to contribute more fully. She is of just below average ability in maths and English. Jamil has an older brother in secondary school, who collects her from school daily.

To adopt a UBC approach, gaining an understanding of each pupil is fundamental. To create *desirable change* in your pupils' behaviour you must acknowledge that it is influenced by your philosophy, your teacher-pupil relationship and awareness, and your teacher vigilance.

Firstly, recognize that your philosophy of education influences your understanding of that pupil and the behaviour and actions you take. So, again reflect on this and how you see the purpose of education. Do you believe that all children can do well or that some choose not to do well, or do not have the capacity to do well? Do you believe in growth mindset and Feurerstein's 'believe to achieve' adage? It is you who truly influences your classroom – you are that decisive element.

Secondly, you need to understand how to address pupils' needs collaboratively – the social constructivist approach. The relationship with others, especially positive pupil-teacher relationships, needs to be present. Relationships and the personality of the teacher influence the learning environment and pupil achievement (Hattie 2003). Consistent and thoughtful teachers, who regulate their own emotions, are more focused and effective at maintaining relationships with their pupils (Sutton et al. 2009), whereas teachers who respond with more extreme negative emotions, such as screaming and yelling, escalate a situation and alienate pupils, making it more difficult to repair relationships. Pupils need to know you still like them and it is the behaviour you do not like. In my NQT year my headteacher sagely told me to 'Tell them off with a glint in your eye!' That little twinkle in your eye will maintain the essential pupil-teacher relationship.

Understanding that a pupil's behaviour is motivated extrinsically or intrinsically and fulfils a need clarifies your role, which is to identify that specific need, as you would in English or maths, and *close the gap*. The pupil's relationship with others, and with self, builds a sense of trust, respect and rapport and allows them to strive to fulfil their potential (the humanist approach).

Lastly, your awareness or vigilance through keen observation is key in gaining an understanding of the behaviour. Adopting a 'lighthouse effect' (habitual scanning) ensures you are aware of what is going on in the classroom. Developing this 360-degree vision (McBer 2000) will enable you to spot anomalies or antecedents in pupil's behaviour patterns (and perpetuate the myth that teachers really do have eyes in the back of their heads!). This information gathering is part of understanding the unique child. Avoid 'jumping' to ill-formed conclusions (especially after meeting a parent, teenage brother, and so on), labelling a pupil a 'problem child' and deciding that, for example, home life, social class, genetics, diagnosed problems such as ADHD, or parents themselves, are the cause of the problem.

Identifying the behaviour

You have noticed that after half-term Jamil has complained of stomach ache on Friday mornings and asks to go to the medical room or toilet. This has been occurring before the spelling test and more recently she has begun to disrupt others on her table and fails to finish all her work on time upon her return.

Now keep asking yourself why this behaviour is occurring and observe Jamil's behaviour more closely until you begin to understand the primary cause. Now analyse this behaviour. The, sometimes more observable, secondary behaviours, such as asking to leave the room or arguing and disturbing others, are a result of the core issue. Now you need to know the cause of this primary behaviour, so ask her: 'Jamil, I've noticed that you have been complaining about stomach ache for a few weeks just before the spelling test. Why's that?' or 'I noticed you haven't been finishing all your work recently. Anything the matter?'

The positive relationship you have built with Jamil will hopefully enable her to feel she can openly respond. However, simply knowing she doesn't like spelling tests or sitting next to Charlotte and Ahmed won't enable you to identify and address the 'core problem' and so move forward. So you probe a little deeper 'What is it about the test you don't like?', 'Why don't you like sitting at your table?'

When *understanding behaviour collaboratively* your beliefs and values will affect the degree to which you view a behaviour as acceptable or unacceptable and how you address it. The nature and degree of behaviour exhibited are often identified through the school behaviour policy. Adhere to the policy and apply a consistent approach within your classroom. In certain cases you may decide you need to enlist additional support, internally, through colleagues, mentors and parents, or through outside agencies.

Levels of behaviour

Most behaviour concerns will undoubtedly centre on learning and safety. These behaviours vary:

- *Low-level*: affects the pupils themselves, for example, humming, tapping, interrupting and mumbling or other off-task behaviours;

- *Mid-level*: affects the learning of others in the class, for example, swinging on a chair to knock others, regularly shouting out, defying an instruction, or destroying their own or others' work;
- *High-level*: affects the safety and well-being of themselves and others, for example, throwing chairs or scissors; biting and kicking; or self-harming.

Understanding the appropriate response for the level of behaviour is necessary, because a low-level behaviour inappropriately addressed can quickly escalate to mid- or high-level disruption. Low-level behaviours are most frequent and teachers often report these as the ones that induce most stress. I would advise you 'wade in the shallows', and use subtle redirections, rather than dive into the deep end. Use nonverbal prompts (the teacher 'look' or 'point') and proximity (wandering with intent!), and gradually increase the intensity of the intervention if needed. Your focus on what is central to your role as a teacher, namely to teach, ensures pedagogy is the driving force and not managing behaviour. Again, pedagogy trumps not only curriculum (Chapter 4) but also behaviour management.

To accurately identify the core behaviour you must recognize how flexible and inclusive you are. This may be reflected in your use of language – for example, the use of 'must' or 'will' ('All children *must* bring in a healthy snack or all children *will* read to an adult every night') demonstrates inflexibility and perhaps a lack of appreciation of the home environment. Your choice of language may not apply to some pupils or leave them feeling a failure (they do not have healthy options at home or perhaps their parents are unable to support their reading), and can induce stress for both you and the pupil.

Greater self-awareness and actively reviewing the language you use will check how fair, realistic and inclusive you are. High expectations should be maintained but balanced with avoiding unnecessary confrontation and alienation.

 REFLECT

Take a moment to think of a pupil who exhibits a behaviour you do not want.

Your choice of language can either escalate or de-escalate the situation. For example, you may hold a belief that all children *must* sit still when listening to you (an inflexible belief), so you ask the pupil 'Why can't you sit still?' This pupil may respond negatively and the situation remains unresolved.

However, if you use neutral phrases, such as, 'I've noticed you fidget on the carpet. How do you find sitting and listening like that?' Here you are being non-judgemental and inviting a response, as well as putting the pupil's behaviour on the table for the next stage of UBC process.

Collaboratively moving forward

As you have established a positive relationship with Jamil she reveals she gets little support at home with her spelling and her mum is shouting at her brother a lot. She also tells you her brother has been 'taking it out on her'. You now have the necessary infor-mation to take the correct action. You may initiate greater home-school links and sup-port and set realistic, more manageable work targets. Most importantly, you monitor and evaluate your actions or intervention. 'Does Jamil still complain of stomach ache on Friday mornings?' If yes, you need more information, so return to the understand-ing *element of this approach and gather more information about Jamil and continue to build trust, empathy and respect to enable her to 'open up' and express her concerns.*

Successful collaboration requires a secure, safe and nurturing environment. If solutions are reached through an open and non-judgemental approach there is an increased likelihood the intervention will be effective. The teacher is not imposing their views or values, with the potential of a power struggle, but is genuinely working with the pupil to address their needs and close the gap.

Together, through sensitive and non-confrontational discussion, a solution may be reached. Your verbal and nonverbal communication will affect how successful your collaboration is. Aim to create a rapport and 'conversation', for example: 'Why do you think that's happening?'; 'Anything else bothering you?' and consider how and why the pupil may respond. Despite your efforts the pupil may 'close down' the conversation, in which case you need to reflect upon how you might encourage them to 'open up' to get to the core of the problem.

This approach will actively promote the pupil to think about their behaviour and how others see them. If you are to promote metacognition in learning and high-er-order thinking skills, this is a natural step for you and the pupil. Ask the pupil to identify the kinds of behaviours they like or ones that others may respect and admire. The level of complexity of thought should be differentiated for both pupil age and stage of development in terms of cognitive 'content' and the language used. This is now an intrinsic process rather than extrinsically imposed by the teacher. Outstanding teachers do have insight into the reasons for ongoing behaviour, why pupils act the way they do and what will motivate or obstruct learning (McBer 2000).

At first, the collaborative conversation with a pupil with challenging behaviour is a challenge in itself. A pupil may have lost their faith and trust. Because no one has addressed why this behaviour manifests, various rewards and sanctions are irrelevant to their developmental needs and may have compounded the problem further. Collaboration, very much akin to developing a dialogic classroom, takes time and confidence in the belief that this is the right approach.

Having a positive relationship with parents is essential in supporting a pupil. Ensure the parents feel connected and that they understand how to support the school and their child and feel they have the skills to do so (see Chapter 8 for bar-riers to parental involvement). In addition, pupils with SEND or those who are oppositional or defiant may take extra time and skill to 'move on'.

 REFLECT

Ben is refusing to do his work. After being told repeatedly to get on, he is begin-ning to disturb others. Do you:

* threaten to call for the headteacher;

- move him to a table by himself or 'time out';
- tell him if he doesn't do it now it'll be breaktime;
- sit with him and try to find the barrier that is preventing him working.

Ideally we all choose the fourth option, but realistically in a busy class of 30 pupils and with the multiplicity of demands placed upon us we often opt for the second or third. You told him what to do and modelled the task, and considered he should be able to do it. So, you tell him to stay in breaktime or to take time out. He 'kicks-off' and begins to disrupt the rest of his table and the class. You are now managing a behaviour issue and not addressing learning needs and teaching. Eventually you resort to the first option and call the headteacher. A lose-lose scenario!

Now apply UBC. You know this behaviour has happened before when tackling extended writing tasks (prior *understanding*). You ask Ben what the specific problem is. He responds negatively, so you come away from your focus group and use non-judgemental, neutral language (e.g. 'I notice that you have been…'; 'I've seen how you…') to discuss the barrier to the task (identifying *behaviour*). Ascertain if the cause is underpinned by cognitive, social, emotional, physical or cultural needs. Once you have got to the root of the problem, negotiate actions to overcome it (e.g. how to 'chunk up' the task). Identify resources and support he could use (ICT, wordbanks, dictaphone), or change seating position or work partner. Together you have come up with a solution (*collaboration*). A win-win scenario!

Once you have abstractly worked through the above, use it in your classroom. You may want to use this strategy with a pupil for whom rewards and sanctions aren't that effective – a 'serial low-leveller'. It is far easier to adopt a 'traditional' behaviourist approach and employ known rewards and sanctions, which may offer immediate compliance or a quieter classroom as the 'problem pupil' is having time out. However, their gap is not being closed and with repeated absence from lessons or alienation from class it gets wider. Please acknowledge greater effort and patience is needed to succeed with this approach but longer-term rewards (and ultimately an easier life) will come.

An outstanding teacher shows emotional resilience when dealing with challenging behaviour and keeps calm. A clear sense of purpose will fuel your conviction about the value of your role (McBer 2000).

Remember, there are times when an event transpires that would be best handled with, or by, another colleague. Part of effective classroom management is realizing that you do not have the resources to meet the needs of every pupil, every time. Ask for help!

Being a positive role model

In order to establish an effective classroom environment, and have equally effective classroom management, you must be the role model who paves the way. Your identity and clarity of philosophy will guide you so that you are indubitably professional and demonstrate the qualities and attitudes you wish to engender in your pupils.

CHECKLIST for being a positive role model

Walk the talk

You are a role model and for 195 days a year, for the best part of each day, you have an impact on the lives of your pupils. Therefore you have to do more than *talk the talk* and *walk the walk*: actively and mindfully *walk the talk*. Be aware that attitudes, choices, actions, attire and even the contents of your shopping basket (the number of times I have been 'caught' buying chocolate and prosecco for my aunt!) influence your pupils. Be the best you can so the pupils can aspire to be the best they can.

Self-talk

When you face difficult decisions, allow pupils to see how you work through problems and find solutions. Actively model metacognition and articulate your thinking. This will demonstrate that process explicitly, from which they can model their own responses.

Celebrate mistakes

Remember no one is perfect. When you make a mistake, demonstrate 'it's okay' (think growth mindset) and how you move forward. This: a) shows mistakes are part of learning/life; b) promotes resilience; c) creates a platform for deeper learning; and d) demonstrates strategies to overcome problems.

Keep your word

Follow through with your intentions or goals as this teaches pupils perseverance and self-discipline which can promote an 'I can do' attitude. Keeping your word builds respect and trust, and so relationships. Be consistent in word and action!

Hidden signals

Pupils pick up on nonverbal cues, the hidden curriculum, the classroom atmosphere and not just the content of a well-planned lesson. Make sure those subtle signs guide your pupils in positive ways.

Have interests

If you haven't got a hobby I would advise you get one. I know, time pressures and the demands of the job hold us back and you are probably thinking 'That's simply unrealistic with the planning, marking, tracking . . .'. However, having a hobby or interest will benefit you by providing, for example, a creative or physical outlet. For your pupils, you may be elevated beyond 'teacher that lives in the cupboard!!' to a more rounded, skilled, exciting individual (unless you are happy to 'live in the cupboard'?).

A thought . . . 'It ought to be an integral part of our teacher preparation to discuss the qualities that are indispensable for our teaching practice, even though we know that these qualities are created by that practice itself' (Freire 1998). As Freire sagaciously notes, it is only through practice that we become the teacher we wish to be, so use your perfect jacket to define yourself and be the positive role model.

References

DCSF (2009) *Learning behaviour: lessons learned,* chaired by Alan Steer, http://webarchive.nationalarchives.gov.uk/20130401151715/https://www.education.gov.uk/publications/eOrderingDownload/DCSF-Learning-Behaviour.pdf.

DfE (2010) *The importance of teaching: the schools White Paper.* London: DfE.

DfE (2012) *Teachers' standards,* www.gov.uk/government/uploads/system/uploads/attachment_data/file/301107/Teachers__Standards.pdf.

DfE (2014) *Behaviour and discipline in schools, advice for headteachers and school staff.* London: DfE.

Elton, Lord (1989) *Discipline in schools: report of the Committee of Enquiry chaired by Lord Elton.* London: HMSO.

Freire, P. (1998) *Pedagogy of Freedom.* Lanham, MD: Rowman & Littlefield Publishers, Inc.

Griggs, T. (2001) Teaching as acting: considering acting as a epistemology and its use in teaching and teacher preparation, *Teacher education quarterly,* spring.

Hattie, J. (2003) *Distinguishing expert teachers from novice and experienced teachers. Teachers make a difference: what is the research evidence?* Australian Council for Educational Research Annual Conference on Building Teacher Quality, www.det.nsw.edu.au/proflearn/docs/pdf/qt_hattie.pdf.

Hattie, J. (2011) *Visible learning for teachers: maximising impact on learning.* London: Routledge.

Hogan, K. and Stubbs, R. (2003) *Can't get through 8 barriers to communication.* Los Angeles: Pelican Publishing Company.

Lemov, D. (2010) *Teach like a champion: 49 techniques that put students on the path to college.* San Francisco: Jossey-Bass.

Maslow, A. (1966) *Psychology of science.* New York: Harper & Row.

McBer, H. (2000) *Research into teacher effectiveness: a model of teaching effectiveness.* A Report for Department for Education and Employment, Hay Group. London: HMSO.

Mehrabian, A. (1971) *Silent messages.* Wadsworth, CA: Belmont.

Ofsted (2015) *School inspection handbook,* www.gov.uk/government/ofsted.

Sayeski, L.K. and Brown, R.M. (2011) Developing a classroom management plan using a tiered approach, *Teaching Exceptional Children,* 44(1): 8–17.

Stipek, D. (2002) *Motivation to learn: integrating theory and practice,* 4th edn. Needham Heights, MA: Allyn & Bacon.

Sutton, R.E. et al. (2009) Teachers' emotion regulation and classroom management, *Theory into Practice,* 48(2): 130–37.

Williams, D. (1997) *Communication skills in practice: a practical guide for health professionals.* London: Jessica Kingsley.

Williams, H. (2012) Fair pairs and three part praise – developing the sustained use of differential reinforcement of alternative behaviour, *Educational Psychology in Practice* 28(3): 299–313.

Summary of the motivation level

Your perfect jacket

Your jacket fits perfectly; pockets are filled fruitfully, and it has become original, individual and communicates, very explicitly, who *you* are, your personality and your professionalism. The jacket has transcended beyond its original conception and function and become a symbol of *you*. It is an invaluable and trusted resource and feels good in any environment and whomsoever you are with. Your perfect jacket is robust yet looks and feels great and you are beginning to wonder whether you could ever do without it.

Your professional knowledge

This level has defined creativity, addressed the physical, social and emotional aspects within learning environments, including effective TA deployment and parental and wider community involvement. This level has also looked at behaviour considered as *prevention as intervention* through effective pedagogy, teacher presence and a more collaborative approach, actively involving the pupil.

Your professional development and action plan

Identify your areas of strength and development and connect the content of this Level to the key themes. Reflect upon the extent to which you have achieved each statement. To support your journey to outstanding, rate each key theme statement 1–5 (1 not confident to 5 most confident) to form action points.

Table 9.1 Key themes confidence rating – the motivation level has prompted you to . . . .

Key theme	Confidence level
Consider how your *teacher identity and philosophy* influences: your own creativity; your organization and classroom ethos; your approach to behaviour in school	1 2 3 4 5
Reflect upon how your understanding of the *purpose of education* reflects in: how you perceive creativity in the curriculum; how you establish your learning environment; how you address behaviour	1 2 3 4 5
Consider how your focus on *well-being for you and your pupils* reflects in: how you respond to the demands the curriculum and creativity; how you organize your classroom systems; your routines, support and responses to individual needs	1 2 3 4 5
Evaluate how you *meet the needs of the unique child* through: your understanding and skill in creativity; classroom organization, use of support and parent involvement; a collaborative approach to behaviour	1 2 3 4 5
Appreciate how your awareness of *creating an enabling and empowering environment* reflects in: how you support the development of creativity and risk-taking; your organization of physical space, resources and people; management of your classroom through routines, rules and approaches	1 2 3 4 5
Reflect how your own *self-awareness* and *critical self-reflection* enhances: how you develop your own creativity and that of your pupils; your classroom organization and approaches; your support, interactions and response to enable each pupil to develop their potential	1 2 3 4 5
Identify your need for *continuous development as a lifelong learner* in relation to: your understanding of creative teaching and teaching creatively; the development of the physical, social and emotional aspects of the learning environment; your understanding of behaviour, learning theory and communication.	1 2 3 4 5
Total score	

Reflecting upon the above, identify key areas you wish to address. This activity will serve as an action plan (Table 9.2) to bring about a desirable change, with a particular focus on motivation, in your teaching.

Table 9.2 Action plan.

Desirable change	Perceived barrier/ risk	Time/support/ training required	Timescale
This could be focused on developing *your own creativity; developing your learning environment; effective TA deployment; or aspects of behaviour for learning*	List these and consider whether they are significant or insignificant	Identify support that might help you to address these barriers/risks, e.g., '*I need support when developing my use of . . .*' or '*I need set aside a specific time to . . .*'	These may be more immediate, e.g., '*By the end of the week I will . . .*' or longer term, e.g., '*By the end of the year I will have . . .*'

To attain outstanding you have to believe in yourself, your pupils and the purpose of education. To emphasize my point I will finish this level with a quote from a creative genius (I have two small boys so of course Disney is magical!).

> *Somehow I can't believe that there are any heights that can't be scaled by a [person] who knows the secrets of making dreams come true. This special secret, it seems to me, can be summarized in four Cs. They are curiosity, confidence, courage, and constancy, and the greatest of all is confidence. When you believe in a thing, believe in it all the way, implicitly and unquestionably.*
>
> Walt Disney

PART 4

Reflection level – excel!

10

Extending and excelling: reflection and change

The function of education is to teach one to think intensively and to think critically. Intelligence plus character; that is the goal of true education.

Martin Luther King, Jr

Our coat hook! The emphasis is now on becoming a reflective practitioner, and as such *you* must decide whether the 'jacket' is one you want to keep. You may hang it up and view it from afar, assessing whether or not it really is a most 'perfect jacket'. You and your environment will change and as they do you will have to ask yourself, does it still fit? Does it fulfil all your needs? Does it express who you are? Will it protect you from the elements?

This chapter identifies ways to extend your practice and excel through reflective practice. Embedding reflection into your teacher identity (it's just what I do and who I am!) is key. Take a moment to consider the hierarchy presented within the book. For each stage would you be able to fully develop your understanding without using reflection? Reflection has been purposefully placed at the apex of the pyramid, as it should trickle down and seep into each level. Education is preparing your children for their futures, therefore your role is to, as Martin Luther King notes, equip them with moral character and the ability to critically view the world to create desirable change. To achieve this for your pupils you must first be that role model.

The key themes in this chapter prompt you to:

- articulate your *teacher identity and philosophy* and identify how it has been influenced;
- clarify your understanding of the *purpose of education* and how this is reflected in your philosophy;
- reflect how your focus on *well-being for you and your pupils* underpins your beliefs and values;
- identify how your teacher identity, professional efficacy and the culture of your classroom *meet the needs of the unique child;*

- evaluate how *creating an enabling and empowering environment* supports your ability to embrace teacher as researcher and critical pedagogy;
- consider how your *self-awareness* and *critical self-reflection* have become an integral part of your practice and enhance being a reflective practitioner;
- clarify how your understanding of teacher identity, professional efficacy, mastery and developing a supportive learning culture has focused your need for *continuous development as a lifelong learner.*

This chapter addresses the following *Teachers' standards* (DfE 2012):

3 Demonstrate good subject and curriculum knowledge.
8 Fulfil wider professional responsibilities.

The reflective journey: becoming consciously-competent

Your journey toward outstanding teaching moves through phases of development, either based on *conscious* or *unconscious* decision-making. The initial stages could be viewed as being *unconsciously-incompetent*, as we are unaware of the complexity and demands of teaching and learning. We realize just how much there is to learn and do, and so we become *consciously-incompetent*. As we successfully address areas for development we become *consciously-competent* and finally, when experience and knowledge are fully embedded and mastery achieved, we become *unconsciously-competent.*

Right now your goal is to become *consciously-competent* and reflective teaching is the vehicle to enable this. You are then able to make professional decisions that are informed and articulated confidently. Conscious-competence requires challenge, as you must critically reflect on your practice in relation to theory. For example, 'Did my response to Omar's outburst help him gain emotional regulation skills?'; 'Did I extend the learning as fully as I could within that lesson?'; 'Did my response to Scarlett's mother reflect my knowledge of child development or my personal opinion?'; 'Am I helping my pupils to construct their own knowledge or am I expecting them to memorize information?'; 'Did I celebrate Sanjiit's musical "intelligence"?'

Effective educational decisions or responses cannot be made without knowing how and why we respond the way we do. Even though this information is not always straightforward, it is your professional responsibility to make sense of it to inform your practice.

EXTEND . . . Becoming a reflective practitioner

Critical reflection on practice is a requirement of the relationship between theory and practice. Otherwise theory becomes simply 'blah, blah, blah', and practice, pure activism.

Paulo Freire, 1998a

To be an outstanding teacher you must embrace critical reflection and, as Freire (1998a) states, connect the theory to the practice. This adds gravitas to your decision-making and produces less reactionary, more proactive and informed approaches and responses. Essentially you understand more fully and 'see' why something is as it is.

The move toward reflective practice was initiated by Dewey's philosophy and developed in his seminal text *How We Think* (1933), which focused on experience, interaction and reflection. Its philosophical roots lay in phenomenology (a focus on lived experiences and personal consciousness) and in critical theory (a focus on the development of a critical consciousness), and writers, such as Boud, Kolb and Schön have developed these concepts into models which promote reflective thinking.

Whether an experienced, expert teacher or trainee, beginning teacher, the benefit of effective reflective practice can be profound. It is a process through which a deeper understanding of your teaching style can be formed as you take greater responsibility for your teaching and its outcomes. It is the synergy between experience and reflection that grows as you take on the role as your own observer. There are, however, degrees of reflection and its positive impact is only possible if there is a willingness to question and deepen your way of thinking and adopt the role of critical friend (Would a close and valued friend say you look great in every outfit you try on, regardless, or would they be honest and advise and suggest alternatives when required?).

Through reflection we can begin to challenge some of deeper, social and cultural thoughts, feelings and reactions (as discussed in Chapter 1). However, as Mezirow (2000) argues, reflection is only of value when it leads to transformation or 'desirable change' that we seek in our practice. This change will only happen if you take charge of your reflection and plan steps to address identified issues.

This is easier said than done as each individual's readiness and ability to reflect is different. If we therefore view reflective practice as a continuum we can see how we might progress toward more transformational reflection. At one end there is *reflection*, whereby something is simply 'thought about' after the event and tends to be superficial. Then we move to *critical reflection*, whereby we begin to ask 'why?' and so critique and challenge our beliefs, values and approaches. At the opposite end is *reflexivity*, which is an 'in the moment', dynamic and intuitive process fuelled by high levels of self-awareness, analysis and metacognition. Here reflection is embedded into teacher identity.

The respective abilities of 'beginning' and 'expert' teachers are relevant here. There should be a developmental readiness to fruitfully engage in reflection (Griffin 2003; Hobbs 2007) at the outset and to develop its depths. New teachers may lack the necessary mastery or tacit knowledge gained through experience and therefore be more inclined to reflect superficially. In addition, the ability to order the issues in terms of importance and to prioritize is likely to be limited. The heady and complex demands of teaching may tempt us to apply rules, procedures and policy to the letter as there is a sense of certainty and safety when certain actions can be 'ticked off' or routines adhered to. These teachers seek 'safety' in controlled classrooms and their tried-and-tested or 'defensive pedagogical practices' (Hayes 2006; McNeil 2009).

Reflective practice adds a level of uncertainty as we may be forced to question and deconstruct our thinking and deep-seated approaches or dominant cultures. Nevertheless, as teachers become more confident, experienced and expert in their practice, they developed the skill of being able to reflect upon, challenge and adapt, perhaps even intuitively, and so transform their practice. Here we find a paradox of teaching: the more expert a teacher becomes, the more responsive they are to contexts and situations, the more adept they are at making instantaneous and often imaginative decisions – yet this knowledge cannot be readily quantified and therefore it can easily go unacknowledged and underestimated by that teacher. It is part of their toolkit: 'It's just what I do!' (*unconsciously-competent*).

To move along the continuum to extend and excel your practice requires: 1) self-awareness; 2) self-improvement; and 3) empowerment.

1 Self-awareness

Self-awareness requires you to think of yourself, your experiences, expectations, beliefs, values and biases. Understanding and having clarity of teacher identity and philosophy is central as attitudes, behaviour and decisions are determined by it (Hayes 2006). A heightened sense of self-awareness enables you to set aside personal values and opinions, and focus objectively on evidence in a professional manner. A keen sense of teacher-self will also act as a 'buffer' to the many changes the educational system experiences. To refine and deepen your teacher identity requires you to examine and re-examine why teaching is your chosen career and ask yourself 'What can I, or do I, bring to the profession personally?'

Developing self-awareness as an element of reflective practice promotes positive changes in your pedagogical practice, and refines and enhances your teacher toolkit. This improvement should be both intentional and mindful. However, challenges and changes can induce a sense of reticence or fear in some teachers, especially if teacher identity, philosophy or professionalism is questioned or contradicted (Harwell 2003).

Remember, you are that influential role model, therefore establishing yourself as the lead-learner who engages in thoughtful, reflective self-development will communicate and form your classroom culture.

 REFLECT

Think of a recent specific and memorable incident within school in which you were centrally involved. Pinpoint the most dominant characteristics you revealed, for example, knowledgeable or accepting. Now reflect on your:

- *dreamer spots* (parts you would like to develop);
- *blind spots* (parts you do not often face up to);
- *public display* (parts you publicly present);
- *untapped reservoir* (parts you think might be there) (Pollard 2008: 119).

It would be beneficial to do this exercise with a friend or colleague. This sharing will deepen your understanding as you explain your perceptions and it will provide support.

Models for reflection

Reflective teachers are enquiring at every stage of the process. Your reflection may stem from:

- a particularly good or bad experience;
- school or pupil performance;
- lesson evaluations;
- lesson observations;
- reading research articles;
- news related to educational issues;
- small-scale personal enquiries;
- discussion with colleagues;
- your own observations.

Models for reflection need to be applied purposefully, flexibly and judiciously, otherwise reflection becomes an exercise rather than a vehicle to deliver lasting, desirable change. The models of reflection most commonly cited are as follows.

Schön's (1983) *reflective practitioner* model focused on how professionals think in action. He identified ways in which professionals could become aware of their implicit knowledge and learn from their experience. His main concern was to facilitate the development of reflective practitioners rather than describe the process of reflection per se. Schön's notion of 'professional artistry' suggests professional practice could be developed through a spiral of action and reflection, where the practitioner acts, reflects on the action and plans new action, which is informed by the results of the reflection. The spiral is continuous, and can be interrupted and incomplete, and the reflection will not always solve problems. It could even cause problems. It does however help bring uncertainties to the surface, and provides a means of looking for solutions. This is the basis of critical reflection, which forms an important part of reflective practice.

Reflection-on-action (after-the-event thinking) consciously reviews, describes, analyses and evaluates past practice to gain insight to improve future practice. It requires:

- thinking about something that has happened;
- thinking what you would do differently next time;
- taking time to act on reflection.

Reflection-in-action (thinking while doing) examines experiences and responses as they occur. It requires:

- thinking on your feet;
- thinking about what to do next;
- acting straight away.

Kolb's four stages (1984), introduced in Chapter 2, propose the development of reflection in practice. This involves:

- *Experience*: the actions taken;
- *Observations* and reflections: review and reflection on the above;
- *Development* of ideas: identifying the learning from the experience;
- *Testing ideas* in practice: planning the steps and putting them into practice.

Gibbs' reflective cycle (1988) developed from Kolb, recommends that theory and practice should enrich each other in a cycle, namely:

- *Description*: What happened? Non-judgemental, solely descriptive.
- *Feelings*: What were your reactions and feelings?
- *Evaluation*: What was good or bad about the experience? Make value judgements.
- *Analysis*: What sense can you make of the situation? Draw on outside experiences to help you.
- *Conclusions*: What can be concluded from the experience and analysis?
- *Action plan*:What are you going to do differently in this type of situation next time? What steps are you going to take on next?

Other models include **Boud et al.** (1985), who advocate describing a critical incident in a non-judgemental way, identifying resultant positive and negative feelings and 'discharging' the negative feelings, which may obstruct the reflection. The incident is evaluated through association (relating new data to what is known); integration (seeking relationships between the data); validation (determining the authenticity of the new ideas and looking for inconsistencies or contradictions); and appropriation (making the new knowledge one's own).

    Rolfe et al. (2001) use a simpler three Ws to stimulate reflection; namely What? (description); so What? (interpretation) and now What? (action and consequence).

    Use critical incidents, case studies, reflective journals/diaries, reflective dialogical exercises (with peers or mentors), role play and practical exercises (Schön, refers to these as 'practicums') to develop reflective practice. Daily reflections will enable you to categorize patterns or trends in your teaching, pupils' responses and your related feelings that may not be immediately obvious from just one reflection.

 REFLECT

Choose a critical incident, take a model of reflection that most appeals, and work through the process. For example, based on Gibbs' model, describe the incident using Table 10.1.

Table 10.1 Gibbs' model of reflection

What happened? *Using specific and relevant detail, give a concise description*	
What were your reactions and feelings? *How did you feel and what did you think prior to, during and after the experience?*	
What was good or bad about the experience? *What went well or badly during the experience (what did and didn't work)?*	
What went well or badly: explain why? *What do you think was the consequence of this?* *How could you have changed the outcome?*	
What should or could you have done differently? *What have you learnt from the experience?* *Did this identify areas of strength and weakness?*	
What steps are you going to take next? *How are you going to address areas for development?*	

Again, discuss the incident, as this promotes further self-reflection. Using colleagues with experience and expertise will enable you to collaboratively reflect on how this can inform your practice, how you can more comprehensively capture what you have learned, and how to develop new perspectives to impact positively on your practice and on your pupils' success.

2 Self-improvement

Self-improvement is about learning from experiences and wanting to improve specific aspects. Developing teacher efficacy and mastery is addressed through improving your practice and seeing research and undertaking specific areas for CPD as part of this. Mastery in teaching enables us to move beyond simple reflection. However, Foer (2011) points to the term *ok plateau* to describe an autopilot state when tasks have been mastered habitually (as discussed in the mindfulness section in Chapter 1), and at this point improvement/development stops or slows despite having the necessary skills. This correlates with the reduced mentoring support provided in the first year or so of teaching. Moreover, improvement requires change and sometimes when developments in either curriculum or pedagogy are either too fast or require significant reflection it can induce fear and reticence in teachers.

Therefore, being receptive and having a willingness to step out of a comfort zone, alongside continuing to develop your professional efficacy and mastery, is central to successful change. It is a journey, not only to secure the foundations of teaching and learning, but also to integrate new subject and pedagogic knowledge into your identity and philosophy.

Teacher as researcher

It's not all about 'big' research! Conducting research in school, no matter how small a scale, provides a counterbalance to the dominant culture or 'taken for granted thinking' (Snoek and Moens 2011) and prevents a teacher or school slipping into complacency or experiencing a plateauing of performance which can eventually result in inadequate practice.

Research is part of my day job. Consider the process of lesson planning and assessment (Chapters 5 and 6) whereby you design, implement, observe, analyse, assess and modify in light of data. This active engagement with information informs learning goals and targets, making the teaching and learning effective. If the data gathered from effective AfL is seen as high quality and interpreted analytically and critically then accurate decisions can be made, therefore you are teacher as an active researcher. Teacher as researcher is simply a more intentional and system-atic version of what is already happening.

In this role you decide what to study. This often starts with a 'wondering' ('I wonder if . . .'). These wonderings evolve into 'pondering' ('If I change/remove/introduce . . .'). The research question emerges and can be framed as a 'What happens when . . . ?,' 'How . . . ?,' or 'What is . . . ?' question. This is often a cyclical process that focuses on *understanding* an aspect of education that stimulates further questions.

The teacher as researcher model is a powerful tool for your development, however, the school culture may affect how you move forward. For example, an infor-mal culture may not support you taking a leadership role with colleagues; equally a very structured environment may not have the flexibility or the risk-taking approach that the research requires. Negotiation, communication and collaboration with key members of staff about your ideas will better enable you to embark on research.

 REFLECT

Slow down and pause to examine, analyse and enquire about the complexities of teaching. Your analysis of significant incidents will provide 'eureka' moments, which challenge and alter your teacher identity and philosophy, hopefully for the better.

Before embarking on your research and answering those nagging 'wonder-ings', structure them into a question to focus your mind. Now consider:

- What contribution will this make to my practice and potentially the school?
- What data am I looking for (pupils' work, photographs, digital recordings)?
- How will I collect data (interviews, questionnaires, group discussions, surveys, observations, digital recording, document analysis, enlist TA or colleague)?

- How effective and practical are these data collection strategies (answer the research question, time, cost, transcribing)?
- Where should I collate the data (using a research journal to 'write-up' fieldnotes, add thoughts, observations, reflections, quotes, descriptions, including dates and times, anomalies, conversations and interactions)?
- How will I analyse the data (categorizing, frequency, with colleagues/pupils)?
- How will I learn from my findings (sharing data with colleagues, presenting a 10-minute summary, concept mapping, report, personal log)?
- What impact will this have on my pupils' learning outcomes?
- What new questions arise? This will point you or your colleagues in a new research direction.

Another focus can be drawn from current educational issues, either local or national. Refer to online sources, such as the BBC and newspaper websites or search for articles related to the subject matter that interests you. Aim to be objective and identify the argument for and against the key issue. Reflect on where you stand and what has influenced you.

- Was there a political influence on decision-making regarding this issue?
- Did you feel that it reflected appropriate educational practice or concerns?
- Did educationalists make a sufficient contribution?

Continuing professional development

> *It's really not possible for someone to imagine himself/herself as a subject in the process of becoming without having at the same time a disposition for change. And change of which she/he is not merely the victim but the subject.*
>
> Paulo Freire, 1998a

By definition, reflective teachers think about their own performance and progress and that of their pupils. They must be, as Freire (1998a) reflects, open to change and take responsibility for their ongoing development, and develop a sense of 'urgency'. This is about a self-critical process of reflection and gradually, but consistently, raising the level of challenge to achieve outstandingness.

CPD denotes and promotes an ongoing, career-long process of learning and refinement of expertise. It enhances professionalism and raises morale if teachers have direct involvement and ownership, and increases motivation and commitment to pupils' learning where teachers implement these improvements in practice.

 CHECKLIST for professional development

- Have a positive effect on pupil learning outcomes.
- Demonstrate a connection between CPD and changes in practitioner knowledge and skills (deepening and sharpening).

- Keep up with developments in the individual fields/subjects, and in education generally.
- Generate and contribute new knowledge and/or innovation to the school.

The school development or improvement plan has a clear part to play in teachers' CPD activities. Similarly, national priorities play a part and to a lesser degree personal interests (Hustler et al. 2003). Ideally CPD and performance management should flow directly from, and feed into, school improvement planning.

CPD support

A *collegiate approach*, whereby peer observation is undertaken in a focused, mutually respectful, enquiring way, with preparation time and follow-up discussion, can be a powerful form of CPD for both the observed and the observer. The term 'co-coaching', used in the national framework for mentoring and coaching (DfES 2005) is akin to this process.

There are many experienced teachers who deliver great lessons, day after day. What they do is ingrained in their professional practice so deeply that they would struggle to explain why they are so effective; they are unconsciously-competent. To distinguish what is special about their pedagogy can contribute to professional development. In addition, consider how you can use local peer and mentor support and networks.

Online support and organizations

Teaching Schools (www.gov.uk/teaching-schools-a-guide-for-potential-applicants#-continuing-professional-development) establishes outstanding schools to work with others to provide high-quality training and development.

The Teacher Effectiveness Programme (TEEP) (www.teep.org.uk), set up in 2002 by the Gatsby Charity Foundation, and under the custodianship of the Specialist Schools and Academies Trust (SSAT), has developed a model of effective teaching and learning drawn from research and best practice.

'TeachMeets' (http://teachertoolkit.me/teachmeets/) offers online and face-to-face support across the UK. Events are organized currently around London for practising teachers.

A *self-led approach* using a reflective journal is explored Mary Louise Holly (1989) in her book *Writing to grow: keeping a personal-professional Journal*.

CPD is about personal development and career fulfillment. Solomon and Tresman (1999) argue that it makes a connection with the 'self' and teacher identity and their practice and professionalism.

However, this can only be realized in a supportive environment, which embraces a learning culture for all.

 REFLECT

From your reflection of a critical incident earlier in the chapter, can you identify area(s) for CPD? Discuss this with a colleague or mentor to add insight and support.

3 *Empowerment within a supportive learning culture*

Changing your behaviour and being in control of making these changes is easier in a supportive learning culture. If all members of the school community are seen as learners and mistakes are valued, risk-taking, development and innovation are easier. Findings indicate that teachers working in schools with 'more supportive' professional environments continued to improve significantly after three years, while teachers in the least supportive schools actually declined in their effectiveness (Sutton Trust 2014).

If teacher identity, philosophy and professional efficacy are addressed, the barriers to growth and change can more easily be overcome. However, that barrier of accountability still remains. Judgements about the quality of teaching, *Teachers' standards*, Ofsted, PRP, as well as appraisal should ideally enhance not diminish best practice. Interlocking both the need to measure and the need for support could be resolved in Leahy and Wiliam's (2012) notion of *supportive accountability*. The central idea is the creation of structures that, while making teachers accountable for developing their practice, provide the support for them to do this. A supportive culture of appraisal is a process that is done *with* not *to* the teacher. They suggest a model of structured monthly meetings with the focus on specific elements of practice and with pupil achievement as the central goal. This reframes coaching, mentoring and lesson observations as developmental not judgemental.

However, for some teachers, any approach to appraisal may be difficult as they see the critical element inextricably linked to them as a person. It therefore feels as if there is something wrong with them personally if they engage in critical analysis of their teaching. To address this, a growth culture needs to be fostered which views the aspects of practice that need improving as positives and platforms for development. Through understanding emotional responses to criticism, generated either from within yourself or externally through mentors, tutors or managers, you become more open to change. More fundamentally, you must know yourself first, define your teacher identity and have a willingness to want desirable change to happen.

Of crucial importance is the value attached to reflection and development by your school. A supportive culture will make the individual teacher feel instrumental in the growth of their learning community as well as feeling a sense of personal development and achievement. A supportive learning culture will not label certain teachers as 'naturally gifted' or a 'born teacher' but believe that all teachers can aspire to be outstanding and, with support, will achieve this.

 REFLECT

Does your school encourage you to be critical, professionally challenging, self-aware, embrace transformation and change? Or is reflective practice seen as bland and mechanical with teachers disinclined to ask awkward questions, leading to strategic compliance (Flores and Day 2006) as the dominant approach within the school remaining unchallenged?

EXCEL . . . Finally becoming an 'agent of change'

Moral purpose without change agentry is martyrdom; change agentry without moral purpose is change for the sake of change. In combination, not only are they effective in getting things done, but they are good at getting the right things done.

Michael G. Fullan, 1993

Contemplate Fullan's notion that teachers need to be 'agents of change' underpinned with a moral purpose drawn from educational goals we aspire to. Think about a change you have noticed in school, for example introducing a new reading scheme, developing growth mindset or new playground equipment. Consider to what extent the teachers were instrumental in this change. Was this change simply for the sake of change, as Fullan notes, or driven by clear educational philosophy and goals? Did staff engage in critical pedagogic discussions with relevance to the impact of the new initiative?

Identifying the role of critical pedagogy can add a deeper dimension to your philosophy and practice. Through embracing critical pedagogy, teaching becomes more than simply effective pedagogy and toolkits. It approaches educational issues analytically, with the focus on empowering and aspiring to social transformation, whereby all voices are heard equally and social injustices are addressed. Critical pedagogy connects classroom learning with society. It requires us to navigate the choppy waters of standards and accountability with democracy and transformation as the goal. This focuses on understanding the purpose of education and refines philosophy.

Freire (1998b) refers to the notion of 'banking', which describes teachers as depositors of information and the pupils as the depositees. Critical pedagogues resist being 'depositors' who are simply transmitters of knowledge and combine reflection and practice. Viewing professionalism beyond the transmission model of the 'competent' teacher requires us to seek alternatives. The 'reflective teacher' perceives teaching as more than practical skills and evaluates their teaching, perhaps drawing on their theoretical understanding with a view to improving and develop their teaching. Another model is the 'enquiring teacher' in which research underpins practice as such, and classroom observations inform professional decisions. Another model is the *transformative teacher* who is a true *agent of change* (Menter 2010). These teachers are those critical pedagogues who examine the world and its processes (Dillard 1997) and seek to address inequality.

As described at the beginning of this chapter, your skill in reflection grows along a continuum, and likewise these models can also be placed on a continuum. At one end we place the *competent teacher* and at the other the *transformative*. In the middle is the *reflective* and *enquiring* teacher. As with all things developmental it takes time and experience to move along the continuum, and progress is never smooth and unhindered. Indeed you may not want to be a transformational teacher and are very happy in the middle. However, to enhance what we do we can blend together the very best from each. We can take the substantive knowledge of the competent teacher; the understanding of theory and willingness to engage in active research of the reflective and enquiring teacher; and finally the critical and more philosophical attributes of the transformative teacher and blend them together.

A final thought . . . Professor Debra Myhill, from Exeter University, argues that a teacher's ability to reflect on their performance and to change is crucial, but so is a healthy scepticism toward national policy. She advocated an element of 'creative subversion', whereby teachers should neither passively comply with government initiatives, nor simply refuse to implement them. Instead they should 'adapt them creatively', drawing on their abilities as a reflective practitioner. This will avoid the nodding-dog syndrome and desperately trying to fit a quart into a pint pot when you know it will never go!

The glass ceiling of outstanding teaching should be shattered so that you can excel and really stand out. Restrictions can be *internally* (perhaps generated through fears or experiences) or *externally* imposed (perhaps through performativity and accountability driven by Ofsted or *Teachers' standards*). To break through, you need the strong foundations of knowing yourself, your children and your subjects, effective pedagogy, an extensive toolkit within the right learning environment and your ability to critically reflect on your practice.

References

Boud, D., Keogh, R. and Walker, D. (1985) *Promoting reflection in learning: a model*, in D. Boud, R. Keogh and D. Walker (eds) *Reflection: turning experience into learning*. London: Kogan Page.

Dewey, J. (1933) *How we think*. Boston, MA: DC Heath & Co.

DfE (2012) *Teachers' standards*, www.gov.uk/government/uploads/system/uploads/attachment_data/file/301107/Teachers__Standards.pdf.

DfES (2005) *Higher standards, better schools for all*. Nottingham: DfES.

Dillard, C. B. (1997) Placing student language, literacy, and culture at the center of teacher education reform, in J.E. King, E.R. Hollins and W.C. Hayman (eds) *Preparing teachers for cultural diversity*, pp. 85–96. New York: Teachers College Press.

Flores, M.A. and Day, C. (2006) Contexts which shape and reshape new teachers' identities: a multi-perspective study, *Teacher and Teacher Education*, 22: 219–32.

Foer, J. (2011) *Moonwalking with Einstein: the art and science of remembering everything*. London: Penguin Books.

Freire, P. (1998a) *Pedagogy of Freedom*. Lanham, MD: Rowman & Littlefield Publishers, Inc.

Freire, P. (1998b) The 'banking' concept of education, in A.M. Freire and D. Macedo (eds) *The Paulo Freire reader*, pp. 67–79. New York: Continuum.

Fullan, M.G. (1993) Why teachers must become change agents, *The Professional Teacher*, 50(6): 12–17.

Gibbs, G. (1988) *Learning by doing: a guide to teaching and learning methods*. Oxford: Further Education Unit, Oxford Polytechnic.

Griffin, M (2003) Using critical incidents to promote and assess reflective thinking in preservice teachers, *Reflective Practice*, 4(2): 207–20.

Harwell, S.H. (2003) *Teacher professional development: it's not an event, It's a Process*. Waco, TX: CORD.

Hayes, D. (2006) Telling stories: sustaining improvement in schools operating under adverse conditions, *Improving School*, 9: 203.

Hobbs, V. (2007) Faking it or hating it: can reflective practice be forced? *Reflective Practice*, 8(3): 405–17.

Holly, M.L. (1989) *Writing to grow: keeping a personal-professional Journal*. London: Heinemann/Cassell.

Hustler, D., McNamara, O., Jarvis, J., Londra, M. and Campbell, A. (2003) *Teachers' perceptions of continuing professional development, institute of education*. Manchester: Manchester Metropolitan University, John Howson Education Data Services, DfES, HMSO.

Kolb, D. A. (1984) *Experiential learning: experience as the source of learning and development*. Upper Saddle River, NJ: Prentice-Hall.

Leahy, S. and Wiliam, D. (2012) *From teachers to schools: scaling up professional development for formative assessment*, in J. Gardner (ed.) *Assessment and learning*, pp. 49–71. London: Sage.

McNeil, L. (2009) *Standardisation, defensive teaching and the problem of control*, in A. Darder, M. Baltodana and R. Torres (eds) *Critical pedagogy reader*, 384–96. New York: Routledge.

Menter, I. (2010) *Teachers-formation, training and identity: A literature review*, Newcastle: Creativity Culture & Education.

Mezirow, J. (2000) Learning to think like an adult: core concepts of transformation theory, in J. Mezirow and Associates (eds) *Learning as transformation*. San Francisco: Jossey-Bass.

Pollard, A. (2008) *Reflective teaching: evidence-informed professional practice*, 3rd edn. London: Bloomsbury.

Rolfe, G., Freshwater, D. and Jasper, M. (2001) *Critical reflection in nursing and the helping professions: a user's guide,*. Basingstoke: Palgrave Macmillan.

Schön, D.A. (1983) *The reflective practitioner: how professionals think in action*. London: Temple Smith.

Snoek, M. and Moens, E. (2011) The impact of teacher research on teacher learning in academic training schools in the Netherlands, *Professional Development in Education*, 37(5): 817–35.

Sutton Trust, Education Endowment Foundation (EEF) (2014) *Teaching and learning Toolkit*, https://educationendowmentfoundation.org.uk/uploads/toolkit/EEF_Teaching_and_learning_toolkit_Feb_2014.pdf.

Summary of the reflection level and conclusion

Your perfect jacket

Your 'perfect jacket' is now perfect for you. It fits, it's filled and it's fabulous! However, as you journey to outstandingness (and beyond!) you may find that just one jacket is not quite enough! Although it fulfils your role as an outstanding teacher more than adequately, it might fall short of equipping you to lead, innovate and inspire as your career develops. You may now consider finding and fitting a 'perfect wardrobe', judiciously selected to meet the increasingly diverse needs you encounter.

Your professional knowledge

You have scaled the pyramid and at the apex you have been guided to become more critically reflective. Reflection trickles down and seeps into each and every layer of the pyramid. You cannot truly know yourself without reflecting upon your beliefs, values and behaviours. Likewise, you cannot refine your strategies and enhance your toolkit without analysis. If reflective practice is embraced, you will move toward your goal of outstandingness.

However, as Charles Handy observes in *The Empty Raincoat*, there is a paradox of success: namely, that which enabled you to attain such status won't necessarily keep you there. He explains this in terms of a *Sigmoid Curve*, which sums up life itself. In the shape of an elongated *S* the start of the curve is slow, experimental and fraught with setbacks. It then gradually rises upwards as you master skills, gain knowledge and achieve successes, but this trajectory does not remain constant; it begins to fall and the trend is then sadly downward. At the point at which it falls is where a second sigmoid curve should be introduced, and when that begins to decline a third, and so on. The secret of success is to introduce the next curve before the inevitable decline of the last. This requires knowing when, how and what *significant desirable change* you need to make to prevent this decline. It is through, as Friere (1998) says, *being open to the process of knowing and sensitive to the experience of teaching as an art; being pushed forward by the challenges that prevent bureaucratizing practice;*

accepting limitations, yet always conscious of the necessary effort to overcome them that will enable you to continue to rise onwards and upwards.

Further reading

Handy, C. (1995) *The empty raincoat, making sense of the future.* New York: Arrow Books.

Your professional development and action plan

Identify your areas of strength and development and connect the content of this level to the key themes. Reflect upon the extent to which you have achieved each statement. To support your journey to outstandingness, rate each key theme statement 1–5 (1 not confident to 5 most confident) to form actions points (Table 10.2).

Table 10.2 Key themes confidence rating – the reflection level has prompted you to . . . .

Key theme	Confidence level
Reflect upon your *teacher identity and philosophy* and identify what may have influenced this	1 2 3 4 5
Clarify your understanding of the *purpose of education* and how this is reflected in your philosophy	1 2 3 4 5
Reflect how your focus on *well-being for you and your pupils* underpins your beliefs and values	1 2 3 4 5
Identify how your teacher identity, professional efficacy and the culture of your classroom *meet the needs of the unique child.*	1 2 3 4 5
Evaluate how *creating an enabling and empowering environment* supports your ability to embrace teacher as researcher and critical reflection	1 2 3 4 5
Consider how your own *self-awareness* and *critical self-reflection* has become an integral part of your practice and continues to enhance you as a practitioner	1 2 3 4 5
Clarify how your understanding of teacher identity, professional efficacy, mastery and developing a supportive learning culture has focused your need for *continuous development as a life-long learner*	1 2 3 4 5
Total score	

This final action plan (Table 10.3) draws upon reflection to bring about *desirable change* in your teaching and ensure at the point one sigmoid curves declines you are committed to starting another, so you continue to progress. Up, up and away!

Table 10.3 Action plan.

Desirable change	Perceived barrier/risk	Time/support/ training required	Timescale
This could be focused on *using models to enhance your ability to critically reflect; identifying how teacher as research can be integrated into your practice; become more aware and analytical of educational policy*	List these and consider whether they are significant or insignificant	Identify support that might help you to address these barriers/risks, e.g., '*I will develop my use of a daily reflective journal to . . .*' or '*To set aside time to use the models of reflection effectively to . . .*'.	These may be immediate, e.g., '*By the end of each I will reflect upon key points of the day . . .*' or longer term, e.g., '*By the end of the term I will undertake an area of research to enhance . . .*'

I would like to finish this book with a dearly loved excerpt from Dr Seuss:

Oh, The places you will go
You have brains in your head.
You have feet in your shoes.
You can steer yourself
any direction you choose.
Out their things happen
and frequently do
to people as brainy
 and footsy as you.
You'll be on your way up!
You'll be seeing great sights!
You'll join high fliers
who soar to high heights
On and on you will hike.
And I know you'll hike far
and face up to your problems
whatever they are.
And will you succeed?
Yes! You will, indeed!
(98 and ¾ per cent guaranteed.)
You're off to Great Places!
Today is your day!
Your mountain is waiting.
So. . . get on your way!
Dr Seuss 2012

You have chosen teaching as your mountain, which will require you to believe in your own ability to grow and to view barriers and challenges as opportunities to develop. Your self-awareness and reflection, underpinned by your clarity of philosophy, beliefs and values, will enable you to succeed. So don your perfect jacket and embark on your journey upwards toward outstandingness.

Remember, outstanding teachers really can change lives!

Index

ESSENTIAL PRIMARY SCIENCE 2/e

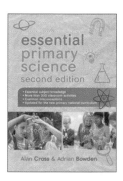

Alan Cross and Adrian Bowden

2014
9780335263349 - Paperback

eBook also available

If you are teaching - or learning - to teach primary science, this is the toolkit to support you!

Highly respected and widely used, Essential Primary Science 2E blends essential subject knowledge with a vast array of teacher activities. Updated and revised throughout to reflect the requirements of the new National Curriculum, it covers the essential knowledge and understanding that you need; plus it offers over 200 great ideas for teaching primary science at KSI and KS2 - so no more late nights thinking up creative new ways to teach key concepts!

Written in a friendly and supportive style this new edition offers:

- Over 200 original and new activities to complement the new curriculum, ready for you to try out in the classroom
- Tips on how to ensure each lesson includes both practical and investigative elements
- Suggestions on how to make your lessons engaging, memorable and inclusive
- How to deal with learners' common scientific misconceptions in each topic
- Two new chapters on working scientifically and how to tackle assessment
- New up-to-date web links to quality free resources

Drawing on their own extensive teaching experience and understanding of the new National Curriculum, the authors provide the essential guide to teaching primary science for both trainee teachers and qualified teachers who are not science specialists.

www.openup.co.uk

OPEN UNIVERSITY PRESS
McGraw - Hill Education

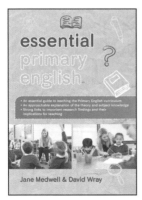

Essential Primary English

Medwell and Wray

ISBN: 9780335262007 (Paperback)
eISBN: 9780335262014

2016

This book is an essential guide to teaching the Primary English curriculum, offering guidance on how to teach the subject, as well as covering the theory and subject knowledge that underpins it. Covering the whole of the Primary English curriculum the book focuses in particular on less-developed aspects such as the development of spoken language, the nature and development of comprehension and the teaching and learning of grammar.

Key features include:

- Practical teaching sequences, strategies and activities
- Classroom cameos suggest ways of delivering content through meaningful activities
- Essential 'Subject Knowledge' boxes present brief exposés of essential knowledge
- Subject Knowledge Quizzes enable you to self-check your knowledge
- 'Insights from Research' boxes outline underpinning theory and research

www.mheducation.co.uk

Essential Primary Grammar

Myhill, Jones, Watson and Lines

ISBN: 9780335262380 (Paperback)
eISBN: 9780335262397

2016

Essential Primary Grammar is an invaluable resource to ensure that you are firmly equipped to teach grammar. It helps you get to grips with your knowledge of grammar for the national curriculum – including the spelling, punctuation and grammar test – as well as providing you with some tried and tested ways to teach grammar. Underpinned by a series of research studies which have investigated the teaching of grammar, it will support you in how to teach grammar in creative and meaningful ways whilst supporting you in developing your own fundamental knowledge of grammar.

Key features include:

- Easy-to-read chapters which systematically focus on grammatical subject knowledge at word, phrase and clause level
- Guidance in each chapter addressing typical grammar problems or misconceptions, and some grammar jokes
- Inspiring suggestions for teaching activities to help children develop grammatical knowledge in meaningful learning contexts
- Reference to authentic children's books to illuminate the grammatical explanations and suggested teaching activities
- Ideas on how high quality talk about grammar and texts can be fostered in the classrooms

www.mheducation.co.uk

ESSENTIAL PRIMARY MATHEMATICS

Rickard

ISBN: 9780335247028 (Paperback)
eISBN: 9780335247035

2013

If you are teaching or learning to teach primary mathematics, this is the toolkit to support you! Not only does it cover the essential knowledge and understanding that you and your pupils need to know, it also offers 176 great ideas for teaching primary mathematics - adaptable for use within different areas of mathematics and for different ages and abilities.

- Think deeply about mathematics and to challenge themselves
- Develop mathematical independence
- Engage in mathematical talk

www.mheducation.co.uk